# OPERA AND ITS SYMBOLS

# Opera

## AND ITS SYMBOLS

The Unity of Words, Music, and Staging

R O B E R T   D O N I N G T O N

Yale University Press   New Haven & London

For my dear Judith

Published with assistance from the foundation established in memory of Calvin Chapin of the Class of 1788, Yale College.

Designed by Richard Hendel.
Set in Joanna type by Tseng Information Systems, Durham, North Carolina.
Printed in the United States of America by Murray Printing Company, Westford, Massachusetts.
Musical examples prepared by Scott Tilley.

Library of Congress
Cataloging-in-Publication Data
Donington, Robert.
     Opera and its symbols: the unity of
  words, music, and staging /
  Robert Donington.
        p.   cm.
     Includes bibliographical references.
     ISBN 0–300–04713–4 (alk. paper)
     1. Opera.   2. Symbolism in music.
  I. Title. ML 1700.D665   1990
  782.1—dc20   89–39530
                    CIP
                    MN

The paper in this book meets the guidelines of permanence and durability of the Committee on Production Guidelines for Book Longevity of the Council on Library Resources.

10 9 8 7 6 5

Frontispiece: The third act of Wieland Wagner's production of Tristan und Isolde (1962), a landmark of the spare 'neo-Bayreuth' style of staging Richard Wagner's operas.

# CONTENTS

# ILLUSTRATIONS

# ACKNOWLEDGEMENTS

I am happy to acknowledge some very constructive criticism from Patrick Carnegy, as well as some quite inspired editing by Harry Haskell of Yale University Press. I also wish to thank Joyce Maxwell for her incomparable typing, and likewise Sue Kellett for some much appreciated assistance.

To many other friends and colleagues I should like to express my gratitude in terms more general but nonetheless heartfelt. To my wife, Judith, I should not know how to express it anyhow, but it goes very deep.

# PART ONE PRINCIPLES

# INTRODUCTION

When Thomas Carlyle wrote in his *Sartor Resartus* (Boston, 1836) that 'boundless as is the domain of man, it is but a small fractional proportion of it that he rules with Consciousness and by Forethought', and when he added that 'it is through *symbols* that man, consciously or unconsciously, lives, works and has his being', he was not introducing any novel concepts of philosophy, since there have been thinkers at least since Plato who would have put the matter not much differently. But he was certainly drawing attention to an aspect of experience which Freud and Jung subsequently explored very much farther, with results which, whether we like them or not, have conditioned our ideas of human behaviour in many crucial areas ever since.

In this book, the area which concerns me is opera, and that for two reasons. The first is that in opera, where the promptings of irrational imagination are at their most uninhibited and the restraints of naturalism are at their least intrusive, symbols both conscious and unconscious particularly abound. Almost as immediately as dreams, and far more coherently, opera offers a royal road into the unconscious, drawing as it does on regions of the psyche where consciousness has little power to penetrate. But insofar as we can pick out in the very twilight between the conscious and the unconscious some further understanding of what is being symbolized, we may gain a little more insight into the workings of the psyche itself on these hermeneutic levels.

My other reason is that we may also learn something of interest about that intimate relationship between words, music and staging which makes of opera so special a case. It is this which so sweeps us along in the theatre, with a pleasure as keen as anything in the realm of art. I rate this level no less highly than the more unconscious levels which also contribute to our experience. But here I shall be concerned particularly with layers which may underlie our conscious experience, giving it an added glow.

The presence of the music as an integral constituent of the drama is not only unnaturalistic but also time-consuming, circumscribing even as it intensifies the elaboration of the plot. Opera is impelled to deal in the great generalities of human passion and conflict rather than in the singularities of the situations and the characters—with whose fortunes we identify, perhaps, all the more suspensefully because we sense in them attributes in which we each of us in our measure share. What we share is that complex network of instinctual and psychological dispositions to which we sometimes give the name of archetypes. Opera is a great purveyor of archetypal images.

Archetypes are by their nature elusive, shifting, hard to pin down or even to define. I shall bring to bear on them here some experience of depth-psychology which may be useful and is certainly appropriate. I am aware of the difficulties and the imponderabilities of this problematic discipline, but I shall try to keep my sense of proportion and, what is equally important, my awareness of the musical elements in the great partnership of operatic symbolism. They are at least as crucial as the poetical and the theatrical elements, and I shall not fail to introduce them here.

Even when we least notice that they so much as exist, the symbols surrounding us may set up a magnetic field influencing those very thoughts and actions where we most fondly suppose that conscious control is in full command. But conscious control, invaluable and indeed indispensable as it may be, never is in full command. Unconscious imperatives always condition our conscious intentions. They may commonly be very helpful, and that indeed is my premise and my incentive throughout the present book. But they cannot be negligible.

I have expressed similar thoughts in previous books, especially *Wagner's 'Ring' and Its Symbols* (London, 1963) and my wider-ranging *Rise of Opera* (London, 1981). But I have reconsidered everything here, and it is in this new presentation, at once contracted and expanded, that I shall now hope to have my contribution assessed.

# A TOTALITY OF SYMBOLS

## SYMBOLS IN OPERA

There are two ways in which symbols may make their entry into opera.

One way is unplanned and results from the innately image-forming disposition of the human psyche. It is not in our nature to come up with images which mean nothing. The meanings may be more or less fragmentary or coherent, trivial or significant, but something will be welling up even in the most unpromising material, and far more interestingly when the material is shaped by a superior intellect and a keener vision: in a word, by genius. For however autonomous the material, it is still only the material, and will need to be worked over with conscious craftsmanship. The artist may not know *why* he does it the way he does, but he must certainly know *how*. His deeper sources are indeed unconscious, his methods are in part conditioned from the unconscious too; but if he knows his craft, the results are bound to be more or less significantly symbolical, and if all goes well, his symbols may be of the most intense fascination. If he does not know his craft, his symbols may be just baffling and frustrating. But for good or for bad, unconscious symbols will lie barely hidden beneath the conscious images. Verdi is a splendid case in point: his operas contain an element of consciously political allegory, of course, but beneath that lies a symbolical potency of amazing force. And in some measure and in some manner, this autonomous formation of symbols always happens.

The second way in which symbols may make their entry into opera does not always happen, and is indeed comparatively rare. Here there is planning for the purpose, and the symbols themselves may be largely, though never wholly, conscious and deliberate. Wagner presents an admirable example throughout his work, or Debussy in *Pelléas et Mélisande*, Monteverdi in *Orfeo*, or Mozart in *The Magic Flute*. In such cases the librettist certainly—and, I feel sure, in many cases the composer also—knows not only how but why. The unconscious still crucially contributes to the formation of the symbols, but the conscious contributes crucially as well.

This distinction between the possibilities of inadvertent and intentional symbolism is very far from absolute, but it may help us with regard to certain notorious difficulties in the sphere of opera. What, for example, is really happening when we find ourselves in the theatre enjoying an opera of which the libretto, dispassionately considered, may strike us as improbable to the brink of absurdity? The music, of course, may be better than the words, but I doubt if that offers a very adequate explanation. It is the opera we are enjoying, not only the music. I think there has got to be something reasonably good about any words which can be composed in good music on the scale of opera.

Are the words then perhaps more meaningful than they appear? Are they hinting at veiled symbols of the autonomous variety which may or may not be of great significance, but at all events are not absurd? Some unsuspected intimation of our basic hopes and fears, our comical follies and our tragic mortality? Some devious reminder that life is seldom what it seems, and that realities like the birth-trauma and the Oedipal conflict are certainly latent. They may well be conjured into dim illumination by characters and situations on stage which seemingly have nothing to say about them, yet are so curiously evocative that we accept them uncritically in the theatre, judge them critically only in prospect or in retrospect: in a word, we enjoy the opera.

Let me add at once that the less crude and fragmented the images in which the symbolical under-meanings are showing through, the better the opera is likely to be and the keener the enjoyment we are likely to be taking in it. But if the opera is moving us at all, we must I think be getting the feeling, if not necessarily the thought, that it all adds up to some sort of meaningfulness emotionally and intuitively, never mind whether it looks that way on cold consideration or not. What would cold consideration have to say about the scenario of *Rigoletto*, for example? Or of *Il trovatore*? Not to mention *Tosca*? Or even, to take a more deliberate instance of surface triviality veiling profound significance, *The Magic Flute*? In every such case, I think we are getting the benefit of unsuspected associations beyond the visible exigencies of the plot and the audible suitability of the music for deepening our experience of that plot.

THE PERSONAL AND THE ARCHETYPAL

Association is another extraordinary faculty of the human mind, and this too may operate consciously or unconsciously, or in some uncanny compound of the two. In the case of opera, it is, I suppose, unconscious association which as a rule is most significantly at work.

There can be personal association, especially from early childhood, though if ever this was conscious it is likely to have been subsequently repressed into unconsciousness. There can be archetypal association, that is to say, association with the behaviour patterns, the mythological themes, the congenital fantasies and the instinctual responses inherited from the collective experience of our species, though little if any of this can ever have emerged undisguisedly across the threshold of consciousness.

We do not, in short, think of ourselves as renewing the patterns of the past when we fall into hope or fear or love or hate or any other of the immemorial predicaments of our human state. We are just contained in them for better and for worse; but this containment is not something we have personally invented. Our basic human potentialities are in us from the start: only our individual versions are personal. They are exceedingly important, but they are not so unprecedented or so isolated as they may appear. Somewhere beneath the threshold of consciousness, we know obscurely that we are animals of this kind; and when archetypal material is presented to us artistically, we get some of the sensations of familiarity without any awareness of its unseen causes. We are gripped; we are absorbed; we are in all probability delighted, although there may also be some very real element of uncanny fear. It is from this blend of conflicting impressions that the sense of purification by catharsis may in certain circumstances arise. Confrontation with archetypal material is likely to be cathartic. Confrontation with the archetypes is the chief business of opera, spontaneously or deliberately as the case may be, and in mediocre specimens scarcely less inescapably than in the finest masterpieces. That is just the nature of the beast.

Thus it is that an opera may come over to us as meaningful even when the intellectual pretensions of its libretto are far from impressive. Something may stir in us which is not literally recognition but is nevertheless akin to recognition. The images may affect us like vague presences of we know not what; it seems they might concern us more nearly if only we could put a name and a context to them. We cannot, and it does not occur to us to try, but nevertheless we are strangely moved. When, on the other hand, the opera is of a higher intellectual calibre, and above all when the opera is composed to music of a higher inspiration, then we may respond with profounder comprehension, and even as our heads are contented, so too our hearts are warmed.

A COMMON LANGUAGE OF SYMBOLS

In the theatre, it would be quite inappropriate to ask what deeper meanings underlie the symbols, and even in the study it is by no means obligatory. The symbols will communicate on their own account, subject only to our responsiveness at the receiving end. There is no such thing as an arbitrary symbol. If it is arbitrary it is not a symbol. Images are variable; symbols are constant, arising as they do from whatever in our human nature is most universal and most enduring. There are in myth and fairy tale and legend and ritual such perennial similarities that they seem to have a common symbolical vocabulary. We do not get proof of it, but we do get a great sense of pattern.

Conscious symbolism, provided that it keeps in touch with its unconscious source-springs, can perhaps go the farthest of any. Words, music and staging combine inseparably to produce all that is best in opera. If, however, as happens frequently today, the staging falls out of line, a clash of styles may result which detracts from the totality of the symbolism. I shall have more to say on this point in the following chapters.

Words can obviously be symbolical; music in my opinion also; staging has possibilities which today are better relished than understood. But in opera it is the partnership of these different components which counts, and they do need to blend together as a matter of intrinsic style. In this partnership, words are the most articulate component, music the most expressive, and staging the most localizing.

I shall have most of all to say about the words; but for the moment it may be sufficient to point out that in the theatre the chief practical difficulty is that we never do pick up all of the words even if we know the language (and translation, though often desirable, is always at a cost). The best remedy is to do some homework ahead of time on the libretto. For the rest, we may just hope to keep in touch, as Puccini put it, 'from the evidence of the situation'.[1]

It is for the music to express what the words articulate. Hanslick (1854) and Stravinsky (1942) doubted if music can express anything beyond itself. Deryck Cooke, on the contrary, in his critically vulnerable but suggestive *Language of Music* (1958), started as I think very properly from the observable behaviour of the harmonic series, including the somewhat complex perception of it by the human ear. This behaviour arises from a verifiable constant of our objective universe, namely, periodic vibration, which within the range of audible frequencies is what we hear as tone. Where there are tones there is a tonal pull, regardless of whether it is or is not organized by keys or modes. There are other elements besides tone in music, and wide varieties of usage, but my point is simply that the conditions for musical as for other symbolism are not mere taste or fashion, but arise from the enduring properties of matter, together with the age-old acclimatization of the human psyche to the properties of matter.

But how? The literature is extensive;[2] but for my present purpose I am interested in a recent suggestion by David Burrows (1987), based on a seminal observation by the child psychologist Donald Winnicott (whose junior assistant I was many years ago). A baby may use a beloved doll or even a tatty old rag as a dearly valued 'transitional object' to help mediate between its initially narcissistic identification with the universe and its emerging awareness that there is also an external reality which can be grasped and colonized. What if music, among so much else that it can do for us, may be serving as just such a transitional object between our residual narcissism and our awareness, limited at best, that there really are people and objects out there, not merely projections of ourselves but actualities with whom or which it is possible to relate?

Outwardly, there are the objective acoustics and tangible instruments of music. Inwardly, there are the subjective emotions and intangible experiences of music. Across this polarity there is relationship. Symbols can build up, some few of which I shall hope to suggest in my musical examples to follow. And so it is that music, which inevitably somewhat obscures the words in opera, far more importantly enhances them by means of that singular directness of feeling and of intuition which it can both induce and inflect. That is indeed the incomparable advantage of opera.

To this illimitable interface of words and music, staging brings a certain local and temporal stability. Words and music usually survive intact, but staging is ephemeral, and certain problems arise as a consequence.

We have discovered the advantages of performing early music under its own original conditions. With stage production we hold curiously old-fashioned views, masquerading as modernism. There was a time when it was considered that Shakespeare, though a good dramatist, could be made acceptable to a later generation only by radical alterations to the text. Now it is merely believed that a modern twist to the production is necessary in order to bring an earlier opera to the comprehension of a modern audience. It is, I think, a self-defeating proposition, severing as it does the indivisible unity of style required among all the components of a single opera.

Thus it is currently regarded as unacceptable, indeed as wantonly behind the times, to use Rimsky-Korsakov's cleaned-up score of *Boris Godunov*, though there is much to be said for it in the theatre, or would be if we did not on balance prefer to preserve all that robust awkwardness which is ultimately part of Musorgsky's vision and character. Yet we accept *Rigoletto* with the Mafia grafted onto it by Jonathan Miller (see fig. 10). We accept the *Ring* blown up by Patrice Chéreau into a Marxist morality (fig. 1). And that was not all. In spite of every gradation in the music, Chéreau kept Act I of *Die Walküre* so light throughout that the moonlight breaking in no less symbolically than romantically at the

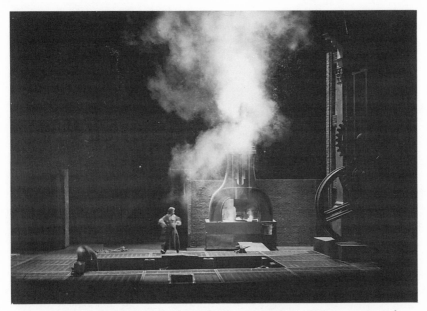

1. Patrice Chéreau's Marxist vision of Siegfried at Bayreuth in 1976: a controversial production that substituted an irrelevant modernist symbolism for Wagner's explicitly prescribed archetypal imagery.

end could make no appreciable contrast. He protracted the fight in Act II long after the music had passed on to other themes. He permitted one character to be filmed in emphatic close-up while the leitmotif of another character was ringing out in the orchestra. He showed, in fact, the well-intentioned but unavoidable ineptness of one by whom the special requirements of opera were little known and less regarded.

It was not all loss, of course, nor was Chéreau's vision totally unwarranted by Wagner's very complicated intentions. I remember my own keen astonishment on first reading Shaw's Perfect Wagnerite as a very young man and coming to the delighted conclusion that Wagner did after all mean something! And so he does, although I later realized that what Shaw thought Wagner meant in the direction of socialist propaganda amounts at the most to a very small proportion of what Wagner did mean. I think our intuitions will always tell us that. All the same, Chéreau's socialist preoccupations did get quite seriously in the way, and so did his vaunted inexperience with the entire musical dimension.

It is the first and foremost requirement for a stage director that in addition to his visual gifts he shall know and love the music, and above all trust it to do its own work without tendentious insinuations or excessive stage business of whatever kind. To instance one blatant breach of this elementary principle: a director who puts mimed action on the stage during the overture is not trusting the music. He is denying contemptuously the composer's own judgement in regard to the music. He is depriving us, moreover, of that wonderful moment for which we should have been waiting, when the curtain does go up to reveal whatever new world of the imagination the stage has been holding in store for us. I have seen, at Covent Garden, Chicago gangsters with tommy guns running about during the overture to Act I of *Die Walküre*, diluting that marvellous score with alien fantasies, as if Hunding and his (in Wagner) unseen men-at-arms would be not enough of a menace without this untoward reminder of the very differently motivated violence of a later age and a nastier environment. We learn plenty from the music about Siegmund's outer plight and inner desperation, and more especially about the weather. If you cannot hear it that way in the music, you are not hearing the music but only wondering what else of greater interest you might be able to think up to underpin the music. I am not saying that this was fatal to the Wagnerian experience, but it was quite an obstacle.

A good case where a director's imagination added valuably to an opera which in an unimaginative production can move very heavily was Andrei Serban's *Turandot* at Los Angeles in 1984 and at Covent Garden in 1987. Puccini's opera is a fairy tale of the wildest fantasy, which needs (and in this production got) an equally fantastical presentation, way beyond anything the stage directions literally indicate. But this is at a quite opposite extreme from Wagner, whose stage directions do sufficiently indicate the fairyland of his own desiring and demand the closest of attention as well as the liveliest of imagination. It is always a matter of reading the given necessities of the case correctly. In most cases, reticence is more to the point than exuberance. And in all cases the moderating influence of the music tends to slow things down and require that the production have a matching spaciousness and dignity.

In opera, too little stage business is almost always better than too much. Each movement and gesture will count for so much the more if it is withheld until it is demanded by an event palpable in the drama and pinpointed by the music. So a good ear for music is indeed essential; and to bring in a director who is not musical on the misguided assumption that he can give a new freshness to the old conventions is a mistaken enterprise from the start. The old conventions, in spite of their artificialities, worked a great deal better than the new trickery. It is not, however, to innovation that I am objecting. It is to incompatibility.

The total symbolism which is opera will not add up unless the staging is basically compatible in style with the words and the music.

Let me put it that opera presents us with a threefold challenge which has to be met as one. Stage directions, when they are present, must be treated with the same respect as all other aspects of the score. I do not mean this pedantically; but the spirit of the relationship must be willing. Not only is this a matter of artistic suitability. It is a matter of psychological communication, which is why I am laying such stress upon it here.

Changing the period of the production in the fashionable attempt to relate the images to modern expectations is almost bound to be counterproductive. Valid symbols will relate to us just as they are, whether presented in the timeless distillations of myth and fairy tale or tied to a specific time and place, implying social and artistic conventions which will jar disturbingly if the time and place of the production are shifted. Original stagings can be suggestively compared at the London Theatre Museum and elsewhere, and contemporary paintings may also be a help. Timeless settings were well exemplified by Wieland Wagner's Bayreuth productions under the influence of Adolphe Appia (so curtly excluded while Cosima Wagner still reigned), although they could be faulted as a little too consistently on the dark side and a little too sparing with actual stage properties (see frontispiece). No need for that circus horse who so disgraced himself and destroyed all illusion on the instant at one Covent Garden *Götterdämmerung* by adding prematurely to the flood of waters, since when that particular symbol has in my experience been left very properly to the imagination. But we do need a ring and a spear and a sword around which, aided by the music, we in the audience can focus our perception of their underlying meanings.

Of Peter Stein's Cardiff production of *Otello* for the Welsh National Opera in 1986 (fig. 2), Patrick Carnegy wrote: 'The spectator has the feeling that a sequence of pictures has sprung into three-dimensional animation, though in a style that is surreal rather than naturalistic'. Fair

2. Peter Stein's 1986 staging of Verdi's Otello for the Welsh National Opera departed from the naturalistic look of earlier productions (compare fig. 12), but on a deeper level remained faithful to the opera's inspired blending of music, text and action.

enough, since 'the use of physical space, lighting, groupings and the entire choreography of the action are consistently embedded in the raw material of music and text'.[1] I too was very favourably impressed by this production, which just goes to confirm that it is not necessarily naturalistic fidelity but some deeper compatibility which counts for most. But when Carnegy adds that 'historical accuracy can best be captured by deliberately distancing it', I hesitate to agree. Wagner, for example, has already distanced the Ring by a mythological ambience almost as remote from his own times as it is from ours; if we do some further distancing on our own account, we may just blur the focal planes. The scenery here is so exceptionally significant that it really amounts to part of the plot. Imagination is of course required, but so is a fairly scrupulous realization of Wagner's admittedly difficult stage directions, with décor and costumes all designed to be congruous with the assumptions of that crucial mythology. The Magic Flute likewise needs at least a vaguely Egyptian touch; Aida more emphatically so; Der Freischütz has to sport some enjoyable suggestion of spooky nineteenth-century Gothic.

And if some of that ambience on stage may seem a little unfamiliar to a modern audience, what else do we go to the theatre for? It is not the familiarity but the otherness of a consistent symbolical totality which is the challenge of a great work of art. Long live the otherness.

By contrast with Peter Stein's scrupulous sensibility, Mike Ashman produced what I would call an unscrupulous *Flying Dutchman* at Covent Garden in 1986. Michael Tanner, a far from unadventurous critic, wrote, 'In no production of any work that I have seen for the theatre has the creator's intention been so systematically and brutally undermined'. He instanced the scenic ugliness, the harsh strip-lighting, the caricaturing of capitalism in Daland and his friends, the high jinks with Senta and her Dutchman, who appeared 'tossed on a piece of meccano [a child's construction toy] to make his point to Senta that his existence is a restless affair'.[2] (That is interesting, because this was of course an attempt at symbolism, not by a real symbol but by a cooked-up fake.) Useless to protest in such a case that since Ashman has experienced the symbols that way, it must be possible and in some sense legitimate to experience the symbols that way. I do not think that Ashman has experienced the symbols.

## SOCIAL MISSION AND ARTISTIC IMPULSE

It can of course happen: think of Ibsen; think of Shaw. But there are considerable possibilities for self-deception. It can also happen that an artist imagines social implications, or is determined to bring them in, because of a pressure stemming perhaps from childhood deprivations real or imaginary which carry over unassuageably into social indignations. Not that there are no valid grounds for protest; but there may still be a hidden reservoir of unconscious compulsion topping up an inflated conscience, and exacerbating a resentment which is not so much unjustified as misplaced, since it has really more to do with the inner state of the director's psyche than with the outer state of the world. Then it is that the chip may show up on the shoulder and fine talent be diverted to productions of which the overt or the covert intention is apparently to shock. There are I think artists around, fine artists, who cannot at bottom feel that they exist at all unless they are giving us such shocks that we cannot fail to notice them. For better or for worse, we do. But either way we should not mistake it for the sober norm.

There is really no substitute for the sober norm. We do not want dull stagings and we do not want unenterprising stagings, but we do want stagings which place each opera in its natural setting. Our own contemporary climate is exceptionally harsh and threatening—schizoid may not be too strong a word for it—and I believe this climate may be predisposing our directors unconsciously but all the more obsessively towards harsh and anxious productions. It is the prerogative and perhaps the duty of artists to portray their intuitions about the way things really are, by means of works which are contemporary with ourselves in every aspect of their content and of their presentation alike. It is not within the prerogative of artists to prepare slanted productions of previous works with a view to bringing them into contemporary perspective. The only perspective which can be right is the perspective of the work itself, seen without prejudice and not through Marxist spectacles or any other form of biased preconception. We do not want biased productions. We want straight productions. Any slant *imposed* upon the work in question is a wrong slant and harmful to its built-in significance.

A director who claims that the work in question is no more than the raw material for his own self-expression is the victim of a narcissistic delusion. The words do most to define the opera, the music does most to meld the opera, but it is the whole which is the opera. To defraud us of that whole by inappropriate production is to cheat us of the opera. Above all is this the case for the younger generation, who may have had no more normal experience of the work with which to make their own comparisons. We owe it to them and indeed to ourselves to put straightforward productions on offer too. Experimental productions on some occasions, yes, perhaps; but not to the exclusion of ordinary productions. I am all in favour of a lunatic fringe, but not of a lunatic core. There is altogether too much of this fashionable gimmickry going on at present for my peace of mind. It is, I fancy, just a little sick.

## THE UNITY OF SYMBOLS

Where dancing is required, or movements and gestures which without being dance may call for a degree of stylization akin to dance, some period accuracy is again required. A minuet for Lully does need to be a minuet and not some mincing modern fill-in. Modern lighting, on the other hand—since I am not suggesting that we should go back to oil lamps and candles for Monteverdi, nor to gas lighting for Meyerbeer—can find many fresh ways of illuminating and even creating decor which may enhance without contradicting the symbols of an older opera. For always it is the unity of symbols which concerns us, and hence the need through all dimensions to tell them as they are. A symbol is not so much something an artist can invent as something an artist can find: a potentiality which he can actualize in an infinity of inspired realizations; but it still has to be that symbol and not something else again.

From around the turn of the century onwards, directors like Gordon Craig, Harley Granville-Barker and Adolphe Appia were in revolt, as they saw it, against theatrical literalness and dull conventionality. They experimented with lighting and with curtains, including mist curtains made of gauze; with multiple levels and with great staircases and with tubular steel scaffolding (known then as 'constructionism'); with elevator stages and revolving stages; with the backdrop and the cyclorama and the projected image and the cloud machine and much else that is available though by no means new today: to say nothing of old-fashioned flies and flats and hoists and trapdoors, all of them still perfectly useful in their proper places. The only stage illusion no longer at our command, so far as I am aware, is the simulation of actual perspective, which needs some seventy feet of stage depth in order to carry the eye to an appropriate vanishing point: many baroque theatres had it; ours do not.

It is also interesting that early in this century Freud's exploration of the unconscious was already inviting surrealist experiments in the theatre, admirable when surreal images really are allowed to float up in their customary dream-like incalculability, catastrophic when it is calculated that the images must needs have Freudian implications which can be clarified by blatantly Freudian images on stage, spelling out what may indeed be implied but not in consciousness. The unconscious never spells anything out. The unconscious never commits itself to any one definitive presentation. We should not attempt to be definitive on the stage, but rest content with the flexible significance and boundless suggestiveness which real symbols offer.

Colours are themselves suggestive: black for darkness and evil and hidden machinations; white for openness and goodness and purity of heart; gold, the metal of the sun, for the royal and the glorious, so that golden hair is proper for heroes but black for villains. Silver is for the moon, and relates to the feminine rather than to the masculine side of life. Blue is for the spirit, and purple for the transforming principle (ecclesiastics are traditionally in touch with this). Green is for the safe and the fertile, red for passion and for danger (many animals and plants exploit this colour-coding in self-defence). Colour, like lighting generally, is of enormous importance in its emotional effects.

The hazard with an adventurous but wayward director is not that he will be short on suggestive associations, but that they may not be appropriate associations. They may be too personal and not collective enough, telling us more about the director than about the opera. If, on the other hand, his stage is bare, or if it is cluttered (as one current fashion appears to have it) with an array of movable tubular chairs, then bareness or clutter will be the association aroused, appropriately or not. A bare stage is better than a cluttered stage and less liable to get in the way of whatever the work itself is offering of collective association and archetypal imagery. But I must confess to a certain nostalgia for those unaffectedly pictorial presentations on which the eye could so agreeably fasten and the imagination feed. They may sometimes have been naive but they were seldom inappropriate, and on the whole they gave us a lot of harmless pleasure.

### STAGING THE SYMBOLS AS THEY ARE

I conclude this discussion of visual symbolism on stage with an instructive instance from that notable French school of symbolist poetry whose aspiration it was to suggest without defining the illimitable fluctuations of our human moods.

When Maeterlinck set up his *Pelléas et Mélisande* with woods and wells and vaults and caverns and a cast of characters not one of whom could find his way through to any vital purpose in life, and when Debussy composed these characters and situations in a score as faithful to the poetry as it is enchanting in sound, we cannot suppose that other symbols or none at all would do just as well. The wood which so imprisons them all comes straight down from Dante, who at the start of his *Inferno* found himself 'in the middle of the journey of our life in a dark wood, because the straight way was lost': one of poetry's greatest moments; and most of us would recognize that nightmare sense of lost direction. It would not have been at all the same symbol if Dante had put himself, let us say, on a desolate mountaintop, still less into one of those fashionably neutral interiors of our day which may be equally desolate but are not equally suggestive. That wood is repeatedly on the minds of all the characters, and already it invokes the main dilemma, which is indeed the lost and hopeless state of those who have never really dared to live.

Then again, a well is intrinsically reminiscent of the unfathomable abysses of the deep unconscious: values, it is true, may be drawn up from there as water from a well is drawn up; but equally values may be swallowed up like Mélisande's crown and her wedding ring when she wished to repress the painful knowledge of what they meant to her. The crown adorns the head, where we tend to feel that consciousness and the ego are particularly focused. A ring is likewise an unbroken circle and may likewise be of durable gold, evocative perhaps of permanence and commitment and sterling fidelity. To lose both of them in the course of one opera bodes nobody any good.

Those eerie vaults and dismal caverns likewise feel dangerous enough, and confirm our sense of unconscious forces building up towards the tragedy. And all this imagery was deliberately meant by Maeterlinck and by Debussy to be not less evocative than undefined. So what am I to say about Louis Sprosser's recent production at Edinburgh in which the characters were squalidly downgraded and the most crucial visual images were discarded to the point of stylistic vacuum? What can then remain of symbolical significance? And with what irony did the conductor go to no less pains to *restore* Debussy's musical intentions than the director to *negate* Maeterlinck's poetical intentions? It is only directors who habitually delude themselves that a past masterpiece cannot reach a modern audience except by being modernized, or that older thoughts cannot be revitalized except by being given a new and trendy twist. Thinking has in any case not all that much to do with it. Feeling and intuition are the normal channels. We do not want the director to stage what he may think the symbols mean. We just want him to stage the symbols.

# PART TWO PRACTICE

## SOPHISTICATED SYMBOLS
## AT THE START OF OPERA

I have now arrived at ground which I have covered exten-
sively in my *Rise of Opera*. Here I shall merely recall in the briefest possible
way how opera started at a period—the late Renaissance—when deliberate as opposed to spontaneous symbolism was at the very height of
fashion, not to mention of sophistication.[1] All the protagonists of classical mythology survived or returned to carry (as is the normal habit of
their kind) the projections of just those aspects of our own personali-
ties which we are least able or least willing to recognize directly within
ourselves.

There had been Dante in his Platonic mood urging us to 'consider
the teaching which is concealed beneath the strange verses'.[2] There had
been Boccaccio, in his graver role as an antiquarian intermediary, rec-
ommending the artist to 'conceal truth in a legendary and fitting covering'.[3] There was Ronsard, whose influence on Rinuccini and Chiabrera
and Striggio, the earliest librettists of opera, was direct and acknowledged, instructing the poet to 'dissemble and conceal fables, fitly, and
disguise well the truth of things with a fabulous cloak', so as to 'make
enter into the minds of ordinary people, by agreeable and colourful
fables, the secrets which they could not understand when the truth
is too openly disclosed'.[4] There was Sir John Harrison, in the preface
to his translation (London, 1591) of Ariosto's *Orlando furioso*, comparing
the poets of antiquity who 'have indeed wrapped as it were in their
writings diverse and sundry meanings which they call the senses or
mysteries thereof . . . and these same sences that comprehend so excellent a knowledge we call the Allegorie, which Plutarch defineth to be
when one thing is told, and by that another is understood'.

Boccaccio and Ronsard, Ariosto and Harrison stood in a line of which
the philosophical involvements were Neoplatonic and the intuitive implications, on one view of it, were psychological. Under the patronage
of Ficino, that prime leader of Renaissance Neoplatonism, a curious

cult was set up to honour the legendary Orpheus, no less enthusiasti-
cally than unhistorically, as by divine inspiration a sort of proto-Plato.[5]
One of Ficino's more wayward pupils, Pico della Mirandola, actually
described the spurious but highly regarded Orphic Hymns as in appearance 'the merest fables and trifles', but in reality outstanding examples
of how 'divine matters, when written at all, must be covered beneath
enigmatic veils and poetical dissimulations'.[6]

Divine matters are archetypal matters, such as thrive in opera and
have done from the very start. But there is a yet more direct connection. Poliziano was a precocious young protégé of Ficino who, during
his distinguished career at the Florentine court, was commissioned to
instruct Botticelli (ten years his own senior) on the art of including
deliberate Neoplatonic symbolism in his painting. (The famous Primavera
is a well-documented example, to which Poliziano's poem 'La giostra'
notably contributed.) Poliziano's small but celebrated pastoral drama
Orfeo did not only bequeath to opera the poetical form in which the
earliest librettos are fashioned; it also made a favoured hero of Orpheus
himself, whose mythological musicianship and hermeneutic reputation
rendered him an especially appropriate protagonist in opera, and more
particularly in that most influential group of very early operas which
pursue his legend.[7] Deliberate symbolism and hermeneutic implication
were built into the very preparations for opera. Opera did not for long
develop in that deliberately symbolical manner. But it did so begin; and
something of what shaped its beginning has perhaps clung to it by force
of example ever since. No opera, at any rate, is without its quotient at
least of spontaneous symbols.

## THE MUSICAL DIMENSION

Meanwhile, much was needed and much was happening
along the musical dimension. It seems to me probable that modulation
through the keys was a prerequisite as it was certainly a concomitant
of the start of opera; for in very broad terms, modes differ in the absolute, transition is restricted and stability is of the essence, whereas keys
merely differ in relation to one another, transition is unrestricted and
mobility is of the essence. Opera is drama unfolding as much in the
music as in the words, and its music must be very free to move.

In 1525, Bembo argued that in poetry the sound is not only a carrier
for the sense but is part of the sense.[8] In 1588, Zarlino associated high
notes and rapid tempos with excitement, low notes and slow tempos

with relaxation, and intermediate states with moderation.[9] These are all potential constituents of musical symbolism, which Zarlino required to be matched to the sense of the poetry, and thus on Bembo's principles to the sound as well. Morley, pirating Zarlino a generation later, insisted that 'you must have a care that when your matter signifieth high heaven, and such like, you make your musicke ascend; and by the contrarie where your dittie speaketh of descending loweness, depth, hell and other such, you must make your musicke descend'.[10] And if that applied too literally might seem a little naive, just think how odd it would feel if *Das Rheingold* began high up in the orchestra, or if *Lohengrin* did not.

Zarlino's one-time pupil Galilei argued misleadingly that polyphony confuses the meanings of musical symbols by interweaving them concurrently in different pitches, directions, speeds and rhythms.[11] In fact, we do not hear the strands of counterpoint as cancelling one another out but as adding up to a sort of glorious overview; but true it is that opera could not have arisen from a collectivity of madrigalists, but only from a confrontation of soloists. The reciting style of solo vocal music which we call monody can mainly be credited to Bardi's circle (subsequently termed 'Camerata') under the advice and guidance of Mei, who had likewise contrasted 'acuteness and gravity' of pitch, together with a 'middle' level in between, as well as 'swiftness and slowness of measure and rhythm'.[12] Galilei suggested learning from the stylized speech of actors in the theatre 'with what voice regarding acuteness and gravity, with what quantity of sound, with what sorts of accentuation and gestures, with how much speed and slowness they talk' when representing different characters and situations.[13] All this presupposes a symbolic as well as a semantic use of sounds.

The influential *Balet comique de la royne* (Paris, 1581) not only credited the immediate source of its scenario to the Neoplatonic popularizer Natale Conti, but printed his explanation, among others, of its hidden meanings.[14] At Florence in 1589, Bardi,[15] on being put in chief command of the sensational court interludes of that year, drew directly on Plato[16] for their eventful scenario, the very characteristic climax of which may be summed up as reconciliation. Stage designs by Buontalenti survive, with engravings after them by Caracci.[17] One of these (fig. 3), showing the allegorical figure of Necessity holding the cosmic spindle (which is, I suppose, the symbol for her central role as the axis for all our human destiny), is quite unmistakably copied from, or from the same source as, the picture on page 304 of the much-illustrated second edition (Venice, 1571) of another conveniently available Neoplatonic textbook, Cartari's *Imagini* of 1556 (the Warburg Institute in London has a

3. Neoplatonic imagery suffused the famous Florentine interludes of 1589. In this engraving after a stage design by Bernardo Buontalenti, the allegorical figure of Necessity exhibits her cosmic spindle, symbolizing her guiding role in human affairs.

copy). Equally fashionable was Giraldi's *De deis gentium* of 1548, while the distinguished head of the line, Boccaccio's formidable *Genealogia deorum gentilium* (Venice, 1472, but manuscript copies date from 1371 at latest) was still in highly respected currency. So acceptable and indeed customary was it to bring calculated symbolism into the ambitious entertainments to which opera shortly afterwards became the still more ambitious sequel.[18]

Opera itself lies to the credit not of Bardi's circle but of Corsi's, with Rinuccini (the chief poet in 1589) indisputably its first librettist[19] and Peri its first composer, claiming novelty as he did for 'a harmoniousness, which going beyond that of ordinary speech, fell so much short of the melodiousness of song, that it took on the form of something in the middle'.[20] This indeed was the nature and the origin of recitative, that open-ended modification of the reciting style to express not only feeling in a given situation but drama in a developing situation. Very early opera virtually was recitative of a highly expressive variety. And the symbolical potentialities of recitative do arise precisely from its open-endedness: where the drama leads, the music is at liberty to follow.

The earliest opera was *Dafne*[21] (Florence, 1597/98), [22] for which Peri's music is lost but the fine libretto by Rinuccini survives. It requires our attention here for certain images which we shall find recurring both deliberately in other Neoplatonic operas and intuitively in some later operas.

Conti wrote, for example, that 'the sun is God, whom the Greeks call Apollo'; for 'what reveals truth more than the sun, and disperses all darkness of night from human states?'[23] And here is Apollo teasing Cupid and asking him whether he intends to 'uncover his eyes or strike in the dark'. The reference is to Plato's *Symposium*, where there are two Venuses: a celestial Venus whose Cupid has open eyes for heavenly love; and an earthly Venus whose Cupid has his eyes blindfolded for sensual love.[24] So Cupid, boasting of 'what a blind archer can do', shoots Apollo, causing him to fall blindly in love with the nymph Dafne. But she pleads that she 'is a mortal, not a goddess from heaven'; and prompt to his Neoplatonic cue, Apollo answers that 'if such light glows in mortal beauty, heaven's no longer pleases me'. She escapes him by being turned into a laurel tree. And Apollo in his bitter sexual frustration vows to make of her laurel leaves garlands for those poets and others whose patron he is as leader of the muses.[25]

A man's muse may be his symbol for that feminine component within his own psyche which, whether for help or for hindrance, relates to the formidable archetype of which Goethe, in the famous last line of his *Faust*, wrote: 'Das Ewig-weibliche zieht uns hinan', the eternal feminine draws us on. But we must not project the archetype of femininity too blindly onto the beloved woman, or we shall not see her as she really is. She will not be able to live up to our inflated expectations, nor will she deserve the disillusionment into which we may next swing over. Hence the practical importance of distinguishing the eternal archetype from the mortal woman.

It is this hard but valuable lesson which I think that Apollo is being depicted by the poetry as learning here. The myth itself implies it, with that sureness of perception which traditional wisdom so often has to offer. Rinuccini picks it up with the uncanny certainty of the poet's vision. Disciple of Ronsard and of Chiabrera as he was, he would certainly have known how to veil a deeper meaning beneath the enchanting surface of his poetry. I do not suggest that he aimed directly at a psychological conclusion. I do suggest that the psychological conclusion is implicit in the poetry. The deeper meaning is the archetypal meaning, which speaks for itself. An added touch of sophistication shows in the references to Plato, which many in his contemporary audience would no doubt have recognized; and by common consent Plato intended his use of myth to be allegorical. I think myself, as Jung did, that those so-phisticated Neoplatonists may have known pretty much what they were talking about. The language may not be psychological but the insights are.

It is not difficult for an audience to share in the archetypal sugges-tiveness of such poetic imagery. I think most of us would find Apollo's dilemma dramatically acceptable. It has a curiously convincing feel. How far any archetypal implications impinge on us must always depend upon how open our own intuitions are, and that must be very much of a variable. But insofar as we are taking artistic pleasure, we are prob-ably getting some intimation of what that pleasure is subliminally about. The magic of a fairy tale has nothing to do with thinking. We do not have to think. We have only to go along consentingly with the fairy tale, refraining from intellectual scorn.

From the sustained flattery of 'le roi soleil' over the centuries, through the Masonic ceremony half veiled and half revealed in Mozart's *Magic Flute*, the radiantly self-explanatory symbolism of the sun shines out everywhere in true Neoplatonic radiance, long after the Neoplatonism here so evident had ceased to be a ruling influence. It does not surprise me to find one of those evidently well-read nymphs in the *Euridice* (Flo-rence, 1600) of Rinuccini and Peri, of which most fortunately the music does survive, quoting line 9 of Petrarch's deliberately allegorical 'Due rose fresche': 'The sun does not see a like pair of lovers'; nor to hear Orfeo on his way down to the underworld lamenting 'the fatal slopes, shadowy fearful fields where you may never see the flashes and gleams of the stars and the sun'.[26] Rinuccini had Orfeo address his Euridice as 'la donna mia', my woman, but in the score this has become 'l'anima mia', my soul, as if to underline the double meaning; for it is precisely her ambiguity and Orfeo's confusion in this respect that Orfeo, like Apollo, is confronting. Is she mortal? Is she archetypal? In all probability she stands for a bit of each.

I think a corresponding ambivalence can be heard in the music (ex. 1). The tritone, standing without harmonic commitment as it does at the very centre of the tonal structure, can lead you this way or that way and is a very emblem of uncertainty, unease and, it may be, grief: a musical analogue, in short, for a dramatic emotion, and as such quite typical. We shall see quite a lot more of it from time to time in the following pages.

(a) DAFNE (the messenger)

Sco - lo - ri - to il bel vol - to, e bei sem - bian - ti

*The beautiful face grew pale, and the beautiful features*

(b) ORFEO

Ohi - mé, Ohi - mé, Che su l'au-ro - ra giun-

*Ah me!        Ah me!        What dawn brought down to its*

se all 'oc - ca - so il Sol_____ de gl'oc - chi mi - ei

*setting        the Sun of my eyes?*

**Example 1**

Jacopo Peri, *Euridice* (Florence, 1600). Grievous tritones, (a) for the
Messenger's narrative of Euridice's death; (b) for Orfeo's anguish.

## MONTEVERDI'S FIRST OPERA

The start of opera took place in originality and talent; but its continuation came at the hands of genius.

When Monteverdi took up that great and fashionable story, with a new libretto by Striggio, for their *Orfeo* (Mantua, 1607), he brought to opera for the first time a mastery which carries entire conviction in the theatre today.[1] We do not praise him for originality but for inspiration. Both the poetical symbolism of the libretto and the musical idioms of the score are along lines very similar to precedent, but I suggest that both of them, the libretto as well as the music, went deeper in.

The libretto focuses on that prototypal Neoplatonic image of the sun symbolizing mental and spiritual (on the analogy of literal and physical) illumination. 'May your burning torch be like a rising sun to bring tranquil days to these lovers', sings the chorus to Hymen, god of marriage. The metaphor is phallic, but there is the usual Neoplatonic double-take. Ficino had long ago called the sun 'everywhere the image of the divine truth and goodness', and described this as 'an Orphic mystery', adding very pertinently that Plato's Socrates 'took refuge in moral philosophy so that with its help the mind, dispelling the bodily clouds, may become more tranquil and at once receive the light of the divine sun that shines at all times and everywhere'.[2] So too a nymph now calls on the Muses to 'tear away the dark veil of every cloud'. The chorus chimes in with 'let the sun see your dancing, prettier than that of the stars to the moon at dark night'.

I recall that by Orphic doctrine 'the sun is god, and the moon'; for 'god is day and night'.[3] I think that this doctrine must convey an intuitive understanding of two constants of our human destiny: first, that the masculine numinosity of the sun is complemented by the feminine numinosity of the moon; and second, that we most certainly have our dark side as well as our light side, and that for the soundest of psychological reasons we have somehow to accept both these polar opposites as parts of that curious package deal which is a human being.

So consistent are these Orphic images that I think they constitute a hermeneutic invitation, to which we shall respond not by any rational curiosity, but rather by a sense of deepened magic. We do not ask the meaning of these lovely poetical conceits; we just get the feeling that they are meaningful—not a nonsense, but an illumination. And to this magic and this illumination the music adds immeasurably; for that is the very method and virtue of opera.

And now, returning to the central image, here is Orfeo quoting, like Rinuccini's nymph, Petrarch on 'the sun which circles all things and looks at all things from the star-strewn circuits: say, have you seen a more happy and fortunate lover?' Euridice replies in words no less happy; but the music makes its own sinister comment by setting them to that same tritone interval which example 1 has already shown us as a musical symbol having potential for menace or for grief. There is no grief here as yet, but there is going to be, and then we shall find the menacing tritones coming back in force (ex. 2).

*I will not say what may be*
*(in your joy, Orfeo, my joy!)*

**Example 2**
Monteverdi, *Orfeo* (Mantua, 1607), Act I. Euridice's words of joy set to the tritone in premonition of later grief.

In Act II, Orfeo is still being 'made happy by the sun through which my nights have day'; and here is one of those Arcadian shepherds softening us up in rippling triple metre and bright C major when Sylvia the messenger runs in, C natural in the bass twists horribly to C-sharp for a six-three triad in A major—and happiness collapses. Her lines, closely resembling Rinuccini's for Peri at the same spot, are so weighted by elisions (Bembo would have approved) that they can scarcely move: 'Ahi

**Example 3**

Monteverdi, *Orfeo*, Act II. The last of the shepherds' rejoicing and the modulation which brings the Messenger's bad news.

caso acerbo! Ahi fat' empio e crudele! Ahi stelle ingiuriose! Ahi cielo avaro' (Ah bitter chance! Ah wicked and cruel fate! Ah wrongful stars! Ah covetous heaven!). And in the music, those hateful tritones return to remind us how ambiguous was the future latent in that previous happiness. Poetical and musical symbols go hand in hand (ex. 3).

The shepherds have no more heart for rhyming, though trying hard for C major again while the messenger pulls us back remorselessly through E major and A major. Then, as Orfeo begins to take it in that his Euridice is dead, E major slips straight into G minor and E-flat major straight into E major as if the whole rational order of tonality were in disarray. The messenger relates how Euridice was stung by that odious snake, and 'at once her lovely face grew pale and the light faded from her eyes with which she put the sun to shame'.[4] Now the shepherds, too, weigh their music down with tritone lamentings; but Orfeo gathers all his courage, and with a descending line of melody (such as Zarlino would undoubtedly have recommended) he resolves to make his down-

## Example 4

Monteverdi, *Orfeo*, Act II. The irrational progressions symbolizing musically the horror of the emotional situation as Orfeo tries to take in the Messenger's fatal announcement.

ward way into the dark caverns of the underworld in search of her. 'Farewell, earth, farewell sky and sun'. And down we and the music go with him (ex. 4).

'The scene changes'—no doubt impressively—to show Caronte (Charon) guarding that River Styx which no dead man can avoid crossing nor living man cross.[5] Orfeo is a living man; but it is part of his legend that he can charm most things out of their proper courses, and now he sets himself with the utmost operatic suitability to charm the action forward in that astonishing 'Possente spirto'. And Caronte, in the middle of explaining why he cannot possibly yield, yields—to sleep. So Orfeo grabs his boat and over he goes. Proserpina, queen of the underworld, persuades Pluto to relent, but with the fair warning: 'Before he draws his feet from this abyss, let him never turn to her his eager eyes, for a single look shall be the cause of her eternal loss'. He turns; and even as he sees her, she vanishes, singing, 'By too much love do you then lose me?' And we, on this human level and to such heartfelt music, are deeply moved (ex. 5).

But for another level, I looked Euridice up in Conti, who explains that some call her 'that soul [anima] which is married to Orpheus or the body

4. *Orpheus and the Muses, a woodcut from the 1637 edition of Natale Conti's much-studied Mythologiae. Conti's Neoplatonic interpretations of the classical myths strongly influenced Monteverdi and his contemporaries.*

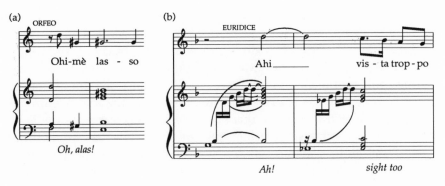

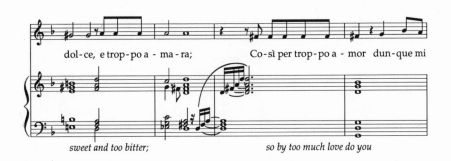

**Example 5**

Monteverdi, Orfeo, Act IV. Symbolic tritones, (a) for Orfeo's grief;
(b) for Euridice's despair.

[*corpori*]'.[6] If Striggio had not at this point been reading Conti (fig. 4), as he might have been, he had certainly been reading the score of Peri's *Euridice*; for this Orfeo too calls Euridice 'my soul [*anima mia*]', promising that 'to you I dedicate my lyre and my song, as before I offered my burning spirit on the altar of my heart'. In short, since she can no longer be his mistress, she shall be his muse. Contemporary audiences might very possibly have recalled that same lesson being learnt by Apollo in connection with his lost Dafne; and almost certainly they would think of Dante in that famous vision when, after losing Beatrice, he vowed that 'my spirit should go hence to behold the glory of my lady', and did so at the distant end of the vast poem of inner exploration to which her image, muse-like, inspired him.[7]

If Orfeo had not looked round while he was still within the transforming influence of his underworld adventure, he would have learned nothing of all this and merely slipped back to Arcadia no wiser than he was before. Now that he braces himself to face his own grief through further tritones and harmonic side-slips—E major to D major to E-flat major—his father Apollo 'descends in a cloud singing', no doubt in direct response.

'Do you not know that no joy down here endures?' sings Apollo. 'Therefore, if you wish to enjoy immortal life, come with me to heaven which invites you'. This invitation itself may be understood on a combination of levels. Literally, there is no doubt whatsoever that down here we are mortal, whereas up there it is at least conceivable that there might be life everlasting. Symbolically, the invitation may be to whatever increase of intuitive awareness the hermeneutic aspect of the libretto may be holding out for those of us with eyes to see and ears to hear. At all events, there can be no real future for Orfeo or for anyone else in Arcadia. The Arcadian fantasy resembles, and may in fact be derived from, that perennial but debilitating nostalgia for the actual or imagined bliss of childhood, which cannot and ought not to last when the time has come for adult growth and development.

I might put it that Apollo has himself achieved some such growth and development in that part of his myth which taught him so painfully that the mortal woman we may desire is not the same as the immortal archetype we must not too persistently project onto her, since confused misunderstandings are liable to result from such unreal expectations. Apollo is certainly in a position to pass on this hard-won insight to Orfeo, since Orfeo through his own suffering now appears to be in a condition to take advantage of it. But here it is that an entire shift of emphasis was introduced between the text as published independently by Rinuccini and the libretto as actually set to music by Monteverdi. Explanations for this change have been advanced from various directions; but in my view it was the deliberate intention to reinforce the Neoplatonic moral and the hermeneutic conclusion to the story.[8]

At all events, there are no furious Maenads assailing Orfeo now; no sundered limbs; no rescue of the severed head to prophesy—appropriately enough—in Apollo's temple: nothing, in short, of the various traditional endings to the myth. Instead, when Orfeo pleads, 'Shall I never again see the sweet radiance of my beloved Euridice?' Apollo answers, 'You will look with love upon her fair semblance in the sun and the stars'. Not the mortal woman: the immortal archetype. And with that Apollo and Orfeo rise together in their cloud machine, duetting cheerfully as they go.

### THE DECLINE IN NEOPLATONIC SYMBOLISM

That deliberately Neoplatonic symbolism which gave so exalted a start to opera was now about to decline.[9] Already Rinuccini's libretto for Monteverdi's lost *Arianna* (Mantua, 1608) mingles humanity and even comedy with a presumably Neoplatonic conclusion, since Bacchus invites that deserving heroine 'to the eternal sky', where 'the brightest stars will make of your beautiful hair a garland of gold, glorious reward of a soul which despises, for the sake of heavenly desire, mortal beauty'. But we have presently the evidence of that much-quoted letter of 9 December 1616 from Monteverdi to Striggio, objecting to composing a piece having winds for characters, for 'how can I, by such means, move the passions? Ariadne moved us because she was a woman, and similarly Orpheus because he was a man, not a wind'.[10]

It would evidently not have occurred to Monteverdi that these characters he set so humanely to music might move us all the more because they are symbols too: but they do; and neither Ronsard nor Chiabrera nor Rinuccini nor Striggio would have had any difficulty in telling us why. But by now the whole mental ambience of opera was on the change.

## MONTEVERDI'S LAST OPERA

There is no Neoplatonic undertow that I can detect to that triumphantly human opera of Monteverdi's old age, *L'incoronazione di Poppea* (Venice, 1642). But there may be a sort of fairy-tale radiance glowing through, not deliberately, but from the spontaneous levels of the imagination which can so valuably colour the inspiration of a great artist.

Busenello based his ostensibly historical libretto broadly on Tacitus and Suetonius.[11] In history, Nero became emperor through the murderous intrigues of his mother, Agrippina, and was in turn seduced into murderous behaviour by Poppea. Part of Poppea's erotic fascination for Nero was that she so resembled his mother, for whom, as Suetonius slyly lets it out to us, he displayed and tried to consummate an incestuous passion. In the opera this is all greatly glamorized and softened down; but we are still left conniving at conduct which is to say the least of it reprehensible. And when I say reprehensible, I do not mean reprehensible because it is sensuous. I mean reprehensible because it is murderous.

The only real problem with regard to *Poppea* is how its perfectly respectable authors allowed themselves to present for our enjoyment quite so cynical a plot, which of course we do enjoy without the slightest sense of incongruity. In a recent article, Ellen Rosand has seen the solution in the edifying moral contrast we are meant to appreciate between the infamy of Nero and the nobility of Seneca, his chief victim and complementary opposite; and I think perhaps we do appreciate it.[12] We certainly admire the tragic plight and relish the vocal excellence of the worthy Seneca. But it is the unworthy Nero and his boon companions and his fascinating mistress who really have our conscious sympathy and draw our unconscious identifications. It is here that I think the uncovenanted symbolism of fairy tale may be welling up to influence our responses.

In a fairy tale, murder may be a literal crime but a symbolical obligation in repudiation of outgrown attitudes and perhaps of obstructive parent-images. Thus it is accepted, for example, that in Grimm no. 6 the children have to be beheaded before they and the Faithful John of its title can come back to life, and the one guilty act there would have been not to commit the guilty act. For in the looking-glass logic of a fairy tale the search is the duty, the ruthless deed is the necessary deed, the prohibitions are the challenge, the obstacles are the test of character, death is for transformation and the royal union is for the ritual union.

In fairy-tale logic, the wrong thing is so often the right thing, but since this cannot be known ahead of time, the test of character is very real.

Not that I doubt the carnal dispositions of this royal couple, nor am I suggesting that this is intentionally a fairy tale. But just the same, we should not in the outside world, I think, be condoning this much treachery and cruelty for the sake of sex. Something from the inside world of the imagination must be welling up to modify and extend our feelings and our intuitions, not less beneficially than inconspicuously. That is what I mean by an aura of fairy tale, lending a certain radiance to an otherwise quite immoral narrative.

### A SYMBOLICAL UNDERCURRENT?

It can only be the archetypal springs of our imagination which so favourably top up the images, having already done so for the authors of the piece. The image which comes into my mind, as the royal couple reach their serene rather than impassioned love duet at the very end, is that perennial symbol for the reconciliation of ourselves with ourselves: the ritual union or sacred marriage. To be made in some manner and in some measure whole, to accept our balance of masculine and feminine components, to join our shadow with our light: such are the aspirations behind so many rituals of initiation and of integration and so many mythological and literary scenarios, right through to Mozart's *Magic Flute* and Tippett's *Midsummer Marriage*. The longing for wholeness is itself an archetype, and I think that the spectacle of so royal a couple uniting in so glamorous a context to such joyful music is enough to evoke the distant echo of that archetype. The ending feels right emotionally because it is right symbolically. For if not that, what else could be permitting us so singular and uncensorious an enjoyment? There are no effects without causes in a work of art.

But it will not escape notice here that I am for the first time introducing an opera in which the main thrust of the symbolism is no longer deliberate but autonomous. The craftsmanship is deliberate and felicitous; the implications are spontaneous and momentous. It is on more levels than one that *Poppea* leaves us in a happy mood (ex. 6).[13]

A setting at least suitably grand and Roman; an aerial machine, perhaps, to underline Cupid's archetypal suggestiveness; and for the love duet, simply the full treatment at its obvious value. Any fairy-tale implications will take good care of themselves; for as always, the director's

## Example 6

Monteverdi, *L'incoronazione di Poppea* (Venice, 1642). Excerpt from the closing duet: if not certainly by Monteverdi, then certainly not unworthy of him.

concern should not be to stage what he may think the symbols mean, but to stage the symbols. In this scene the royal pairing is the symbol, and if it is presented royally, its work is done.

Little rhyme and less reason about so entertaining a sample of operatic high spirits as Cavalli's *Ormindo* (Venice, 1642).[1] Prince Ormindo and Prince Amida are both indifferently encouraged by Queen Erisbe, herself married to old King Ariadeno. After Amida is won back by Princess Sicle, whom he had previously discarded, Erisbe turns more seriously to Ormindo, and farce moves on towards tragedy when Ariadeno, who is not such a fool as he appears to be, soon has Ormindo and Erisbe in prison together. She drinks the supposed poison first; he drains the cup. Ariadeno comes in to gloat, only to discover that Ormindo is his own long-lost son. Literally, it is implausible; symbolically, it makes a curious sort of inadvertent sense.

Prosaically analysed, the implication would be that since Ariadeno is Ormindo's father, and since Erisbe is Ariadeno's wife, Ormindo in desiring her desires unconsciously (it would have to be unconsciously) the woman who now stands revealed in all the forbidden fascination of the mother-relationship. This brings us inadvertently (it would have to be inadvertently) so close to the Oedipal scenario that recognition stirs, not in awareness, but in those deeper caverns of the psyche where that which is archetypal is always in a manner familiar and operative, conditioning our feelings and our intuitions however inaccessibly to our reason and our common sense. For Oedipal desire and Oedipal conflict are archetypal, they are normal, they are apt to loom up of their own accord in any artist's imagination and, one hopes, to work through to some symbolically acceptable resolution. Thus it was that in performance with Muriel Wolf's excellent opera workshop some years ago at the State University of New York in Buffalo, we found it a very moving climax when the tyrant Ariadeno, following a baroque stereotype, turns magnanimous in the last scene and rejoices as the sleeping potion, which is all that has actually been swallowed, wears off. With true fairy-tale propriety, he then yields to his son both his wife and his kingdom.

Maybe this stereotype of the relenting tyrant pleases us because we have such need to forgive ourselves for that buried residue of Oedipal guilt we all harbour and must somehow find a way to tolerate. The happy ending here could hardly be less rational nor feel more right.

### OPERA REFORMED BY REASON

Behind the newly reformed librettos of Zeno and Metastasio lay the classical French drama of Corneille and Racine. It is as if such concentrated types of virtue and of villainy show us the characteristics all humans in their measure share, but separated by some prism of the imagination into characters who add up to a composite portrait of humanity. Order is praised; monarchy is flattered: truly this was the drama, and subsequently the opera, of the Establishment.[2]

Corneille, who had a poor opinion of opera, had a point when he complained in 1650 that 'words which are sung are imperfectly heard by the audience'.[3] It was nevertheless Corneille's admirer Saint-Evremond, exiled in London, who conceded that 'there are things which ought to be sung, things which can be without offending propriety or reason', and we may note the emphasis on reason as if possible a guiding principle. 'Vows, sacrifices and in general everything which concerns the service of the gods', he instances; 'the tender and the grievous passions', and 'the expression of love', and 'the irresolution of a soul in conflict'.[4] It is an interesting list, decidedly on the introverted side: for what concerns the gods concerns the archetypes; love and irresolution are inward states; and with hindsight we may say that Saint-Evremond started up a line of thought here which set the pattern for much subsequent discussion of the proper subjects and the appropriate contexts for opera. Already we find Dryden picking it up in the justly celebrated preface to his failed opera of 1685, *Albion and Albanus*:

> An *Opera* is a poetical Tale or Fiction, represented by Vocal and Instrumental Musick, adorn'd with Scenes, Machines, and Dancing. The suppos'd Persons of this musical Drama, are generally supernatural, as Gods and Goddesses, and Heroes, which at least are descended from them, and are in due time, to be adopted into their Number. The Subject therefore being extended beyond the Limits of Humane Nature, admits of that sort of marvellous and surprizing conduct, which is rejected in other Plays. Humane Impossibilities, are to be receiv'd, as they are in Faith; because where

Gods are introduc'd, a Supreme Power is to be understood; and second Causes are out of doors. Yet propriety is to be observ'd even here. The Gods . . . must all act according to their distinct and peculiar Characters.[5]

Then, as if following on, John Hughes wrote in the preface to his semi-opera *Calypso and Telemachus* (composed by J. E. Galliard and performed at London in 1712) concerning 'the Supernatural and Allegorical Persons, which may on some Occasions be introduced in [opera], tho' not allowed in [spoken] Tragedy', that 'tho' these are Characters form'd beyond the bounds of Nature and Reality, there is a kind of Poetical Nature that presides here, and ought to regulate the Poet's Invention and Conduct'.[6]

Useless then for Dr. Johnson to call Italian opera in England 'an exotic and irrational entertainment, which has always been combated and always has prevailed': it has prevailed because it is irrational; only Dr. Johnson was by his own admission too unmusical to appreciate opera as a total form.[7] Yet Dr. Johnson showed himself very interestingly aware of the archetypes of human behaviour when he called Shakespeare 'the poet that holds up to his readers a faithful mirrour', because 'his characters are not modified by the customs of particular places', but 'act and speak by the influence of those general passions and principles by which all minds are agitated'.[8] That would do very well as a general account of opera.

John Hughes was quoted with approval by Johann Philipp Praetorius in the preface to his own *Calypso* of 1712.[9] Johann Friedrich Offenbach had it in 1757 that 'if the poet in his endeavour to put forward a narrative altogether naturally, strays so supernaturally against plausibility, this stands much more to his praise than to his discredit'.[10] Charles Henri Blainville admired the musician on the very grounds that 'he traces, without knowing it, the beauties which he scarcely understands: like a second Pythian, he falls into a frenzy, he speaks the language of the Gods'.[11] As I once more might put it, the language of the archetypes.

THE FRENCH DEPARTURE

Metastasio perfected the structured libretto of later baroque Italianate opera.[12] But for that French school[13] which ran so differently in parallel, Quinault set the literary pattern.[14] His libretto for Lully's *Amadis* (Paris, 1684) is a chivalric fantasy beneath which fairy-tale re-

**Example 7**

Lully, *Amadis* (Paris, 1684), Act I, scene iii. French recitative, still melodious by contrast with the much drier Italian recitative then evolving, but nevertheless also declamatory. The tritone at the cadence is as symbolically grievous as usual.

semblances to Ariosto and Tasso loom interestingly enough. In its own rather wordy manner it has considerable eloquence, and the music for it is extremely well and enjoyably matched to the many dramatic opportunities afforded. It is none of it so stiff or so formal as it might at first acquaintance be thought. French opera was a very worthy partner to Italian opera in the later baroque period.

We start in a dark wood resembling that *selva oscura* of Dante with which Quinault was assuredly familiar. The benevolent magicians Alquif and Urgande with their troupe are waking from an enchanted sleep, and compare Amadis to 'one still more renowned, still more glorious' —Louis XIV, of course, as he sat there drinking in the expected flattery. We shall need some courage to follow the elder Scotin's engravings after C. Gillot (Prunières's modern edition reproduces them) with those preposterous bustles and that fantastical headgear and the rest of the improbably classical pretensions of this extraordinary convention; but if we want the consistent flavour of it, that is, I suppose, pretty much what we shall have to do.

Act I has Amadis in person wandering through that strange wood to tell us: 'I love, alas; that is enough to make me unhappy'. For his Oriane, believing him unfaithful, is not only unhappy but angry. Florestan, not yet unhappy although he is soon going to be, assures his Corisande that 'if I had loved glory less, you would not have loved me so much'. Love and glory, as so often protagonists in French opera of the period, will in due course be reconciled, but not before providing the plot with some notable misadventures (ex. 7).

In Act II, Arcabonne presents us with a wicked sorceress (the complementary opposite to Urgande); and here too is her brother Arcaläus, who seeks to win glory by killing Amadis, who has killed another brother, Ardan. They retire as Amadis comes on to sing that most celebrated of Lully's airs, 'Bois épais': 'Gloomy wood, redouble your shadows; you cannot be too dense to hide my unhappy love'. And again we shall appreciate it that Quinault intended not merely a literal wood, but one whose shadows are of the spirit too. Corisande enters from the other side, lost and unhappy because her Florestan has been enticed to the rescue of a fraudulent damsel in distress. Amadis is all for going to his aid; Arcaläus brings up a ballet of demons to oppose him (fig. 5), unavailingly until they turn themselves cunningly into nymphs; but when one of these nymphs magically assumes Oriane's shape, Amadis wanders bemusedly off-stage after her, thus repeating Florestan's mistake without a moment's hesitation.

If, that is to say, it really is a mistake. So often in a fairy tale the wrong

5. *Act II of Lully's* Amadis, *as depicted by C. Gillot and engraved by the elder Scotin. The hero, seeking solace for his broken heart in the forest and fighting to aid his friends, is threatened by the evil enchanter Arcaläus and a pack of demons.*

choice turns out to be the right course, because it leads on into perils through which alone a way forward can be found. The present deception looks to me very like what happens to a man who follows a pretty face regardless of consequence or suitability. It is not that the girl may not be worth following: very likely she is. The deception is that she offers such bliss and such fascination as only a projected fantasy can—however deceptively—promise. For then she is standing in for the alluring aspect of the eternal feminine, the dangerous opposite of which is the ensnaring aspect. And the danger is precisely that the fantasy may get so damnably in the way of the reality. As in all such cases, the remedy is to distinguish the woman who may be loved from the archetype which is so liable to be projected. Most human love-relationships do of course go through a stage of considerable mutual projection, which is perfectly natural provided that it remains within reasonable limits, yielding gradually to a shared understanding through which love can truly prosper.

Ariosto or Tasso might have intended some such implications Neoplatonically; Quinault almost certainly not, in spite of his membership since 1674 in the Académie des Inscriptions et Belles Lettres, the body responsible for overseeing the symbolical correctness of court productions. He probably regarded this pivotal scene just as very good theatre, which it is. But its archetypal resonance may still be echoing autonomously through.

In Act III, Arcabonne floats in through the air to assure an eloquent half-chorus of prisoners (the other half being their jailers) of a speedy release in death. But now, in a bass air of superb underworldly power, brother Ardan rises from his tomb to rebuke Arcabonne, 'false sister', for betraying him. She cannot make him out at all, and neither can we, until suddenly Amadis is thrown onto the stage in chains. In Amadis, Arcabonne recognizes the stranger who, in rescuing her previously from one of those troublesome serpent-dragons, had won her heart, but who as it now appears was also Ardan's slayer. So of course she cannot kill him, as Ardan's ghost percipiently foresaw. Instead, she offers Amadis any boon; and he asks for the prisoners to be released. Out they all pour joyfully in dance and song (ex. 8), rather touchingly like the prisoners in *Fidelio*; but Amadis alone remains captive, having I suspect to undergo

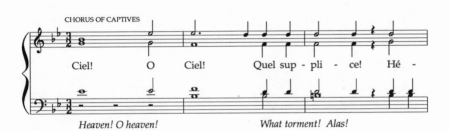

**Example 8**

Lully, *Amadis*, Act III, scenes i–ii. The prison scene: typical French chorus, broad and seemingly (not really) obvious, but with excellent word setting and expressive harmony, reminding me of Carissimi.

(a)

Thy hand, Be-lin-da; dark- - - - - - -ness shades    me; on thy

bo - - som    let me    rest;    more I would__ but Death__ in-

vades me:    Death    is    now    a wel - -come__ guest.

**Example 9**

Purcell, *Dido and Aeneas* (London, 1689). (a) The free and idiosyncratic English recitative, less declamatory than affecting; (b) the
famous lament with the ostinato bass pulling against its emotive
harmonies as if bringing grievous emotion under resolute control:
a symbolical ambivalence which adds profoundly to the beauty of
this justly celebrated scene.

(b)

When I am laid,___ am laid___ in earth, may my wrongs___ cre-ate no trou--ble, no trou-ble in thy breast.

some further symbolical working out before he can really get free. He does, though not through any overt exertions of his own.

What sets matters right is the timely intervention of Urgande, the benevolent enchantress. 'Without anyone knowing where I am, I journey through the world: take care, take care to know Urgande, know and accept'. Something deep in the psyche can guide us if we can somehow open ourselves to the benevolent promptings of which the unconscious is capable when things are going at all well with us. The chorus beautifully responds: 'Understand what has happened, our choice will be right'. We found this ending very moving when the opera department of the University of Iowa mounted my realization of this splendid opera. It was as if we also were being invited to know and accept.

### THE ENGLISH SCENE

English opera should have burgeoned after Blow and Purcell. What an ending to *Dido and Aeneas* (London, 1689), as Dido (like Norma after her, and Brünnhilde) voluntarily mounts her own funeral pyre as if for some uncovenanted transformation through the flames (ex. 9). But English opera was overlaid by Italian opera, imported or, in the case of Handel, domestic. Handel's *Semele* (London, 1744), though not altogether typical, will serve my present purpose very well. 'Not of course an oratorio but an opera', wrote Winton Dean; and indeed it was for Eccles's unperformed opera that Congreve actually wrote this highly mythological libretto.[15]

So here is Semele snatched up, to a rising surge of strings, by an eagle who either is or represents Jove, her celestial lover, and 'endless pleasure, endless love' thereafter 'enjoys above'. Yes, but what is this if not the deceptive glades of Arcadia over again? There is no real future in it. Jealous Juno at all events soon intervenes to break it up. At her contriving Jove, on being sent an erotic dream of Semele, offers her any boon to induce her to embrace him; and thunder is heard on solo timpani to confirm his solemn oath. 'Then cast off this human shape you wear, and since Jove you are, as Jove too appear!' To an accompaniment of rushing scales, he warns her, not even taking time for his da capo repeat; but she in full confidence embarks on long roulades. 'For I'll know what you are', she insists. And there of course we have it. She has to know.

It was Thomas Mann who noticed that Semele's having to know and Elsa's having to ask are one and the same symbolical mythologem.[16] For in *Lohengrin* too the issue is that clinging to blissful fantasy is what we

**Example 10**

Handel, *Semele* (London, 1744), Act I, scene viii. Ino confesses her passion in typical declamatory, late baroque, Italianate recitative.

think we want, but what we really want, if only we can know and accept our innermost need, is to move on towards more independence, more responsibility, more awareness of our own real value in greater maturity and consciousness. But new knowledge on such a level can feel uncommonly painful, because of the drastic shifts in our habitual attitudes it may entail. When Semele sees 'Jupiter descending in a cloud', she sings in terror, 'I burn, I faint, for pity I implore', whereupon 'the cloud bursts, and Semele with the palace instantly disappears'. Ino, reporting this, adds that 'Jove ordain'd I Athamas should wed', which takes care of the human end of the situation (ex. 10); while 'a bright cloud descends' from which 'Apollo, seated in it as the God of Prophecy', and supported by a brilliant symphony with oboes doubling the violins, promises that

> from Semele's ashes a phoenix shall arise,
> The joy of this earth, and delight of the skies:
> A God he shall prove more mighty than Love,
> And sighing and sorrow for ever prevent.

He is in fact alluding to the birth of Bacchus.

The chorus rather cleverly pick him up, putting it that Bacchus 'shall crown the joys of love'. Congreve, however, would certainly have known, and Handel might very probably have known, that there is more to Bacchus than the mere pleasures and hazards of alcohol: Bacchus who was twice born (once from Semele's flames and again from Jove's thigh after being hidden there from Juno's anger); Bacchus who presently took Semele to heaven to share with Ariadne herself that immortality she had so ardently desired, thus turning yet again an erotic fantasy into an archetypal image. It is rather interestingly on record that Congreve possessed a copy of Conti's *Mythologiae*.[17] But all I am suggesting here is that Handel's choral rejoicings sound numinous, as if the birth of Bacchus really matters. Now Handel is Handel, and has indeed his own numinosity; but the mythological context does perhaps add its usual subliminal bonus. A myth arises from something in us which cannot just have gone away, but may still be contributing to each new embodiment its own ineffable aura of rightness. The symbolism here has basically to do with renewal: Bacchus (or Dionysus) is repeatedly reborn and is forever young. And golden-haired Apollo should surely descend in a cloud machine to hold our eyes with all proper radiance, confirming everything that the chorus is meanwhile putting so joyfully into song.

Oh, but I was forgetting that this is officially an oratorio. Not bad going for oratorio. Not bad going for the Age of Reason.

## A BALANCED VISION

For Diderot, 'In the degree to which the mind gains more enlightenment, the heart gains more sensibility'—a very balanced vision of the possibilities.[1] For Algarotti, as for Dryden, 'the intervention of supernatural beings' can give 'an air of probability to the most surprising events' and justify the presence of music as a result of 'every circumstance being thus raised above the level of mortal existence'.[2] For Schiller, it was in opera that 'one truly lets go of that slavish naturalism', relying upon 'the power of music' to justify 'the supernatural through the power of feeling'; while Goethe insisted that 'the more impossible a work of poetry is for reason to assimilate, the better'.[3]

Gluck was thus well in tune with his age when he prescribed, in the famous preface to his *Alceste* of 1767, 'a beautiful simplicity', having already to perfection exemplified it in his noble 'Che farò senza Euridice?' (ex. 11).[4] Yet Boyé was justified in pointing out that the lovely tune would have gone still better to cheerful than it does to melancholy words.[5] The music opens our hearts not because it arouses the emotion of grief in particular but because it arouses emotion in general. On the other hand, Gluck achieved a very specific musical symbol with that frequently admired scene in his *Iphigénie en Tauride* (Paris, 1779) where Orestes is assuring us that he is perfectly all right, perfectly calm, while the syncopated rhythm in the viola part is telling us that, on the contrary, his heart is beating furiously and that without admitting it to himself he is very agitated indeed (ex. 12).[6]

## RECONCILIATION IN MOZART

But the greatest of his age, and one of the greatest in any age, was Mozart.[7] So often, to my delight, his theme is reconciliation: in *Idomeneo* (Munich, 1781),[8] for example, and in *The Abduction from the*

(a)

Chorus

Ah!Se in - tor-no

*Ah! if around*

(b)

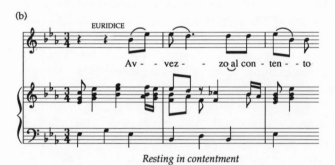

EURIDICE

Av - - vez - - zo al con - ten - - to

*Resting in contentment*

(c) ORPHEUS

Che fa - rò sen-za Eu - ri - di - ce,    do-ve an - drò__ sen-za il mio    ben?__

*What to do without Euridice,      where to go without my love?*

## Example 11

Gluck, *Orfeo ed Euridice* (Vienna, 1762). The big tune (a) anticipated by orchestra and chorus at the start of Act I; (b) evoked in passing by Euridice; (c) achieved by Orfeo in Act III, scene i.

**Example 12**

Gluck, *Iphigénie en Tauride* (Paris, 1779). The famous double-take in Act II.

*Seraglio* (Vienna, 1782), where even wicked Osmin's music 'must never distress the ear';[9] rather flippantly in *Così fan tutte* (Vienna, 1790); but compassionately, above all, in *The Marriage of Figaro* (Vienna, 1786),[10] with the Countess forgiving her erring Count so that one more untoward adventure shall end movingly in reconciliation (ex. 13).[11]

Don Giovanni's problem, on the other hand, is his stony-heartedness, masquerading as passion.[12] It was Shaw who reminded us that Don Juan is not really the man who has possessed many women but the man who has never possessed any woman, being too narcissistic to relate

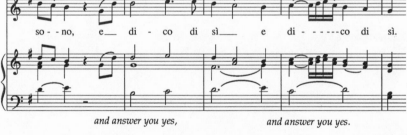

## Example 13

Mozart, *The Marriage of Figaro* (Vienna, 1786). The forgiveness which
leads to reconciliation at the end.

to any. Those whose early fathering and mothering were warm enough
are not so liable to this eternally unavailing search: an actual woman
may suffice, not having to compete so disadvantageously with an unconsciously idealized mother-image; nor need she evoke the mortal fears
which are the obverse of that fatal fascination. For you cannot miss it
that your Don Juan runs no harder after the next woman than he runs
away from the last, especially if she begins to look like threatening his
well-tried defences. As Donna Elvira with her real fidelity and her real
feeling, might look like threatening Don Giovanni's defences by push-
ing his projections and his fantasies aside and letting real life in. And
that, I think, may be why he fights her off so cruelly.

In one earlier example of the legend, there is a typical libertine who
decides nonetheless to marry. As he makes his way to the church to set
up his wedding banns, he stumbles upon a corpse, who regards him
most evilly. Crying 'evil, evil', the hero kicks disdainfully at the corpse,
who bites his foot as if to start eating him; but the hero asks him, if he
is so hungry, to come to the wedding feast. The corpse not only accepts
but returns the invitation for the following midnight. The hero next
meets with an old beggar in the porch of the church and, taking pity
on him, gives him his cloak and his money. The corpse shows up again
to explain that by this act of spontaneous feeling the hero has indeed
saved himself from being devoured alive.

A more sophisticated and literary version was the very well known
and very fine poetical drama of 1630 El burlador de Sevilla, by Tirso de
Molina. Here Christian morality prevails: Don Juan has no doubts of
his own irrevocable damnation, but wins our admiration by his courageous refusal to become anything other than his true reprobate self.
There is a stone statue so revengeful that he will not even grant Don
Juan's request to see a priest in his last moments. All the same, it was
an interesting impulse, coming from so dissolute a character. Breaking
into a hot sweat and a cold fear all at once, he cries: 'My heart inside me
is ice'; but he feels already the pangs of the eternal fire. His icy heart is
not going to stand up to that.

In the Age of Reason, the comic potentialities of the story took prece-
dence, though Molière's free adaptation of 1665 stressed very characteristically the hypocrisy of a recanting Don Juan whose cowardice in
so doing, by a nice touch of irony, is presented as worse morally than
all his previous immoralities. Of many eighteenth-century operas on
the subject, Giuseppe Gazzaniga's Don Giovanni Tenorio (Venice, 1787) is
known to have influenced Da Ponte and Mozart. The difference is that
with Da Ponte and Mozart we do not only laugh.

'Women of every rank', Leporello's preposterous catalogue informs us, 'fat or thin, tall for majesty, small for prettiness, old women for the list's sake, poor girl, rich girl, ugly girl, lovely girl, so long as she's a skirt, you know what happens!' That does not sound like romance. It does sound like compulsion. But at last in the graveyard Don Giovanni shocks that faithful Leporello by boasting of his dealings with Leporello's own woman. And then as the moon breaks through, the statue intervenes: 'Your laughter will end before the dawn', he sings to his imposing trombones, traditional in their associations with the underworld. 'Who spoke?' asks Don Giovanni, understandably startled. 'Ah!' Leporello answers with instant comprehension, 'that must be some spirit from the other world, who knows you from the bottom!'

From the bottom is right. At bottom Don Giovanni is in a bad way, having squandered so much of his true manhood on his unfeeling philanderings. With the extraordinary intuitiveness of legend, and quite ferocious courage, he now stops running away from himself. He asks that man of stone to supper. It may be that at last he is confronting his own stoniness and is even preparing to come to terms with it.

At supper, Donna Elvira breaks in to warn Don Giovanni, who will

**Example 14**

Mozart, *Don Giovanni* (Prague, 1787). Start of the overture, with the massive rhythms and eerie harmonies for the statue, heard subsequently as that 'man of stone' makes his formidable appearance: not quite a leitmotif, but certainly a theme of musical identification and recognition.

6. The icy handshake of the Commendatore's statue consigns the paradoxically loveless philanderer Don Giovanni to his doom. This illustration adorned the title page of the first edition of Mozart's opera, published in 1801.

not be warned; but we are deeply touched if he is not. For, as Leporello puts it straight out, 'he has a heart of stone'. Then in stumps the statue, that other 'man of stone', called such by Leporello as if to make yet clearer the connection we should surely have seen for ourselves by now (ex. 14). Refusing the earthly nourishment of which he has no need, the statue invites Don Giovanni in return to some unearthly nourishment of the spirit. No sooner has he grasped the statue's hand than Don Giovanni feels unmistakably that mortal cold which has always been his unknown enemy (fig. 6). He cannot let go, and down he goes, with full benefit (as I hope) of an old-fashioned trapdoor, and lurid, flaming lights in token of the consuming fire—which may also, on my interpretation, be the transforming fire.

No very obvious sign of reconciliation here. But I am not the first to have noticed that Don Giovanni left no trace of his body behind him, almost as if he might be going to need it again. Rather oddly in these presumably Christian circumstances, the other characters now commit him to the pagan company of 'Persephone and Pluto', in that mythological underworld to which other heroes have descended, returning with some token treasure of new understanding. New understanding for Don Giovanni would be the knowledge that a man of stone is a man of nothing, and that in human relationships, feeling is all. I only hope he may get through to that.

## THE ARCHETYPAL PHILANDERER

Ostensibly, of course, Don Giovanni is damned for ever, and serve him right too for all those sexual misdemeanours. Or so they say. But if sex is damnable, then we are most of us damned. I do not take that view. What may really have brought Don Giovanni down was not his genuine sexuality so much as that element in it which was not genuine at all, but was merely the deprived mother's boy seeking obsessively for the ultimate satisfaction never to be attained, since a baby may or may not enjoy blissful union with mother, but a grown man never.

Nonetheless, that is part of the fantasy which the unconscious may so often weave around our sexual desires, and so long as it remains within normal limits, it should do no harm. It is probably, in fact, a necessary ingredient. But if it colours too insidiously the whole experience, then it may drive a man on into sexual adventures which are the more repetitive in proportion as they are less the outcome of real feeling. It is a common complaint. Recovering from it would be tantamount to a rebirth from the deep abyss, but that does not very often happen, and Don Juan will always stand for the illusory glamour and the manic obsession which are the chronic symptoms of the disease. Da Ponte and Mozart have made a wonderful story of it, and all the better in that our sympathies are so deliciously divided between the leading characters. Are we for Don Giovanni or are we against him? On the whole, undoubtedly we are for him. But he is a pretty troublesome sort of a scallywag all the same, and really not much less cruel than he is courageous. He stands, however, for something incontestably archetypal. That is perhaps his ultimate recommendation.

Many other interpretations, both plausible and bizarre, have been advanced for this extraordinary opera, and for an excellent survey of them, I recommend Rushton (1981). But I feel sure at least that *Don Giovanni* is neither so obvious nor so cynical an opera as it might outwardly appear. As to *Così fan tutte*, I am not quite so positive. I can see that the main relationships could have been more real after than before the satisfactory forgiveness and the characteristic reconciliation. The opera includes some very beautiful music. But no: it is not so touching, nor so compact nor so funny as *Figaro*, nor in any way so searching as *The Magic Flute* which followed it.

THE SEARCH FOR INITIATION

The Magic Flute (Vienna, 1791) is not only a Masonic parable.[1] It
is also in more general terms a prolonged symbolization, in part deliberate and in part intuitive, of that search for wholeness which is so
commonly furthered by ceremonies of initiation and instances of the
sacred marriage throughout the mythological and ritualistic traditions
of our race (fig. 7). It reminds me a little of Pico della Mirandola describing the Orphic Hymns as in appearance 'the merest fables and trifles' for
the good reason that 'divine matters, when written about at all, must be
covered beneath enigmatic veils and poetical dissimulations'.[2] Edward
Dent evidently overlooked this possibility when he called The Magic Flute
'one of the most absurd specimens of that form of literature in which
absurdity is only too often a matter of course'.[3] But Koenigsberger more
perceptively saw here 'a quest of the human soul for both inner harmony and enlightenment', by characters who are 'joint participants in
one being, one psyche or one soul'.[4] That is absolutely right. But in
actual practice it is of course the music which is transporting us to such
hidden depths. No one would be bothering much about Schikaneder if
it were not for Mozart.

We must start by noticing the traditionally and Masonically masculine symbolism of the number three.[5] It appears very prominently in
the music (ex. 15). Tamino, our princely hero, enters carrying a bow,
but 'without an arrow', which in this context probably suggests that
although potentially he is very much of a man, his manhood is by no
means in his effectual possession as yet, and in fact it is going to take
him most of the rest of the opera to acquire it. 'A serpent follows him',
one of those formidable snake-dragons who so often seem to stand in
mythology for some obstructive force of inner resistance and inertia
needing to be overcome, as the Python was overcome by golden-haired
Apollo. Wagner's Siegfried manages his own dragon; but then Siegfried

7. Masonic symbols abound in this imaginary scene by Ignaz Alberti from Mozart's Magic Flute, which appeared in the first (1791) edition of the libretto.

(a)   Adagio

(b)   Allegro

Zu  hil - fe!  Zu hil - fe!  Sonst  bin   ich  ver - lo - ren!

*Oh, help me!   Oh, help me!      Or I shall be lost !*

## Example 15

Mozart, *The Magic Flute* (Vienna, 1791). The triadic motive of three chords, (a) making its immediate and massive impact at the start of the overture; (b) thinned down and despondently in the minor as Tamino cries for help; (c) fleetingly, but recognizably, as the Queen of Night reassures her 'dearest son'; (d) firmly as she sets off in her great aria following; (e) with chromatic distortion as Tamino is turned back from the wrong choice of temple door; (f) diatonically impressive again (and with a numinous modulation) when the priest questions him at the right door; (g) triumphantly in full harmony and bright C major as the chorus greets Sarastro; (h) innocently from the orchestra as Pamina submits herself to him; (i) as the full threefold chord at the turning point of the ceremony; (j) in further triumph from the chorus; (k) yet more radiantly for the final rejoicings. And if that is not quite in Wagner's sense a leitmotif (since it forms no part of a symphonic development), it is certainly coming very near to behaving like one.

(c)  Queen of Night

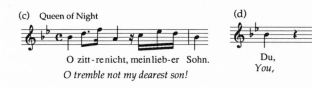

O zitt - re nicht, mein lieb-er  Sohn.
*O tremble not my dearest son!*

(d)

Du,        du,        du
*You,*      *You,*      *You,*

(e)

Priest                    Tamino

Zu - rück!        Zu - rück?        Zu - rück?

*Go back!*        *Go back?*        *Go back?*

(f)

Priest

Wo willst du, kühn-er  Fremd-ling hin?

*Bold stranger, where would you go?*

(g)  Chorus

Es    le - be  Sa-ras - tro,  Sa-ras - tro

*Long life to Sarastro!*

Example 15 continued

(h)

(i)

(j)    Chorus

Tri - umph!    Tri-umph!    Tri - umph!

Tri - umph!

(k)

by that time has forged his own manhood, under token of the sword. Tamino has not yet got as far as that, and he has every reason to cry out for help, on the very motive of the thrice-repeated chord: but in distressful C minor, frightened as he quite reasonably is, and lacking any means by which to defend himself. And so he temporarily abnegates responsibility for himself by fainting away. Quite properly, it seems; for at once from the nearby temple door 'three veiled ladies come out, each with a silver javelin'. And with those three silver weapons, at three jabs from the orchestra, they strike that serpent into three (sic) pieces, having just sung a sort of melodic inversion of the triple triad. We are not, it seems, to be left in any doubt about the symbol. Three.

But three is for masculinity. It seems the young fellow has had to be started on his way towards finding his own masculinity by the very agents of femininity, since the three ladies have certainly been sent by the Queen of Night, and their silver javelins are of her very own moon-metal. She must at bottom want him to grow up. But there is no real difficulty of interpretation about that. She is very much in the role of the good mother-goddess here, and a good mother does push the boy-child off in the manly direction he will have to take if anything worthwhile is to become of him. After all, we do all start from mother, however pressing our need may later be to get away from her.

There is a sense in which initiation always is, as it certainly appears to be here, a movement away from the instinct-world of the mothers towards the spirit-world of the fathers. Goethe's Faust had to make the dangerous underworld journey 'to the mothers' before he could come up with Helen in token of increased consciousness and maturity; for however desirable Helen of Troy may have been in bed, and no doubt she was, that was not for Goethe the main purpose of her symbolism. Much rather was she a stage along the way to that most famous of last lines which (like Wagner) I am so fond of quoting: 'The eternal feminine draws us on.' And so it already appears to be happening to Tamino here.

## STARTING FROM THE MOTHER

As so often in these stories of initiation, we find that a secondary couple is going to be involved, who will not be tested so hard nor arrive so far, but for whom the simpler qualities and the more limited adventures may very well suffice. Here comes Papageno in the feathery livery of the Queen of Night, whose bird-catcher he says he is, with a further hint at her mythological stature, since the Great Mother in her many manifestations is commonly attended by birds. Tamino, recovering, is both surprised and relieved to find the grim serpent dead. 'Is it a fantasy [Phantasie] that I am still alive?' Well, it is certainly a fantasy, though not quite in the sense he intends. Now Papageno thinks it safe to boast that it was he who with his bare hands killed that serpent, which brings back the three ladies to punish him for the lie with a padlock on his lips.

When Loki had his lips sewn up by the Nordic gods, it was for telling not a lie but an unwelcome truth—and true at least it is that the Queen's party is taking on all the action so far. It is the three ladies who now show Tamino the miniature of Pamina, the Queen's own daughter, and draw him on indeed with the promise of 'joy, honour and glory' in reward for rescuing her from 'a wicked demon'. He finds her 'bewitchingly [bezaubernd] beautiful', a 'divine image [Götterbild]', words which suggest something not just attractive but numinous, as of course she will be in channelling for him his image of femininity in addition to complementing him in his mating instincts. Sarastro is denounced as the 'wicked demon' because he has parted Pamina from her mother; but in that he has only been preparing what Tamino himself will have to complete. You can on one level call it separating the image of femininity from the mother-image in which we necessarily first see it. Growing away from mother is part of a man's normal development, and is a necessary stage towards finding a mate who is not just mother's image projected. Neither is she the eternal feminine projected; but that is a distinction which comes later on.

Now, to the sound of thunder, the mountains open (and they must really be seen to open) to show us just how numinous a figure is the Queen of Night herself. Papageno repeatedly calls her 'star-flaming'; her robe, her throne, according to the stage directions, and probably the very heavens behind her are to be seen ablaze with stars. For so, too, was Isis called 'star-crown of Ra-Horus' and 'Queen of the Dekan stars': she whose robe Apuleius had once pictured with 'scattered sparkling stars'. Always, I think, she is in essence that Great Mother of a thousand names. Her sign is positive in this portion of the opera. Later on, her sign will be negative. What of it? The Queen of Night is an archetypal image, and all archetypes are ambivalent, showing now a creative and now a destructive aspect of the same mythologem. Human nature is ambivalent, and all our fabled images for human nature are ambivalent or are paired with complementary opposites which show the other side of them.

What could be more numinous than soaring to high F (two octaves and a fourth above middle C) in that magical coloratura? But it was on an outline of the triadic motive, in B-flat major, that the Queen has bidden Tamino to 'tremble not, my beloved son' (she must mean it symbolically since she cannot mean it biologically here): 'trust a mother's heart' (which for the time being is right enough, since the quest on which she sends him is necessary to his own development). More thunder, and the mountains close over her again. She has evidently some chthonic attributes, connecting her with the underworld as well as with the night. Her resemblance to Hecate rather than to Isis grows stronger, in fact, as the opera proceeds, with all that implies of dark counsels and darker doings. We shall not see so much of her star-flaming radiance at that later stage.

But here and now, it is she, the Queen, who has sent her own three ladies to bring, as her present to Tamino, that very 'magic flute' from which the opera takes its name. The flute is here described as golden (the sun-metal), though later as oaken (the father-tree). It was left with the Queen by Sarastro, I think in token of the manhood which Tamino must inherit through her before he can make it his own; whereas Papageno gets a set of silver bells (the moon-metal). Is Sarastro then such a 'wicked demon'? Of course he is not, but he too is an archetype and ambivalent. His dark shadow perhaps appears symbolically in his black servant, Monostatos, who shows us something of his quality now by getting Pamina alone with the worst possible intentions. But just at that moment Papageno turns up: and since he has never seen a black man before, nor Monostatos a feathered man, each takes the other for the devil in person and runs away.

Papageno returns, having found Pamina. In his role as Tamino's other self, he now has her portrait, which he checks point by point against her lovely person. And surely her role as heroine is to represent Tamino's femininity, the other side of his masculinity as hero. On this level they are complementary aspects of each other, and like the two halves of a divided token are waiting to be united within the single psyche for which their love story is indicative. But that does not make us any the less sympathetic to their love story. On the contrary, it increases our sense of archetypal identification and human concern alike.

Next there is a change of scene (there are a great many changes of scene) and 'the theatre transforms itself into a wood'. Three spirit-boys lead Tamino in, each having 'a silver palm-branch in his hand'. We have been expecting them ever since the three ladies promised our pair of heroes the help of three 'wise' boys, almost as if in hermaphroditic polarity with themselves. 'Be a man', the three boys encourage Tamino, 'and you will conquer manfully'. They do not tell him where to find Pamina, but they are evoking the manliness in him through which he may find her.

MOVING TOWARDS THE FATHER

Three temple doors. On the right: 'Temple of Reason', but an unseen guardian warns Tamino back. On the left: 'Temple of Nature'; same result. The third and central door, as if combining Reason and Nature in one balanced symbol, is inscribed 'Temple of Wisdom', and here an old priest appears, backed by the familiar three chords, but rebuffs Tamino 'while death and vengeance inflame you'. Alone again, Tamino shows his Masonic background (his ultimately Neoplatonic background) by exclaiming: 'Oh, eternal night! When will you lessen? When will my eyes find the light?' Voices within assure him: 'Soon, soon, youngster, or never'. But they also reply to him no less quietly that 'Pamina, Pamina still lives'.

In delight, he bethinks him of his flute, and just as if he were Orpheus, 'wild beasts of every kind come out to hear him'. Yes, 'but only Pamina keeps away!' Now there is an answering signal from Papageno's pan-pipes. He has Pamina with him; but Tamino in his eagerness just misses them; and next Monostatos and the three black slaves loom up. They, too, are sent innocuously dancing off by the sound of Papageno's bells —in symmetry, you might say, with Tamino's flute. It is all at present rather oddly hit-or-miss; but not for much longer now.

A 'strong march with trumpets and drums' and a full chorus are heard 'from within'. The very sound of them somehow resolves Pamina to tell the truth to Sarastro. And on he comes at last, with his train of atten-dants, in a triumphal car drawn by six lions—twice three lions—while the ascending three chords ring out in bright C major from the chorus. Pamina kneels to him, but on the same triadic outline, in G major, he raises her up: 'Without first pressing to the bottom of you, I know more of your heart: you greatly love another'. Then, almost as if, like Hans Sachs, he might have wished it otherwise: 'I will not compel you to love'—yet 'I do not give you freedom'. It would not yet be freedom if he did. She starts: 'My filial duty calls me, for my mother——'; but he breaks in: 'You would have been defrauded of your destiny if I had left you in her hands', for 'a man must guide your heart'. Not, I hope, merely as an antifeminist sentiment, but as an acknowledgement that in this present context of initiation, a woman needs to find her own quota of inner masculinity no less than a man needs to find his own quota of inner femininity.

Tamino is brought in by that egregious Monostatos, who expects re-ward for his hypocritical services but receives instead punishment for his odious stratagem. So our destined couple are at last together. But Sarastro, stern only to be kind, and ascending in G major the usual triad, ordains that 'they must first be purified'.

Act II adds to the orchestra a pair of Mozart's favourite basset horns, which he seems to have associated particularly with Masonic occasions. 'The theatre is a palm-wood, all the trees are silvery, the leaves of gold'. And a yet more solemn version is heard, on wind and brass, of the triadic opening adagio of the opera, here in B-flat, and entitled 'der drei-malige Akkord,' the thrice-repeated chord. Sarastro introduces Tamino as a candidate, blowing three times on his horn and naming Pamina as destined for him by the gods. All show approval by repeating on their horns the thrice-repeated chord, as the stage directions, although not the score, request. The Speaker asks whether Tamino can be expected to survive the ordeal without disaster, adding in his favour: 'He is a Prince'. But true spokesman for the Enlightenment as he is, Sarastro replies: 'Yet more, he is a man'.

After Sarastro and the chorus have sent up a prayer to Isis and Osiris on behalf of the young couple (including yet another 'dreimaliger Ak-kord'), the scene changes to a courtyard by night. Tamino and (to our surprise) Papageno are first unveiled and left in the dark; it thunders three times and each time louder; the Speaker returns with another priest. 'Prince, there is still time to go back—one step farther, and it is too late'. Tamino is resolute. Papageno is not resolute, but is persuaded to chance it by the prospect of a mate after his own kind if all goes well. They must not speak, for 'this is the beginning of the testing time', and I suppose this means that the greatest inner concentration is essen-tial. The priests duet about the wiliness of women; and no sooner have they left, taking their torches with them, than those wily three ladies (but at least they bring back torches) lose no time in telling our brave ones that they are as good as dead. Thunder and lightning, then twice again strong thunder, followed by the 'dreimaliger Akkord' (again in the stage direction only, but no doubt to the same music as so often previously). Down to hell the frustrated ladies go; in come the Speaker and his priestly companion to replace the veils; and the scene changes to a garden, with Pamina asleep, alone.

So Monostatos steals in to have another go. The Queen of Night pops out in front of him, with the usual thunder, from 'the middle trapdoor' (out of three?); gives Pamina a dagger 'sharpened for Sarastro'; and over-rules her protest with the second of those coloratura arias (high F again) which make the Queen herself so unforgettable a personage. She descends; Monostatos is there on the instant to try once more and does get hold of the dagger, but the poor fellow never really has any luck. Sarastro appears from nowhere and thrusts him back.

And we have a good laugh; and Sarastro merely tells Monostatos that since his soul is as black as his face, he had better be off; so, baulked of the daughter, he decides to have a try for the mother. But though I laugh, I feel a shade uneasy too. There was that Set, the dark brother who killed Osiris and his son Horus and tried to possess too his sister-bride Isis: the slain deities were resurrected, but humanity still has its dark side, and in this Egyptian context, I get the slightest shiver down my spine even at this clumsy villain. It can only be to the advantage of the drama, I think, if the singer can give Monostatos just a hint of some such menace behind the fooling. But now Sarastro comforts Pamina a little, though not very much; and they go off together.

So the scene changes. When Papageno craves water, it is brought to him by an apparently ancient hag who announces herself as his sweetheart Papagena, aged 'eighteen years and two minutes' (which he cannot as yet accept). But the three boys promise that when they are seen for the third time, joy will be the reward of courage. And they restore the flute and the bells, besides conjuring up a magical feast. Tamino flutes. Papageno feasts. In answer to the flute, Pamina comes; but Tamino will not speak because of his vow, and Papageno cannot because his mouth is full. She despairs in an aria of haunting sadness, and goes off to seek release in death.

Three drum calls, thrice repeated, have Papageno protesting that not even Sarastro's six lions could drag him from the table; so the six lions appear; so they are tamed by Tamino's flute; so the scene changes. And dizzy though any self-respecting director must be getting by now, he has got to do something imaginative about all these changes, however swiftly with lighting and projections and some modicum of stage machinery. The original audiences expected it and enjoyed it. After all, we are at the pantomime, however high-class, and we too should be in position to enjoy the fact.

On the inside now of a great pyramid, the chorus praises Isis and Osiris and the rays of the sun which drive gloomy night away. In the dark again, Papageno is forgiven for his pusillanimity, but told quite reasonably that he will never attain to heavenly delight. He has never wanted to; but he would like just a glass of wine. It arrives magically, you might almost say ritually, and makes him want . . . want . . . his bells tell him . . . to be blessed with a wife! And suddenly the old hag comes back, but this time he accepts her, and at once she is the young, the beautiful, the one and only Papagena. Yet for the moment, she is snatched away again, and the scene changes!

## THROUGH INITIATION TO INTEGRATION

We see a garden, the three boys, and Pamina well and truly lost; but they save her from suicide by promising her that Tamino loves her still. The scene changes into two mountains, one with a waterfall, the other with fire. Two armed men (unknown to us, but evidently on the father side of things) lead Tamino on, within sight of a pyramid raised high up in the middle. They warn him most solemnly in octaves, supported by the grandest of counterpoint in the orchestra; but their tune (though not their text) is that familiar chorale 'Ach Gott, von Himmel sich darein', to which the three trombones add their last touch of solemnity. It is one of the most impressive scenes in this or any other opera (fig. 8). The warning is that the ordeal by fire, water, air and earth, to be undergone for initiation into the mysteries of Isis, can be entered

8. *A wild, romantic landscape provided the setting for Tamino and Pamina's trial by fire, water, air and earth in Simon Quaglio's design for* The Magic Flute *in Munich, 1818.*

only at the risk of death. Tamino assents, and may now speak to Pamina as she too is brought in. The music (curiously innocent) which he plays on his flute protects them, through the waterfall and the fire and the howling of the wind and the echoing of thunder in the caverns. The couple come through safely, with a short duet and a renewal of the flute playing and more duetting as a door opens for them. The full orchestra and chorus greet them: 'Triumph, triumph, noble pair', and into the temple of Isis they disappear, the triadic theme pervading the chorus in bold C major.

But just as we are expecting the climax of the ceremony, the scene changes back to the garden as before. Of course, this can be regarded as fine theatrical contrast in preparation for the grand finale; but I have never myself quite been able to avoid some passing irritation at yet one more unanticipated delay. It is the long though admittedly very funny scene in which Papageno continually attempts—and as continually postpones—the suicide by hanging to which the loss of Papagena is supposed to be impelling him (not that we ever really think that he will). He pipes hopefully just once, twice, three times more. Those inspired three boys then fly down to tell him to have more sense, we only live once, so 'let your bells ring, that will bring your woman back'. And to that lovely glockenspiel shimmering, supported by woodwind, off fly the three boys in their stage machine to bring Papagena back.

Is it my imagination that Mozart's heart went out to this naive and secondary couple here with especial sympathy? Their pretty, innocent, sentimental scene as each recognizes in the other their very own inwardness, appeals, perhaps, to the child in each of us: 'the buoyant child surviving in the man', as Coleridge had it so beautifully.[6] Long live the child! Still more so do those three boys appeal, triple embodiments as I suggest of the mythical *puer aeternus*, the eternal boy, and trailing clouds of glory as that lovely image always does. In so many ways, The Magic Flute is an innocent entertainment; but innocence transcended, as it was given to Mozart above all other composers to convey.

Off go the innocents. Up come the adversaries: Monostatos, the Queen and the three ladies, all with 'black torches'. Monostatos now insists on having the Queen's word that her daughter shall be his wife. She gives it, upon which the unseen realms comment sardonically with 'rumbling thunder and the sound of water'. But even as the conspirators encourage one another with further boastful menaces, 'the strongest chord is heard; thunder, lightning, storm. At once the whole theatre is transformed into a sun. Sarastro stands raised up; Tamino, Pamina, both in priestly garments. Near them the Egyptian priests on both sides. The three boys carry flowers'.

Immediately the adversaries succumb, singing: 'Broken, broken is our might; we are all of us fallen into everlasting night!' Which, we quite appreciate, is where they properly belong. But what are these dark forces which can erupt or subside, but assuredly never lose their perennial ability to harm or to heal? Are they not a mythological recognition of our own unconscious, where primitive instinct jostles with human potentiality, where infantile retrogressiveness tangles with the urge to grow, where goodness and wickedness and destruction and creation fight it out before welling up to condition the very inwardness of our deeds and our characters? And when Sarastro sings now that 'the rays of the sun dispel the night', is not this the oldest of images for the consciousness which sets us apart from other animals, aware as we are of mortality, capable of reason, and even in our unreason dimly acquainted with what we are and what we do? Did not Apuleius the Platonist, back in the second century, have his Lucius (himself, really) describe his own comparable initiation into the mysteries of Isis as taking him 'close to the boundaries of death', where he saw 'the sun gleaming with bright splendour at the dead of night'?

And so, as the chorus praises Isis for the feminine numinosity, and Osiris for the masculine, in this doubtless Masonic but also self-evident victory of 'beauty and wisdom', I do not think that we could miss such transparent imagery for illumination, for integration—or in this context, had I not better just say, for enlightenment?

DREAMING ALONG

If the Enlightenment retained some of the sobriety of the Age of Reason, the romantic period sought a more dream-like ambience. There had been premonitions, of course, for classical and romantic are perennial opposites in our human constitution. In 1741, J. E. Schlegel wanted his audience 'as we have sometimes seen in our operas'—but which operas at such a date?—'to dream along with its hero'. In 1754, J. A. Hiller called the power of music 'a riddle, which reason will not easily resolve, because it is presented with it only as in a dream'.[1] In 1775, C. M. Wieland put it that 'because music is an ideal language', it is especially apt for mythological characters and situations: Dryden's old association yet again.[2] But when, in 1816, that experienced poet and composer E. T. A. Hoffmann insisted that 'romantic opera is the only true kind, for only in the realms of romance is music at home', we may really take it that we are into the romantic period.[3]

Your true romantic is more than anyone responsive to the constant nearness of the archetypes. There was the romantic Wordsworth insisting upon that 'invisible world' where loom 'the types and symbols of eternity'.[4] There was Coleridge describing 'the translucence of the eternal through and in the temporal', and reminding us that 'man exists . . . how much *below* his own consciousness'.[5] We know (since he told us so) that Coleridge had been reading the Neoplatonist Ficino, for whom 'all things have two aspects, an inner and an outer',[6] just as the romantic Wagner later stressed that 'man's nature is two-fold, an outer and an inner'.[7] So introverted was Coleridge that 'in looking at objects in nature' he seemed to himself 'rather to be seeking, as it were *asking* for, a symbolical language for something within me that already and forever exists, than observing anything new'.[8] The thought is Platonic; the disposition is romantic. And concerning Coleridge's venture with Wordsworth in their seminal *Lyrical Ballads*, there comes his famous pronouncement: 'My indeavours should be directed to persons and characters supernatural, or at least romantic; yet so as to transfer from our inward nature a human interest and a semblance of truth sufficient to procure for these shadows of imagination that willing suspension of disbelief for the moment which constitutes poetic faith'.[9]

But then again 'a poet's heart and intellect should be combined, intimately combined and unified with the great appearances of nature'.[10] We can see what he meant. There is scarcely one vivid descriptive detail in The Rime of the Ancient Mariner which has not been traced to some scientific book about nature, overtly or covertly recalled; nor any touch of the beautifully romantic symbolism which does not come clearly out of that transformed natural description.[11] I even wonder if the albatross of that vivid poem itself shares with the storks, the geese or the swans of common folklore some hint of mother-symbolism, in which case the shooting of it may have been on some level necessary by way of escape and growth of character, although it must all the more have aroused a sense of guilt and a need to work through that sense of guilt, as the Mariner with great difficulty and partial success may well have done. I shall in due course raise a similar speculation over that unlucky swan in Parsifal. At all events, the romantic spirit is very present here.

Is Fidelio (Vienna, 1805, 1806, 1814) a romantic opera? It is certainly what is significantly called a 'rescue opera'. I shall always think that Joseph Kerman and Alan Tyson got very near to the heart of it when they suggested that 'the profounder implications that the story held for [Beethoven's] own psychology will have appeared as the labour progressed; oppressed and isolated by his undeserved deafness, it was easy for him to identify with the unjustly imprisoned Florestan who lay alone in the dark with no apparent hope of rescue'.[12] Perhaps Beethoven identified with Leonora too, the woman whose courage and fidelity did rescue Florestan, rather as Beethoven's muse, his own component of creative femininity, might be thought to have rescued him from the loneliness and the darkness to which the Heiligenstadt Testament and other letters of the time bear such moving witness. Freedom is the burning issue; and on such a theme and for such a score, surely the staging should preserve a corresponding dignity. There is the cold dungeon down below; there is the warm sunshine up above; and it is important to show this contrast of the dark and the light in a production that is not gimmicky, but of the gravest integrity.

### FROM THE DARK TO THE LIGHT

Mattheson had already discussed opera as a fusion of the arts (Zusammenfluss) back in 1739.[13] But Weber went a stage farther in requiring 'a work of art complete in itself, in which all the related parts and contributions are blended together and thus disappear, and somehow, in disappearing, form a new world'—an exaggeration, since they do not actually disappear, but it suited Weber, and Wagner also a little later on.[14] Friedrich Kind, Weber's librettist for Der Freischütz (Berlin, 1821), agreed that 'by the union of all the arts of poetry, music, acting, painting and dancing a great whole could be shaped'.[15] As indeed it could be and was.

Max, the somewhat ambivalent hero of Der Freischütz, finds his marksmanship inexplicably inhibited on the eve of a contest having for its prize Agathe, daughter of the hereditary forester Cuno, whose enviable office is also included in the award. Caspar the dark villain has sold his soul to the devil in return for certain magic bullets, and is now due for death and damnation unless he can find a substitute. Caspar's plan is for Max to be the substitute. He gives Max the last of his magic bullets to bring down an eagle almost invisible in the failing light, and the two of them make a furtive assignment for midnight in the Wolf's Glen. There is furthermore a portrait of one of Cuno's ancestors whom rumour accuses of having got his position by the same illicit bargain; and when we learn that this has come crashing down on the heroine Agathe's head at the very moment at which the eagle was shot, we begin to suspect some sinister connection. But Agathe herself has been visited by a kindly old hermit, of great local repute, who has brought her some consecrated white roses. Both negative and positive aspects of the father-principle would seem to be at work, not of conscious intention, but because the romantic imagination is so naively drawn to just such unwittingly archetypal material.

In the Wolf's Glen (fig. 9), the moon is shining fitfully through scudding clouds. At the back, a cave and a waterfall. Nearer a blasted tree, phosphorescent with putrid funguses. Owls flit by, their eyes as bright as fire; a hidden chorus howls mournfully about 'moon's milk' and 'spider's web wet with blood'. There would seem, on the same autonomous level of the imagination, to be some emphatically negative mother-symbolism in this range of images; but now, with diminished sevenths on tremolando strings, cavernous low notes for clarinets and horns, traditional underworld sonorities for trombones and sinister taps and rolls for timpani, on the stroke of midnight Caspar conjures Samiel, the devil's representative, with three twists of a gleaming skull; and Samiel

9. The Wolf's Glen in Weber's Freischütz, as envisioned by Carl Wilhelm Holdermann for a production in Weimar in 1822. The scene recalls the trinitarian symbolism of Mozart's Magic Flute.

offers him a three years' respite if Max is spared. So Max appears above, and looks down 'as into the pit of hell'; sees but ignores the forbidding ghost of his mother; thinks he sees Agathe about to plunge herself into the waterfall; decides quite rightly that his 'fate calls'; and down he comes.

And now, in this devil's brewing, three appropriate ingredients are dropped into the cauldron: lead (the primary material in alchemy), glass (from broken church windows) and mercury (in alchemy, the transforming principle). Three spent bullets follow; three times, at three pauses in the music, Caspar bows. We are being reminded, I am sure deliberately, of The Magic Flute by all these threes; and so we are when the chorus of invisible spirits, flinging A-flat against its tritone opposite, D major, names the four traditional elements of initiation: fire, earth, water and air (ex. 16). Spectral horses next cross the darkened sky; the two shadowy figures in front are bending over and calling out the number of each newly moulded bullet in harsh speech against the orchestra.

*Through fire and earth and sea and air!*

## Example 16

Weber, *Der Freischütz* (Berlin, 1821), Act II, scene iv. The four elements of initiation—fire, earth, water and air—invoked by the chorus of spirits with a tritone progression in the bass to bring out the spookiness.

At the sixth bullet, lightning flashes and flames belch. At the seventh, Max catches at a branch for support but is clasped instead by the hand of the Black Huntsman (to whom they say great Odin was at length reduced); and no more than Don Giovanni does he seem able to let go.

We learn early in Act III that the seventh bullet is at the devil's command. Out of agitated D major and back across that same tritone into A-flat, Agathe greets the sunshine against a sparkling obbligato for solo cello; but she has dreamt most disturbingly of Max shooting a white dove which turns into a black bird of prey. Cousin Aennchen has dreamt, on the contrary, of a fiery-eyed monster in chains which turns into Nero the faithful watchdog. And down that persistently interfering (and doubtless heavy) ancestral picture comes tumbling again. Worse still, the box of flowers for Agathe's bridal wreath is found to contain black blooms instead of white. But, mercifully, Agathe remembers the hermit's gift and puts herself under token of his protection by wearing his white roses. She now rather strangely suggests that a girl may wear white roses before the altar, or in the coffin. Her wedding, we know, is impending, but her death is not (unless this is meant to hint that her transformation is close at hand). Let me just put it that she seems to have some vague premonition of approaching crisis, and that wearing the white roses was evidently the crucial decision which prepared her for the seeming miracle when, at the great contest, Max is instructed to shoot a white dove just as she runs in crying, 'Do not shoot, Max: I am the dove'. But he has already shot. She falls, but rises again; and Caspar it is who dies. That devil's bullet got turned around after all to good.

Max is condemned for his misdeeds to instant banishment; but with a splendid modulation to E-flat major, the most prominent key of *The Magic Flute*, that venerable old hermit comes quietly in and proposes instead a year's probation, with Agathe and the succession if Max can keep clear of the devil's temptings meanwhile. Chorus, soloists and orchestra agree resoundingly upon this excellent resolution (ex. 17).

Wer legt auf ihn so stren-gen Bann?

Why lies on him so strong a ban ?

**Example 17**
Weber, *Der Freischütz*, Act III, scene vi. The warm modulation
(G minor to E-flat major) which brings on the old hermit for his
long-delayed but all the more effectual entry.

That widespread myth about the dangers of bargaining with the devil has got to mean something. It reminds me of the fantasies of omnipotence which come normally into childhood but which may become dangerous indeed if they persist into adult wishful thinking and narcissist delusions of infallibility. Yet the unconscious trickster in all of us is just as ambivalent as any other archetype, and it is perfectly legitimate to give the devil and his accomplices at least the credit for starting something up. Caspar tempts Max to bring the eagle down, which brings the ancestral portrait down, which lets in both Samiel and the holy hermit; and because Max does not then shirk his unholy encounter, it all ends up in bright C major with the chorus praising the 'kindly guidance' of 'the Father'. They mean, of course, quite conventionally the heavenly father; but all the same it comes in conformably to my narrative.

Weber himself claimed that 'half the opera plays in darkness', where 'these dark forms of the outer world are underlined and strengthened in the musical forms'.[16] But the direction is out of the darkness and into the light, like *The Magic Flute* he so much admired, like *Fidelio*, like Goethe's *Faust* starting as the devil's work but evolving over so many years towards a sort of poetic consciousness and transfiguration. *Der Freischütz* is not in that league, but it stands within the great romantic canon, and very romantically it needs to be produced. Lurid stage properties and projected spectral horsemen and gloomy lighting for the dark doings in the Wolf's Glen; bright lighting for the prosperous country-people, and brighter still for the long-delayed entry of the redeeming hermit: no alien or incongruous images, but plenty of well-directed variety in the illumination, as usual decisive for the variety of mood.

## PARIS A CENTRE OF GRAND OPERA

Spontini took Paris[17] by storm in 1807 with *La Vestale*, that officially virgin priestess who not only lets in a lover but lets out the sacred fire, but is reprieved when Jupiter lights his own fire again with a thunderbolt, thus signifying not only his forgiveness, but also perhaps his very sound view that carnal flames and spiritual ones are not incompatible but complementary.[18]

We best love Rossini, no doubt, for his intoxicating *Barber of Seville* (Rome, 1816); but he is very wonderful in *William Tell* (Paris, 1828), a grand opera which both begins and ends in serenity, making along the way several deliberate changes in the weather to help symbolize changes in the emotional climate.[19]

Bellini really did have his heroine dreaming along in that enchanting *La sonnambula* (Milan, 1831); while in *Norma* (also Milan, 1831), another of those unchaste priestesses who seem to have appealed to some obscurely liberating impulse around this time adds irony to sentiment in her impassioned 'Casta diva', chaste goddess; then redeems herself by entering the transforming fire, as I might suppose it to be (I am sure that Bellini did not).[20] Bellini was naive; Bellini was a natural; and that no doubt was one of the reasons for his being so very good. Never was limpid melody so effortlessly poignant nor creamy harmony so miraculously uncloying (ex. 18).

Also in 1831, at Paris, came *Robert le diable* from that practised librettist, Scribe, and that far from naive composer, Meyerbeer.[21] There is the sinister Bertram, father of Robert, who turns out to be none other than the foul fiend in disguise, intent on thwarting any good intentions on his son's part and more particularly his love for the virtuous princess Isabella. There is a dark wood after Dante—a long way after, but with the same implication of getting lost in it. There is the ballet of fallen nuns trying to entice Robert into stealing a sacred bough, having

Ca - - - - -sta__ Di - - va, ca - -sta

*Chaste goddess,*

Di - va__che i - nar - gen - - - -ti    Que - - - - ste__

*who bathe in silver light*          *these*

sa - - -cre, que - -ste sa - cre, que - ste sa-cre an-ti - -che pian - te,

*ancient, sacred trees,*

## Example 18

Bellini, Norma (Milan, 1831), Act II, scene iv. Cavatina with chorus, 'Casta diva', of all Bellini's bel canto arias perhaps the most famous, and the very type of his languorous yet impressive melody: singer's opera at its wonderful summit.

magical powers, from the statue of their saintly Abbess, who alone had stayed chaste; but when Bertram lets it out that her name was Bertha, the name of Robert's mother, she seems to be looking at him accusingly in his mother's likeness, and he recoils. Yet the next moment a nun aptly called Helen seduces him into the outrageous action, whereupon the nuns reveal themselves for unholy spectres, who now have him in their immoral power. But when he accordingly tries to rape Isabella, she so impedes him with her extensive bel canto that, feeling guilty, he breaks that somewhat phallic emblem which is his magic branch. Rescued again by his devilish father, Robert is turned against him by the mere appearance of a chorus of virtuous monks; prays to heaven; and is rewarded by one of those spectacular Parisian scene changes into the interior of a vast cathedral, and there united belatedly but legitimately with Isabella.

To see your father as the devil and your mother as a saint, or alternatively to see the nuns as devilish and the monks as saintly, certainly verges on the Oedipal; but although this is valid archetypal material, it is presented too chaotically and too ostentatiously here to come out as a great work of art. It is, however, fairly typical of Parisian grand opera of the period, and probably very enjoyable in a sufficiently uninhibited production.

A MAN FOR POWERFUL SITUATIONS

Verdi thought the libretto of *Rigoletto* (Venice, 1851) 'the best, the most effective subject I have ever set to music . . . it has very powerful situations'.[1] Powerful they are: but in more ways, perhaps, than its authors intended or its audiences suspect. For when we learn that Rigoletto keeps his daughter Gilda in such close confinement that the courtiers take her for his mistress, it occurs to me as quite probable that in his unconscious he wishes that she were. Certainly in the outside world we should have to regard so close a tie as constituting psychologically an incestuous situation. But if that is so, it would look as if in holding the ladder bemusedly for Gilda's abduction, some sane part of Rigoletto were colluding inadvertently in seeking for her, and even more importantly, for himself, the liberty which the sick part of him denies. On any more obvious explanation, it would seem to be a very improbable contingency. Old Monterone's curse could then be seen as constellating outwardly the doubts, the suspicions and the hallucinations with which Rigoletto is by now being assailed inwardly: in terms of psychology, a persecutory fantasy; in terms of theatre, a melodramatic masterstroke.

The remainder of the scenario can likewise be taken as a melodramatic extravagance covering up a much more valid and interesting symbolical undercurrent. That highly exaggerated Duke of Mantua, for example, may come across quite luridly in the theatre, but in psychological reality, after all, he is only one more of your preposterous Don Juans persuading himself and others that he is following the most virile of impulses when in actuality he is obeying the least rewarding of compulsions: a mother's boy at bottom, and by no means the fine fellow that he thinks he is. However, he is such good theatre that we are happy to go along with him, not excluding his splendid 'La donna è mobile' (but who is really the fickle one?).

But that bizarre final scene when Gilda gets herself stabbed in place of the Duke she so unreasonably loves? Anthony Ransom has suggested to me a positive explanation along the general lines that since Gilda can be taken as standing on one level as representative of Rigoletto's own inner element of femininity, and since she undoubtedly dies praying for him in the most Christian spirit, her death may be hinting symbolically at the same transformation in the psyche which so many operatic heroines adumbrate from Euridice through Semele through Senta through Brünnhilde. But there is also a more negative possibility. I have seemed to detect throughout this opera some sweet but sickly odour of incest. The stabbing of Gilda may on this level symbolize vicariously and horribly the sexual penetration which both she and Rigoletto might not less urgently than unconsciously desire. Incest in *Die Walküre* is acceptable because it is introduced both compassionately and consciously. Here in

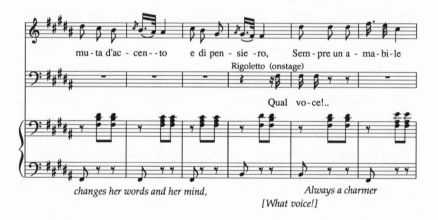

### Example 19

Verdi, *Rigoletto* (Venice, 1851), last scene. The highly operatic stroke of irony when the Duke, whom Rigoletto supposes to be dead in the sack, is heard offstage singing once more that cynical bel canto aria, 'La donna è mobile'. Here the music does not only express the action: the music is the action.

10. Contrasting conceptions of Rigoletto's house, scene of Gilda's abduction in Verdi's opera: above, the traditional setting for the original production of 1851, designed by Giuseppe and Pietro Bertoja; below, Jonathan Miller's recent Mafia-style staging, transferred to New York in the 1930s.

11. The tomb scene from Verdi's Aida, as sketched by Philippe Chaperon in 1901: a touching image of ritual burial and subsequent rebirth.

Rigoletto I feel altogether too much unassimilated unconsciousness slopping around. Cathartic, I grant you; and so much of the music is so uncommonly effective. But I do not think I am alone in finding the end of Rigoletto rather more unsettling than rewarding (ex. 19).

More or less of a Renaissance costume piece is the natural setting here (fig. 10). For any Verdi staging, the production books which he authorized for so many of his operas should be consulted; they illustrate so fully the integral totality in which he conceived words, music and staging, not to mention his anger when his clear and detailed instructions were not satisfactorily carried out. And, of course, Rigoletto, however disturbingly, is a theatrical triumph, and requires like so many romantic operas to be produced with a quite brazen panache.

Il trovatore (Rome, 1853) is a muddle; La traviata (Venice, 1853) is coherent and affecting, with a touch of Oedipal mordancy as father Germont breaks up the young couple. Aida (Cairo, 1871) unfolds exuberantly but ends unexpectedly. Above, the brightly illuminated priests are chant-

*O verdant hillsides,*

*O sweetly smelling banks,*

## Example 20

Verdi, *Aida* (Cairo, 1871), Act III, scene i. Aida's homesick melody is so nostalgic and the oboe accompaniment so plaintive; but the scene is nevertheless much more touching than it is distressful.

ing; below, Aida and Radames are quietly counterpointing in their dark tomb: 'Heaven opens to us'. But, astonishingly, it is the now repentant Amneris who has the last word: 'peace'.

Peace? Or slow murder? Literally, there is courage and fidelity, but also there is cruelty which the quietness of the music in no way expresses. Symbolically then? However you may take it, 'heaven opens to us' implies some manner of renewal. 'Peace' envisages some manner of reconciliation between the rival carriers of femininity. There are potential associations with the stone which closed in Christ's sepulchre; and he certainly rose again. In short, the scene points to some very archetypal images concerning transformation by ritual burial and subsequent rebirth, reflecting our perennial hopes for a new beginning somehow (fig. 11). Whatever Verdi's conscious intentions, his music fairly glows out at us with symbolic hope, subliminally activated but nonetheless satisfying on that account (ex. 20).

## IN DARKNESS AND IN TRAGEDY

The curtain rises for *Otello* (Milan, 1887), without overture, on the fearful storm which gives us, deliberately, the measure of that side of Otello's reckless character (fig. 12).[2] When Iago gets Cassio fighting drunkenly with Roderigo, Otello demotes Cassio with no proper enquiry. Deliberately, too, the storm subsides for the inspired symphonic development which carries the ensuing love scene. And again deliberately symbolical is the music for those three kisses, so poignant that it is almost unbearably moving when we twice again hear it at the other end of the opera, the poignancy redoubled by the fatal difference in the circumstances.

It was Boito the splendid librettist who brought in, as deliberately as could be, that great monologue known as Iago's Credo, spelling out, what Shakespeare no more than implied, that Iago is not so much an evil person as evil personified. 'Your demon drives you', he sings triumphantly as Cassio walks into the trap cunningly prepared for him, 'and I am your demon. Mine, an inexorable deity in which I believe, drives me'. Then, as if to make still clearer his identification with the principle of evil: 'I believe in a cruel God who created me in his own image', and furthermore, 'I am evil because I am a man'. He is right in that all men carry the potentiality for evil, wrong in that no man is entirely evil. But we recognize the common element. We recognize our unwilling kinship, and are intrigued by it even as we are repelled.

When Iago, without actually saying that Cassio and Desdemona already conceal a guilty intercourse, somehow gets Otello to put the hateful insinuation into words which he believes are coming from himself, it is altogether as if Iago stands symbolically for a part of Otello: the dark part. Again Otello makes no proper enquiry, but is gulled instead by all that clever business with the handkerchief. It would seem that Otello is a man so proudly buttoned into his own conscious personality that he is more than usually vulnerable to invasion from the unconscious. It is from his not knowing that Othello's tragedy arises. Iago is an awesome image for the darkness Otello does not know that he has got.

And Desdemona? At the height of his possession, Otello sings, 'My soul [*anima mia*], I curse you'. And truly I think he has projected his soul into her keeping, so that in killing her he is also killing a part of himself. In Act IV, her very Shakespearian 'Willow, willow' does not perhaps transplant so well into Italian opera; but Boito's 'Ave Maria' prepares us quietly and appropriately for the fearful moment as the high violins and violas die down and the double basses grind in, three octaves below, for Otello's entry through the secret door. So he kisses her awake with the

12. The violent storm that opens Verdi's Otello, emblematic of the Moor's fitfully tempestuous nature. Bagnara's naturalistic décor for the La Scala première in 1887 contrasts with the more surreal settings that Lucio Fanti designed for the recent Welsh National Opera production (see fig. 2).

three kisses we recall so well, rejects her transparently honest plea of innocence, and smothers her. The alarm being raised, Iago is swiftly unmasked, and Otello in belated awareness stabs himself. 'Before I killed you, wife, I kissed you. Now dying, in the shadow in which I lie, a kiss, a kiss, once more a kiss . . .' Here, I think, the symbol is once more one of those which pull two ways: the upward yearning of the reiterated semitones with the sequences rising as kiss follows kiss; but against that, the downward resolution of the unprepared suspensions. For the third time, we hear that urgent harmony and keen scoring, as the orchestra fills in the tonic Otello has not quite got the strength to reach (ex. 21).

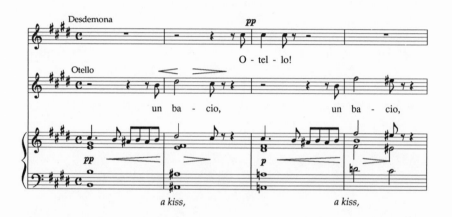

### Example 21

Verdi, *Otello* (Milan, 1887). The unforgettable music for Otello's three kisses, as heard first at the end of Act I, and twice again in the finale of Act IV, the last time left uncompleted in the voice because Otello dies.

Otello being what he was, maybe the anguish was always latent in the ecstasy, and certainly the music speaks, as only music in opera can speak, of but one single unified experience across the long span of all that happened in between. The cathartic effect is very powerful, for we mind so much about Otello and Desdemona. We sense their archetypal implications: we pity their individual tragedy. It was Peter Stein who insisted that 'you only in the theatre can confront yourself with the deep ambiguity of life in a way that is bearable and gives you hope and strength'; and 'this is the so-called cathartic element', by which, though 'everything is black on stage, at the end the effect of the manner in which it is presented is that you are absolutely convinced that it is worth going on'.[3] And in just such a manner did his production of *Otello* (Cardiff, 1986) convince me, rooted as it was in the profoundest implications not only of the text but of the music too (see fig. 2).

### IN LIGHTNESS AND IN LAUGHTER

Sly is the comedy in that enchanting *Falstaff* (Milan, 1893), but never for one moment malicious.[4] When Falstaff is singing so touchingly to Mistress Ford about his slender youth, we feel a sudden sympathy for the fat old lecher which does wonders for the balance of the drama. When young Fenton and his Nanetta are seen and heard by us (but not by the others) spooning and duetting behind that convenient screen, it is like some joyful counterpoint telling us about love and renewal and the fruitful cycle of the generations. When Falstaff meets his renewed assignment at midnight disguised as the Black Huntsman (to whom we have already had occasion to recall that great Odin has been reduced), but feeling more than a little apprehensive in such creepy surroundings, he is betrayed by the treacherous Mistress Ford to the taunts and blows of a ballet of children pretending to be fairies—whom for a mortal so much as to set eyes on is certain death. But so haunting is Verdi's music that we too have fallen under the spell of the ancient forest and the moonlit night. More (and more grown-up) spirits and demons add their violence to the rough jest, until Bardolph's hood slips and Falstaff at once perceives that red nose shining like a beacon. So eloquent is his outburst that it wins him a friendly 'bravo', and that part of the jest gives way to a more complex sequel.

Ford, thinking he is marrying Nanetta to horrid old Dr. Caius, bestows on him a veiled figure, and cheerfully agrees while he is at it to marry a second couple; but so soon as they are all unveiled, Dr.

Caius finds himself ridiculously with Bardolph, and Fenton sentimentally with Nanetta. It was, of course, those merry wives of Windsor who had taken the whole matter in hand and refused to countenance Ford's totally unacceptable intention. He is greatly shocked, but soon shows the good grace to accept the joke as being this time against himself. When Nanetta asks for his pardon and blessing, he calls down heaven's on the happy pair; and our hearts rejoice at the happiness and—need I say it?—at the reconciliation. Falstaff, claiming disarmingly that his is the wit which 'creates the wit of others', calls for a chorus to sing that lightest of vocal fugues, 'All in the world's for laughter' (ex. 22). And so in lightness and in laughter Verdi ended one of the two careers in nineteenth-century opera which mattered most. Wagner's, need I add it, was the other.

*All in the world's for laughter.*     *Man is born as a jester.*

## Example 22

Verdi, *Falstaff* (Milan, 1893). The witty fugue which ends Verdi's last opera in lightness and in laughter.

## THE ARCHETYPE OF REDEMPTION

Wagner, unusually aware of his own symbolical intentions, focused them throughout his life around a single theme, his name for which was redemption.[1] Already in *The Flying Dutchman* (Dresden, 1843), Senta forecasts the predestined pattern in that haunting ballad (ex. 23), a symbol in melody which Bellini could have done no better; and like the other side of that pattern, her Dutchman, ghost that he is, brings to her more force of personality, because he is more archetypal, than any of the merely mortal characters around them. The sea from which he comes is a traditional image for the deep and deeply ambivalent unconscious. He may himself stand in for an ability which the human unconscious has for throwing up new potentialities for growth, provided that our intuitions are in a condition to accept them; if not, then no such acceptance occurs until perhaps the next opportunity arises—seven years on? In the music, at all events, the chromatic unease, with its confident romantic surge, keeps that numinous ocean present to our minds all through. We should also, I think, actually see on the stage some hint of rigging to suggest both the arrival of the eerie vessel and its

*Yet to the pale man redemption may one day come,*

**Example 23**
Wagner, *The Flying Dutchman* (Dresden, 1843). The dream-like assurance of Senta's Ballad.

13. Senta, one of many *Wagner* heroines seeking redemption, hurls herself into the ocean in the final scene from the first production of The Flying Dutchman (Dresden, 1843).

sinking at the end (fig. 13), in a sunset radiance to match the redeeming transformation so unmistakably heard in that uplifting plagal cadence in the music.

On 19 October 1858, Wagner wrote to Liszt about Mathilde Wesendonk, who as he says 'dared to throw herself into a sea of suffering so that she should be able to say to me, "I love you!" No one who does not know all her tenderness can judge how much she has had to suffer. We were spared nothing—but as a consequence I am redeemed and she is blessedly happy because she is aware of it'. That is a fairly disingenuous statement; but it does show us how aware Wagner was of needing this relationship with a woman which he called redemption. The woman herself must in each case have had that in her on which Wagner's projection of the eternal feminine could fasten; and real feeling for the woman herself would also come in, probably a great deal of real feeling in the case of Mathilde.[2] But actual woman or fictional heroine, she will be required to carry Wagner's fantasy of being redeemed; and so we shall see it all the way through to Kundry, who starts by putting Parsifal to the test and ends by being redeemed by Parsifal. This way up or that way up, it is redemption all along the line.

In *Tannhäuser* (Dresden, 1845), sensuous and spiritual love are differentiated like the two Venuses in Plato's *Symposium*. Wagner brings his errant hero back from Rome in fine vocal form, but otherwise so broken down by guilt and remorse that it almost seems as if Wagner himself felt that his censorious old father-figure of a pope might after all have got a point. But Elisabeth, when dead, takes on the redeeming function made visible in that beautiful image of the pilgrim's staff putting forth

### Example 24

Wagner, *Tannhäuser* (Dresden, 1845), Overture. The Pilgrims' March set against the brash lure of Venusberg in a simple but effective combination which is as much a counterpoint of drama as it is of music: an entirely operatic device of which Wagner later made much more complicated and sophisticated uses.

new shoots. And indeed so far as I am concerned it is this image which redeems the opera's considerable shortcomings—although, of course, its beauties are very considerable as well (ex. 24).

## THE FORBIDDEN QUESTION
## WHICH MUST BE ASKED

Wagner claimed for *Tannhäuser* that 'my declamation is song and my song is declamation',[3] which reminds me of Berardi in 1681 ('singing one speaks and speaking one sings')[4] or Brossard in 1701 ('as if one declaimed in singing, or as if one sang in declaiming').[5] *Lohengrin* (Weimar, 1850) is even more flexible and impetuous than *Tannhäuser*, although not as yet with quite the continuity and flexibility of the subsequent music-dramas.[6] But it is a fabulous outpouring: surely the grand opera to end all grand operas.

Those high divided violins immediately acquaint us not only with the mountain heights but also with the high moral tone of the elevated brotherhood which guards the Holy Grail. Elsa first relates her prophetic dream (a little like Senta with that fey ballad) and then sees it materialize as Lohengrin is drawn in by the swan, wins the judicial combat, and marries Elsa on condition of her never questioning him. And, of course, the great question about *Lohengrin* is why Elsa must never question Lohengrin.

Wagner himself explained that Lohengrin 'sought for a woman who would believe in him; who would not ask who he was or where he came from . . . who would love him unconditionally. For this reason he had to conceal his higher nature'; for 'what he yearned for was not admiration and worship, but the one thing which could release him from his loneliness and satisfy his longing: love, to be loved, to be understood by means of love'.[7] Revealing as this certainly is, it is not altogether satisfactory. It is normal for a baby to want to be loved unconditionally; but insofar as that legitimate expectation has been met by good enough parenting, he may not need to cling in adult life to what has then all the unreality of wishful fantasy. And to conceal your nature, higher or otherwise, is tantamount to inviting projections of the very kind which Elsa puts on to Lohengrin as her perfect knight in shining armour, exactly as she has told us that she had already dreamed about him. There never was really any future in that.

These questions which are not to be asked but which do get asked are very interesting. It was here that Thomas Mann drew the parallel between Elsa and that incautious Semele, from whose indiscretion the great god Bacchus nevertheless was born.[8] It is an open secret of fairy-tale interpretation that the forbidden deed may be the necessary deed in order that a static situation, however agreeable, may open out into some real possibility for growth. Ortrud is here the villainess whose formidable ambitions and honeyed words precipitate the crisis. So back comes (and must be seen to come) that magic swan; and Ortrud defiantly reveals him for none other than Elsa's brother Gottfried, whom she had falsely accused Elsa of murdering. Maybe Elsa in her dreamy way really had repressed something of her own masculine component; but Ortrud's story is that she had herself bewitched Gottfried in vengeance against the people for deserting their old pagan gods. That is interesting too, because it sets Ortrud firmly among those dark powers which, like Mozart's Queen of Night, may be for you or against you, or more probably a little of each, since there are forces on our dark underside which can work either way.

So Elsa in losing a dream-lover regains an actual brother.[9] The entire situation is left curiously open-ended; but for the sequel, where asking questions comes in again but from the opposite angle, we must wait until Parsifal, a generation back for the holy brotherhood, but for Wagner several operas and much eventful development ahead.

### WAGNER IN TRANSITION

Between Lohengrin and the Ring, Wagner went through one of those transitions, by no means uncommon around the age of forty, between the first half and the second half of life, when tacit assumptions may be as tacitly questioned, and new development arrived at not without accompanying stress and uncertainty. Wagner's prose writings during those years when his music was in abeyance (although his poetry was not) must have been invaluable to him in working some of the stress out of his system and some of the uncertainty out of his thinking: for us it is rather a case, perhaps, of 'easy writing's curst hard reading';[10] for, as Jack Stein put it so perceptively many years ago, 'in spite of his extensive theorizing, Wagner was primarily an intuitive artist'.[11]

For my present purpose, the following hints from Wagner's Opera and Drama of 1851 and from several of the important letters of the period, while not conclusive of anything, are nevertheless suggestive. For example: 'As an artist, my intuitions had compelling certainty', whereas various 'consciously conceived ideas' had to give way before 'the exquisite unconsciousness of artistic creation'. And then again, wishing 'to bring the unconscious part of human nature into consciousness', Wagner spoke of myth as being 'true for all time' and of 'its meaning, however condensed', as being 'inexhaustible through the ages'. He returned much later, in the first sentence of his *Religion and Art* of 1880, to 'the allegorical value of the mythological symbols' for those who can see beyond the 'literal truth' to 'the deep truth' within. He warned us rather pointedly against 'the reader who substitutes his own ideas for those of the poet'. He explained that he wanted 'to work not through a display of intentions, but through a display of things instinctual'.[12]

Myth is true for all time. Symbols explain themselves. So we have seen that Wordsworth and Coleridge had it, and Carlyle, who in *Sartor Resartus* wrote about 'the true force' being 'an unconscious force', adding as he did, in language recalling those Renaissance Neoplatonists at the very rise of opera: 'In a symbol, there is concealment and yet revelation'.[13] The romantics were especially well aware of it; and Wagner was a romantic of romantics. His symbols reveal their meaning not in spite but because of their mythological imagery. Not even Shaw, who saw Wotan as an Ibsenite pillar of society and Alberich as a top-hatted capitalist, ever suggested *staging* them that way. It is not by naturalistic but by archetypal verisimilitude that Wagner's compassion glows out through those miserable dwarfs and all the rest of the resolutely mythological characters and situations in the *Ring*. The whole object of Wagner's celebrated *Gesamtkunstwerk* was to assimilate words and music and staging in one totality. Since his words and his music are so undeniably romantic, so had his staging better be as well.

By general consent, however, the music is first among equals, *primus inter pares*. And so it was that Carl Dahlhaus was able to write of the listener's 'intuitive grasp of the musical expression, which constituted both the substance of the dramatic action and the composer's self-depiction . . . a musical epic, in which the narrator, commenting on the events and reflecting the emotions, is really the principal character'.[14] Wagner's character, in short; and behind Wagner's character, those enduring archetypes pressing onto the stage for which Wagner's character gave the point of entry. No artist has ever been more accessible to courtship from the archetypes nor given them a more royal welcome. And the means used by Wagner for presenting his truly 'musical epic' may be seen especially in that weaving of leitmotifs into a symphonic texture which he presently evolved to such unprecedented lengths.

Short, combinable and infinitely adaptable, these leitmotifs can make a counterpoint of notes into an interplay of action. A development of motives may become a drama in progress. Do we attach meaning to a motive from the words first heard with it? Or from the actions first seen? And thereafter by reminiscence? By all these, perhaps; but I think that basically the connection is more direct and more reliable. Leitmotifs are musical symbols. All symbols are recognizable in principle, and musical symbols are recognized by musical people. It was Schopenhauer who finally brought Wagner more or less round to the view that 'the other arts . . . speak only of the shadow, but music speaks of the essence of things', yet with 'the greatest definiteness', so that 'we completely understand them in this distilled essence', thereby recovering, without their pain, 'all the feelings of our inmost experience'.[15] Without their pain? Emotion recollected in tranquility?

Anthony Newcomb has rightly objected that to tie labels to Wagner's leitmotifs may be to misrepresent as fixed some variant of what could as well be shown by other variants.[16] I have therefore now used freely descriptive captions as opposed to labels (as I did in *Wagner's 'Ring' and Its Symbols*) for my greatly revised set of examples in the Appendix, hoping to hint in this way at some of the organic, plant-like proliferation which actually goes on. But there is nothing indefinite about the symbols themselves. The sound of a word, argued Bembo the poet, does not just have a meaning: it is a meaning.[17] The sound of a leitmotif does not just get attached to a meaning. It is a meaning; a musical symbol: a unit of musical expression.

## A VARIETY OF INTERPRETATIONS

The Ring (in full at Bayreuth, 1876), Wagner's central master-piece, is particularly susceptible to a variety of interpretations on many levels. One of the most recent critics of my old and now much re-considered *Wagner's 'Ring' and Its Symbols*, the Jungian analyst Sally Kester, remarked very fairly that 'whichever interpretation is selected or what-ever new ones are conjured from the fecund matrix of the imagination depends on the composition of our respective psychic constitutions'.[2] And indeed, 'because of its archetypal basis, the Ring will always tran-scend the sum of all interpretations: the totality of its meaning stands outside time and is not subject to its laws'; which is very much as Wagner put it when he wrote so succinctly that 'myth is true for all time'.[3] But now for my revised consideration.

## FROM NATURE TO NURTURE

First of all, John Deathridge has shown that Wagner's famous account in his autobiography (for 5 September 1853) of the musical ori-gins of the Ring was not so accurate as, doubtless for good psychological motives, he evidently came to believe.[4] He certainly experienced a tra-ditional image for rebirth—on one level, from his own long transitional period—in his vision of being swept along by the waters comprising 'the musical sound of the E-flat major chord, from which arpeggios rose unceasingly'. We know that in 1849 Wagner had already been pondering over 'the moment when man became aware of his distinctness from nature, and thus took the very first step in his development as man, breaking away from the unconsciousness of natural animal life to move over into conscious life'.[5] But this evolutionary second birth did not only happen to man; it also happens to men. Every adult was a baby once.

It is, by common agreement, into some such state of nature that Alberich stumbles, only to be baited unfeelingly and unthinkingly by those three all too enticingly animal mermaids. As in ancient myths of the creation, the sun sinks down through the waters, representing not, it is true, scientifically the origins of the world, but intuitively the origins of consciousness.[6] The dormant gold lights up, like some potential fire of life; and the Rhinemaidens accidentally (but was it such an accident?) let it out that 'he who renounces the power of love' can forge the gold into a ring by which to gain the mastery of the world.

But what sort of world? Money can gain some kinds of mastery, but omnipotence is a mere narcissist's fantasy. And what sort of love? Mermaids' love is known to be lethal, like that retrogressive yearning for the mother-image which can drag a man down into debilitating illusions of unfathomable bliss. Wagner eventually had his Parsifal renounce that kind of love, which is not at all the same thing as renouncing the great principle of love itself. Here he merely noticed to his own surprise that his sympathies kept drifting to the side of Alberich, as opposed to those vain, mean and, let us face it, themselves superlatively unloving Rhinemaidens.

We do not want any actual water here, or any hydraulic machinery or other reminder of our own industrial age. We simply want the rippling lights and perhaps the fan-blown streamers to persuade us of being underwater, not literally but magically, as if in a dream. We should, I think, be allowed some device for getting the Rhinemaidens visibly water-borne, perhaps by tactful cables rather than the cumbersome trolleys of the earliest productions (fig. 14). And we need a few small rocks for Alberich to trip over, and a plausible crag for him to clamber up when he steals the gold. Throughout the *Ring*, back-projections will be particularly useful, and changes of lighting will serve best to illuminate every change of mood.

A MUSICAL COMMENT

So much for the staging here. I come now to a symbol in the music which has caused us commentators a notorious difficulty. (The musical examples in this chapter will be found in the Appendix beginning on p. 193.)

'Only he who renounces love' is carried by appendix example 6, which, so far from sounding either dreary or defiant, has a quietly noble and accepting quality. Now true it is that Alberich accepts his unenviable role as villain of the piece with undeniable courage. Goethe had his Mephistopheles know himself for 'part of that power of which the will is evil but the outcome is good'.[7] Alberich does not know that: he is a very Iago of the underworld. Yet the good outcome is the transforming conflagration at the end of *Götterdämmerung*; and but for Alberich there would have been no such ending. Alberich is cast as a hateful archetype of evil. But if he were not on some deep level ambivalent, he would not be an archetype.

There is, however, a further passage where Siegmund, in Act I of *Die Walküre*, sings this very same motive on the words 'Holiest desire, highest need, yearning love, uttermost need' at the summit of his love scene with Sieglinde; and this is seemingly a paradox. Courage and acceptance are in common, but the characters and the situations are at opposite extremes. Then what about the music itself? Appendix example 6 opens with a rising minor sixth followed by a falling semitone. So does example 26, which is the start of *Tristan und Isolde*. So do numerous baroque slow movements of the sadder sort. And so this melodic shape is found in many other idioms. I think it is an analogue for poignancy, whatever the context; and of course the immediate context in *Das Rheingold*, and again in *Die Walküre*, is moderately diatonic, whereas the context in *Tristan* is to say the least of it chromatic. But poignancy comes through in every case. This is raw material for musical symbolism on the basic level, which makes it particularly difficult to verbalize about it in theory. I have never met with anyone who had any difficulty over it in the theatre. Perhaps the mere mention of love is enough to warrant this sense of nobility in the music.

And now the music becomes harsh and ignoble enough for Alberich's horrible stealing of the gold. It is intended to strike horror, and so it does. I must just repeat on the other side that if it had not been for Alberich, we might still be watching those blessed Rhinemaidens swimming around unprogressively in E-flat major. The state of nature may be all very well for the creatures of nature, but for us humans it is not meant to last.

INTO CONSCIOUSNESS AND CONFLICT

Wotan, Alberich's complementary opposite, is likewise archetypally ambivalent. Impetuous young red-head of a deity as he at present is (directors please note), he is himself in trouble because he has pledged the life-giving Freia to the stupid giants in payment for building

14. The opening of Das Rheingold: above, *Alberich and the Rhinemaidens at the bottom of the river, as seen from the theatre at the Munich première in 1869; opposite, a backstage view of the trolleys on which the mermaids appeared to swim in the 1876 production at Bayreuth.*

him his new castle, Valhalla, outwardly as impregnable as it is inwardly vulnerable. But here at last comes tricky Loge who has half-promised to get him off.[8]

Loge's excuse for causing such anxiety by his late arrival is that he has wandered everywhere in search of something that might be accepted in place of woman's joy and worth. The music comes near to what Alberich sang when he did renounce love. Ambiguity again; for we are right to value woman's love, but Wotan's own casual wanderings, and Wagner's, were nevertheless contaminated with compulsive fantasies which are not the same thing as real love, though it may be hard to distinguish them while the deception lasts. Freia, however, undoubtedly stands for the real power of love and of life itself; and it shocks us when Loge persuades the giants to accept Alberich's illicit gold in place of her. When they take her off as hostage, meanwhile, the stage darkens and the gods wilt. That is the measure of the evil which the ruler of the gods himself is risking, through wilful ambition and ungodly stubbornness.

But now for the trick which Wotan hopes will get him off: setting a thief to catch a thief. So Loge and Wotan are taken down into Alberich's Niebelheim by the music. The sharp hammering of many invisible anvils leads us to the gloomy cavern and the treacherous binding of Alberich, and so we hear them too on the return journey out into the upper air. No great matter for Alberich that he is robbed of his present gold; he can get plenty more of that, having the ring; but when Wotan robs him of the ring as well (and with quite hateful violence), he is undone indeed. He curses the ring and damns all its future wearers to envy, care and death. The music of the curse (app. ex. 19) is a leaping variant of the music of the ring (app. ex. 18), as much as to tell us that the real force is still the force of life itself. But Wotan clings to the ring like a man clinging too hard to what his conscious will would wish his life to be. Erda the Earth-Mother comes up like some saving intuition from his deeper self. He yields, and life goes on again—except for the horrid shock of Fasolt's murder.

But when the gods line up to cross the rainbow bridge, from the waters far below there floats up the plaintive harmony of the Rhinemaidens (app. ex. 9): creamy; poignant; making all the doubtful glory of Valhalla and the deceptive platitudes of society seem of little worth against their timeless seduction. Quite right that they so touch us, for a man whom nature cannot touch is only half a man. But a man sucked down again towards the animal is no man either. That is our human dilemma, and it is no wonder if the gods look momentarily disturbed as they line up to cross the rainbow bridge, to music eloquent of the very genuine if unreliable grandeur of our worldly state. Just the same, I think that rainbow should be visibly projected. There still is hope.

### SIEGMUND THE DOOMED HERO

Stormy weather in the orchestra and agitation in our hearts collude as the curtain rises for *Die Walküre* on a forest chieftain's dwelling, and Siegmund falls in exhausted, sinks by the hearth and is there found by Sieglinde. 'A drink', he cries; and as she brings him drink, their motives counterpoint so companionably, and the strings melt into such a poignant arch of melody, that we feel the whole yearning of their lonely beings poured into that first fateful meeting of their eyes.

It was of this passage (app. ex. 36) that Vaughan Williams, having his earliest encounter with any of Wagner's music-dramas, reported: 'I experienced no surprise, but rather that strange certainty that I had heard it all before. There was a feeling of recognition, as of meeting an old friend, which comes to all of us in the face of great artistic experiences'.[9] It is not literal recognition; it is archetypal recognition. At the age of twelve I had the very same experience, at the very same passage: never having known any Wagner before, I nevertheless felt in boundless delight that I had known it all my short life. A touch of unconscious nostalgia for the mother may be suspected to be topping up an emotion quite so immediate and quite so peremptory: I notice that Martin Gregor-Dellin had some such thought (1980), while Jerrold

Moore (1984, p. 18) drew comparable attention to what Elgar openly acknowledged as 'the influence of the mother'.[10] So much of our later development does depend upon that unavoidable, unassuageable, unallowable yearning, translated as a creative ingredient of our later passions and our later achievements alike. They are nonetheless genuine on that account.

Like Wagner himself, Siegmund has grown through his own deprivations and his own difficulties, which he confides not only to Sieglinde but also to Hunding when that dour chieftain returns, proceeding to question Siegmund until it comes out that he is the clan's most noted enemy. And dourly Hunding offers Siegmund the safe hospitality for the night which his honour—his purely Nordic honour, so he had better be dressed for the part—requires: but for tomorrow, 'look to your weapons'. Since these have been broken in Siegmund's latest fight, he will tomorrow be a weaponless man. Or will he?

As Hunding retires, we see that Sieglinde drops one of those convenient operatic potions into his drink before she follows him. The sinking fire blazes up for a moment, so that we catch a gleam from— yes, the music assures us that it is the sword plunged into the roof-tree, though Siegmund thinks confusedly that it must be some glint left behind from the woman's bright glance. (See app. ex. 15.) Then, against all his expectation, she comes quietly back, leaving Hunding safely drugged asleep for the remainder of the act. And now, with faultless timing and unfailing felicity, they explore each other's memories and misadventures, until they approach the discovery that they are siblings: not only in delighted recognition, but in impassioned love.

Now if *Rigoletto* glanced at incest uncomfortably because unconsciously, *Die Walküre* advances incest as a conscious theme, and invites us to accept it eagerly, as of course we do. That could not happen in the outside world, where incest is not, believe me, a pretty subject. In primitive society, incest is stringently forbidden to ordinary mortals, because of its dangerously backwards pull towards the unconscious animality so recently and so precariously escaped. In mythology, on the other hand, Osiris and his twin sister Isis had intercourse even in their mother's womb: a physiological impossibility which makes it all the clearer that we are meant to take the symbol psychologically. The brother-sister marriages expected of the pharaohs were the far-from-ordinary externalization in ritual form of the same valuable symbol.

The connection between symbolical incest and the ritual union or sacred marriage consists precisely in the turning inwards, representing inner reconciliation under the image of erotic intercourse. That is not only felt to be acceptable but desirable on the highest plane, and is what may ultimately account for our feeling so perfectly happy about the incestuous union of Wotan's children here. It feels all right because it is all right, deriving as it does, like so much of the best of Wagner, from authentically mythological material. There were plenty of incestuous couplings in Nordic mythology, particularly in its more primitive layers, but including descendants of Odin or Wotan on whom Wagner drew, although closing up the generations slightly to make a neater story of it.

That Wagner's intuitions about this subliminal but quite ordinary need to become more united in yourself were exceptionally acute may be confirmed from that notable letter of 18 September 1858 to Mathilde Wesendonk in which he described his yearning 'to find the affirmative, singular marriage of myself to myself' (das Bejahende, Eigener, Sich-mir-Vermählende zu finden). In the symbolism of myth and fairy tale, incest can indeed be an image for finding yourself and thereby becoming more integrated. And certainly in the theatre it does not for one moment occur to us that, taken clinically and externally, this lovely story might have to be seen as something of a pathological case history. It is, of course, nothing of the kind. It is myth and it is fairy tale and it moves us greatly.

Sieglinde has described very suggestively the stranger with the brim of his hat covering one eye—lost, as surely everyone knows, in payment for wisdom drunk at Mimir's well; or, if you have been so ignorantly brought up that you do not know, there is Wotan's grand motive in the orchestra (app. ex. 17) to tell us that it was he who strode into her wedding feast at her forced marriage to Hunding, and thrust a sword into the roof-tree so deeply that no hero could pull it out, though many have tried. As he strode away again with no word, but with a smile for her alone, she knew him for her father, and knew too for which hero that sword was meant. Were you that hero, she ends, and in my arms, all my ill fortune would be remedied. And Siegmund, knowing her now for what his yearning has been seeking all along without his knowing it, has her in his arms at once.

Not the little wicket door by which Siegmund entered, but the whole back of the hut swings open, flooding the hall with sudden moonlight and showing them at last plainly to one another. 'Ah, who goes there, who has come in?' she cries. 'No one goes, but one has come; see, the spring laughs in the hall!' And he sings, very lyrically, the nearest to a formal aria anywhere in this opera, though it does not sound formal but only the natural outgrowth of the situation. Sieglinde shall name him anew, which she does with his own name, Siegmund; and as he pulls out the sword, she also names herself. While the orchestra climaxes magnificently, in full knowledge and full awareness they run out into the forest; and the curtain falls.

But what about the seeming paradox of giving Siegmund, as he claimed his father's sword and his sister-bride, the same noble, resigned and accepting motive (app. ex. 6) which long ago carried the Rhine-maidens' instructions to Alberich on how to forge the ring by renouncing love? I think that motive, which is generally described as a motive of renunciation, might just as well be called a motive of acceptance, since accepting one choice necessarily implies renouncing any other choices. The sadness in the music here might seem misplaced until we realise that Wagner knew (and we too perhaps may know, though Siegmund does not) that his courageous acceptance of love is also going to bring him tragically to his death. That poignant foreknowledge may be what Wagner has put compassionately into the very music for Siegmund's climax of delight and fulfilment. Music in opera does have this uncanny ability to look behind and ahead, giving us an emotional overview of the whole drama in relation to the part. It is one of opera's many advantages.

### THE TRAP CLOSES

When Fricka hounds Wotan to punish Siegmund for the double offence of incest compounded by adultery, Wotan, instead of replying that no Nordic deity, and least of all Fricka, could stand up very well on either charge, merely defends the incest on the general grounds that change is a part of life and that this fresh proof of it is to be congratulated rather than censured.

Wotan knows indeed that change is needed, hemmed in as he is by the runes and bargains carved into the wooden shaft of his own spear. I am reminded of the emotional bargains all of us have begun to make with ourselves long before we have any conscious choice in the matter. Shall we react to our environment with aggression and assertiveness, or with mildness and conciliation? With free emotion, or with guilt and repression? With unhampered warmth, or with involuntary coldness? With what allowable sublimations in work or living to compensate for any unavoidable failures due to our very inhibitions? To question these

early foundations of our own characters is far too alarming—unless, perhaps, there is some brave part of us which might dare to do so, provided
that we can dissociate ourselves from any conscious responsibility in
the matter: some image for what is sometimes known in mythology as
the hero archetype; as it might be, Siegmund.

The weakness here, as Fricka immediately appreciates, is that Wotan
is still trying to have it both ways, giving Siegmund a magic sword without giving away anything of his own wilful authority. It is not really
Siegmund's sword; it is his father's sword, for acting out vicariously his
father's purposes. If Siegmund were a free agent, he might cut through
both spear and bargains, as Siegfried will do in the course of Wotan's
second and more successful attempt at experiencing the hero archetype.
But Siegmund is not a free agent, and indeed we can hear this in the
close musical relationship of appendix examples 32 and 33. So Wotan
yields miserably to Fricka. Our only consolation is that Siegmund dead
will be reborn as Siegfried alive; but he too will die the death, and we
have to look more deeply if we are to understand that as a consequence
the tragedy will come out to some sort of a redeeming conclusion. That
does not, nor should it, diminish meanwhile the sheer pain for us of
these tragic deaths.

Brünnhilde, not yet an important personage in the drama but very
shortly about to be, will not wear Wotan's protestations either. Wotan,
using her blatantly as a carrier for his feminine projections, exposes
his own uneasiness when he wants to keep his present dilemma from
her, for 'if I were to tell it you, should I not then lose the controlling
power of my own will?' Yes, of course that is what he is so mortally
afraid of, although it will have to come to just that in the end, since
that is what Wotan's story means. Her answer, however, confirms how
essentially these characters are and even see themselves as parts of one
another. 'To Wotan's will you are speaking', sings Brünnhilde; for 'what
am I, if I were not your will?' And so he concludes that in sharing his
thoughts with her, 'I take counsel only with myself'. But since he is not
yet ready to reverence his own will on so deep a level, since he still
clings to the illusion of being in full conscious control, he merely forces
his wilfulness on her, thereby doing great violence to both of them.

Sieglinde, with Siegmund close behind her, runs in to a tormented
correlative of the music of their love. She seems half crazed with guilt,
though Siegmund assures her—how rightly—that the real guilt is Hunding's for his forced embraces. She faints; and on a motive expressive
of the deepest sense of destiny, Brünnhilde quietly enters, to foretell

15. *The Ride of the Valkyries from Act III of Wagner's* Walküre, *as depicted by Theodor Pixis in 1871.*

to Siegmund his now approaching end. (See app. ex. 30.) When he refuses the tempting prospect of Valhalla, since Sieglinde cannot come with him, Brünnhilde so melts with compassion that she promises him the victory in spite of Wotan. The ensuing battle needs timing precisely to the music, as Brünnhilde shields Siegmund, Wotan interposes his spear, Siegmund's sword breaks on it and Hunding takes his opportunity to give a fatal thrust, but then falls dead at a mere contemptuous wave of Wotan's hand. Properly directed, it is a shattering experience in music-drama, as swift in action as it has been deliberate in preparation.

But Sieglinde, waking from a nightmare to this nightmare scene, is carried to safety by Brünnhilde, together with the fragments of that broken sword. Wotan, in a red cloud and redder anger, gives violent chase. In Act III, after the resounding Ride of the Valkyries (app. ex. 22; fig. 15), Brünnhilde arrives, telling Sieglinde that since she is now carrying Siegmund's seed (for Siegfried, as the orchestra confirms) she must take courage to escape into the eastern forests where Wotan never goes; and so she does. (See app. ex. 38.) Wotan storms in, red cloud and all, and Brünnhilde confronts him submissively enough, only to be told that by opposing him she has sentenced herself. 'Valkyrie you have ceased to be; now be you henceforth what thus indeed you are'. But what better could she do than be herself? The less divine she becomes, the more human; and the less of a Valkyrie, the more of a woman. That is sheer progress in Brünnhilde's own growth of character.

As the storm and Wotan's anger quieten down, she reminds him that she only did for him what his own love longed to do; so he tells her more bitterly than ever that since she thinks so highly of love, she shall be left asleep on the mountain to be made love to by the first man who finds her (love in two opposite senses, we are bound to notice). But not by a weakling who will bring shame to our race, she next pleads, adding very meaningfully that the Wälsung race could produce no weakling, and that Sieglinde carries a future Wälsung (identified as at app. ex. 16c but instantly repudiated by grandfather Wotan). Then suddenly inspiration seizes her, and she asks to be protected from any but 'one who is fearless and free', by magic flames that no craven would dare to approach. And as suddenly Wotan's thought runs out to hers; for the one who is fearless and free is the one who may yet save him, which Siegmund, being dependent on him, could not do. And so he promises her a bridal fire such as has burned for no bride before. 'Then only one shall free the bride, one more free than I, the god!'

As Wotan sings his moving farewell, and the somnolent, haunting sleep-music (app. ex. 13) opens up in the orchestra, she droops and is laid gently on a mossy bank at that bare mountaintop. Then 'Loge, hear!' —and the flames break out, and the fire-music counterpoints glamorously, irresistibly with the sleep-music into that surging finale. The verbal poetry has been intense and eloquent, but it is no longer needed. The orchestra does all the singing now.

### THE SECOND TIME ROUND
### FOR THE HERO ARCHETYPE

Siegfried, brought up roughly enough in Mime's cave, brings us almost back again to the state of nature; but not quite, as that highly instructive exchange of questions between Mime and Wotan presently confirms. When Wotan in his new role as the Wanderer (and with quite remarkable self-knowledge) compares the dwarfs—the 'black beings' whose home is in the underworld ruled by 'black Alberich'—with the giants on earth and with the gods—'the light beings', dwelling on the heights where 'light Alberich, Wotan, rules the host'—he reveals himself and his old enemy for no other than the light and the dark sides of whatever polarity it is which holds sway over the ever-fluctuating balance of our lives. When Mime, who might have asked it while it was his turn to ask, cannot say by whom the sword can be forged with which Fafner may be killed, Wotan pronounces, 'Only he who has never learned fear', contemptuously leaving Mime's head to him in forfeit.

It is still Mime's unlikely plan to get hold of the ring when Siegfried, we hope, has learned fear in the very act of killing Fafner, who guards it. So Mime gives Siegfried the magic steel to forge again, as only he can; for when Mime forges him a sword, a good sword, he just smashes it on the anvil. Rejecting the solder and shredding the steel, melting it and pouring it into the mould and tempering it and quenching it and hammering it, Siegfried forges his own sword and his own manhood, owing nothing but the raw material of it to his father or his grandfather. And when, with another mighty stroke, not the sword but the anvil is shattered, we know that Siegfried is ready for his own heroic deeds to come.

In Act II, it is black Alberich whose broodings penetrate the orchestra as he waits for his own anticipated opportunity outside Fafner's cave. A strange blue light (not red, now) brings in Wotan, who refuses any longer to treat his old adversary as an enemy, telling him to his great astonishment that he is free to make anything he can of the developing situation. They leave the stage to Siegfried, who—of all unexpected postponements—sings nostalgically and poignantly of Sieglinde, the mother whom he never saw. Perhaps the birds could tell him more about her, if only he could learn their language, into which he tries to enter by cutting a little reed pipe. He is getting warm: back to mother will not serve, but it is perhaps the right point to start from; and soon, to our relief, he throws away that feeble pipe and blows on his horn the traditional challenge, to which Fafner responds at once by trundling out. In his dragon form, he is a close relative to others we have met, and perhaps represents massively the same sort of inner parental opposition to growing up which nostalgia for the mother-image may represent seductively.

I feel confirmed in this view by Thomas Mann, who put it that 'what we have here, rising from the dark depths of the unconscious, is a presentient complex of mother fixation, sexual desire and *Angst*'; for where 'Siegfried's thoughts of his mother slide into eroticism', and previously where Mime was trying to teach Siegfried 'the meaning of fear' and 'the

16. *Siegfried slays the dragon Fafner—representing, perhaps, the hero's fixation on the mother-image—in Act II of* Siegfried, *as designed by Joseph Hoffmann for the first Bayreuth* Ring *in 1876.*

motif of Brünnhilde slumbering in the fire moves through the orchestra like a dark distorted presence—this is pure Freud, pure psychoanalysis'.[11] But when poor Fafner dies (fig. 16), it is the motive of the curse which rings out as he reminds us of that prior cause condemning every owner of the ring to envy, care and death. Or should we not rather say, to everything that life may bring, including envy and care and death as the end; for that is how our life will have to go, if we are really to live it at all.

Fafner's blood so stings that Siegfried puts his hand to his mouth, whereupon the primitive virtue in Fafner evidently passes into Siegfried. So now he can understand the forest bird who tells him, to music almost identical with the music of those other ambivalent representatives of Mother Nature, the Rhinemaidens, where to find the treasure and the ring, and warns him, too, not to listen to Mime's honeyed words —or what would be his honeyed words were it not that he cannot seem to help uttering instead, to our grim amusement, the murderous thoughts he is really having. So when Mime most hospitably offers him the poison, Siegfried jabs him dead; and that splendid bird, speaking (I feel certain) very positively now for Siegfried's emerging instinct, after a few moments of purely feminine teasing leads him off firmly in the right direction.

Act III shows a much chastened Wotan consulting, for the last time, with the enigmatic Erda. 'How can the god conquer his care?' She cannot tell him; but he knows already. 'Anguish grieves me not over the end of the gods, since my own wish wills it', and then with Siegfried in mind (and perhaps Goethe's *das ewig Weibliche*): 'to the eternal young [*dem ewig Jungen*] the god yields in delight'. Nevertheless, Siegfried for his own benefit must learn beyond a doubt who and what it is that stands in his path. And so Wotan—feeling really angry now—interposes his spear, and Siegfried severs it with his sword. As a symbol for overcoming any further dependence by Siegfried on the father-principle, this is significant; as a symbol for ending all the father-god's own blind authority and shallow will, it is crucial. To let his over-forceful ego yield to that deeper totality which is sometimes called, in contrast, the self: that is the choice towards which Wotan's story has been leading him; that is the growth which makes so many of us think of Wotan—or, of course, if you prefer to put it that way, Wagner—as the real hero of the Ring.

And so Siegfried passes through the flames and learns fear—from a sleeping woman! So he cries out for help—to mother! But when, greatly fearing, he kisses Brünnhilde awake, her first greeting is—very traditionally—to the sun and the light. Next she calls him 'awakener of life, conquering light!' When she goes on that she has loved him before he was born, he is more sure than ever that she must be his own mother awakened. But no:

> Your mother will never come back to you.
>    I am yourself
> if you, blessed one, love me.
>    What you do not know
>    I know for you;
>    for I have knowledge
> only—because I love you!
>    O Siegfried! Siegfried!
>    Conquering light!

I think Brünnhilde in effect is telling Siegfried, first, that she is not his mother and that he had better take back from her his projection of the

mother-image; but second, that she can indeed carry for him the projection of his own inner femininity, and in that respect can fairly say: 'I
am yourself'. And third, she can then give him the intuitive knowledge
of the feminine side of himself which a loved woman can reflect for
a man who loves her, thus helping him towards that wholeness which
we have already seen Wagner describing longingly as 'the marriage of
myself to myself'.

But meanwhile Siegfried is a man on fire, as he thinks from those very
flames of life itself through which undoubtedly he passed. Brünnhilde
still does not want him to disturb his reflection in that clear stream
which is her mirror for his feminine image. But when he insists that he
must plunge in now to cool those flames, she too catches fire; and just
as their duet climaxes about 'luminous, loving, laughing death', and the
music tells us deliberately enough what they mean by that, once again
down comes the curtain, as in Act I of *Die Walküre*, not one moment
too soon. Projection of the mother-image; projection of the feminine
component; fulfilment of the sexual instinct: the archetypal sequence
could hardly be more succinctly compressed.

## REDEMPTION AGAIN AS THE RESOLUTION

Brightness was the symbol when Brünnhilde woke to greet
the sun with that radiant pair of sustained chords lifting our spirits from
E minor to C major. Darkness is the symbol now for those three de-
crepit old Norns in the misty wood at the world's end, and for them
the identical mediant relationship is transposed almost unthinkably as
E-flat minor to C-flat major (see app. ex. 24). Truly extremes meet, or
rather stand as polar opposites; and this polarity is further emphasized
by the return of that same elemental arpeggiation which accompanied
the three radiant Rhinemaidens at the start of it all. Swan-maidens, Wish-
maidens, Valkyries, Norns, like Greek Fates or Muses or Graces and
others elsewhere, do seem to come up by threes or multiples of three
as curiously interchangeable or complementary minor representatives
of femininity, emanating as they do from a more primitive level of the
unconscious than Wotan, which is no doubt why the Norns so grumble
here about his having disturbed their ancient wisdom. Their music is of
an eerie, haunting beauty, well suited to their setting in the misty pine
wood at the world's end.

Yes, but why this sudden wave of darkness set up between the radiant ending of *Siegfried* and the joyful scene to follow? Is it possible that the recent happiness of Siegfried and Brünnhilde came a little too suddenly to be altogether solid? That it had, in short, a manic component? The manic state is all too vulnerable to unconscious reactions which can be decidedly self-destructive; and a reaction into unconsciousness is one way of describing the misfortune into which Siegfried is about to fall.

For now, in no less sudden light, Siegfried gives Brünnhilde that fateful ring, rides off on her horse with full benefit of orchestra, and is greeted by Hagen and the magic potion. And so Siegfried forgets Brünnhilde to a horrible distortion of the trill in the middle of their own music; and falls for Gutrune because he is now a man possessed—by a magic potion. Or might we not equally put it that Siegfried is a man possessed—as if by a magic potion—because he has fallen for Gutrune? Magic is for the unconscious. Siegfried has fallen into a state of schizoid amnesia from which he is going to recover only in the last fraught minutes of his life.

Brünnhilde on her rock refuses to let Waltraute collapse the whole necessary development by giving the Rhinemaidens back their ring; and this scene allows Wagner to remind us again of the mythological dimension. Siegfried, transported by some further instant trickery with the magic Tarnhelm, and disguised by it as Gunther—worse, made to be as mean and unfeeling as Gunther is—appears over the back of the mountain: an appalling transformation, symbolically intelligible, but we do not think any the better of him on that account. We share in Brünnhilde's horror as he forces the ring from her finger, and with it her strength; drives her into that bridal cave he should know so well; and only salvages the last shred of his native honour—ambiguously enough on the symbolical level—by setting his drawn sword between them for the night. Incidentally, we may notice the limits of the ring's own magic power, which saved neither Alberich when he was robbed of it, nor Fafner when he succumbed to the curse upon it; nor does it save Brünnhilde here. For this really is a necessary drama, and the one thing the ring, focusing as it does the force of life in all its intrinsic ambivalence, cannot be expected to do is to stop the drama from going on.

It is good mythology and good music-drama again when Alberich finds Hagen watching by the Rhine. 'Are you asleep, Hagen my son? Do you sleep and hear me not, whom rest and sleep betrayed?' And Hagen answers, but as if he is indeed in a dream, 'I hear you, evil dwarf, what have you to tell my sleep?' So evil a pair; and so numinous; for here in Hagen is the very shadow-opposite of Siegfried, as black as the Gunther in him is a kind of nasty grey. But now the dawn grows bright with all those warm horns in canon; and Hagen vociferously summons the clans, with rare and much appreciated humour (for there is no actual danger) as Siegfried magically returns and Gunther with Brünnhilde more sedately by boat. Her fury and the general consternation climax with the swearing of Siegfried's oath against hers on the point of Hagen's spear. For there is the ring on Siegfried's finger, which had been on hers; his denials seem carefree enough, as he sweeps offstage with Gutrune and the company; but thereupon Hagen and Brünnhilde and (more reluctantly) Gunther plot 'Siegfried's death'. Dark is the music, and dark should be the stage, until, in the last few radiant measures of the act, the bridal procession sweeps on in sudden light and beauty, bringing it home to our ears and our eyes how splendid is the glory to which so sombre an ending has just been planned.

For Act III, there are horns to tell us that the hunt is up, but here too is the familiar, flowing arpeggiation of the Rhine, and here are the Rhinemaidens melting our hearts as they always do with those creamy six-three harmonies. Siegfried, lost in more senses than one, almost tosses them back their ring, but grows obstinate when warned that if he does not, he will die that day. When the huntsmen presently find him, Hagen the villain himself starts prompting Siegfried the hero in the way he needs to go—which is towards knowledge of his true self once more. And so Siegfried settles himself down for his famous narrative, that long recapitulation, both musical and dramatic, and in both ways beautifully rounding off the structure. But because we know already of the murder planned, it is for us beauty framed in tragedy.

As memories come flooding back, and Hagen squeezes a herb into another horn for Siegfried to drink his magic amnesia away, more than recapitulation is plainly happening. Integration, rather, and the healing of the fatal split. 'Ah, how hotly then lovely Brünnhilde's arms embraced me!'—Siegfried remembers it all now. Gunther starts up: 'Ah, what am I hearing?' Wotan's two mythical ravens fly out. Hagen, as black as they, has Siegfried turn to look at them and spears him in his undefended back, where consciousness, perhaps, can offer no protection. No better weapon being within reach, Siegfried lunges at Hagen with his shield, but falls back on it helplessly instead. Hagen walks away into the gathering dusk; Gunther and the vassals support the dying hero. In token of renewed self-knowledge, he seems to see Brünnhilde as first he woke her with a kiss. 'Ah, those eyes are open now for ever'.

17. Kurt Eckwall's rendering of Siegfried's funeral march in Götterdämmerung, *as seen* at Bayreuth in 1876.

The great funeral march (fig. 17) concentrates our grief as well as reminding us of Siegfried's true heroic quality, obscured as it has been but not negated by his catastrophic regression. Back in the hall, Hagen makes for the corpse to take the ring, is opposed by Gunther, and kills him: another most violent shock, but at least it reduces the recent duplication of shadow-images. The dead Siegfried now raises his arm in that old mythological gesture of denunciation by the murdered man of his murderer; and this time it is Hagen who steps back defeated.

It is a supernatural gesture, which could not happen literally. But symbolically, it brings to a focus our awareness of a change in the balance of forces. For on the level where all the characters are acting like forces within a single character, Hagen is Siegfried's main complement and shadow-opposite. Their confrontation here is illuminated in the music not by the ambivalent motive of the ring, nor by its uneasy derivative, the motive of the curse, but by the confident motive of the sword (app. ex. 15), always a token for manhood, and since Siegfried forged it again for himself, a token for independent manhood.

As if in response, Brünnhilde arrives to take quiet command. Gutrune, her symbolic double, on learning the truth falls dying to the ground, thus perhaps closing yet another unconscious split. Brünnhilde sings of Siegfried: 'Clear like the sun his light shines on me'; and to the unseen Wotan: 'The purest must betray me, that a woman might grow to knowledge'. And indeed I think that all along, knowledge has been the object of the enterprise. I am not suggesting that Wagner himself made much progress towards a more conscious balance in his outer life: far from it. But I am suggesting that on an inner level of understanding he did advance to an extraordinary symbolical grasp of what our human psychology is really like. I do not imply that this is the whole story of the Ring. But it does enter into it.

Brünnhilde, the ring once more on her finger for the Rhinemaidens to recover when the flames of the funeral fire have purified it, already seems to feel that fire 'fastened on my heart, to embrace him, encompassed by him, in mightiest love to be married to him'; not literally but symbolically now, of course, and as an image for integration such as Wagner so persistently, and on the artistic level so convincingly, sought to achieve. Redemption, again, is how Wagner expressed it in that invaluable letter to Röckel of 25 January 1854, writing that 'only in the union of man and woman does there first exist the true human being', so that 'Siegfried alone . . . is only the half: it is with Brünnhilde that he first comes to be redeemer', for 'ultimately it is suffering, self-immolating woman who becomes the true, conscious redeemer'.

So Brünnhilde rates with Senta and Elisabeth and perhaps with Isolde too as a redeeming heroine. But for redemption to make any sense, one way or another there has got to be a future. And as the long plagal cadence shapes up from the subdominant underside of the harmony, we hear that rare motive (app. ex. 38) which first announced Sieglinde's pregnancy when she was told that she was carrying Siegmund's seed into what was then the future. I do not see how we could be more beautifully assured that there is going to be a future now.[12]

---

THE CONFLICT OF NIGHT AND DAY

The idea of redemption does, I think, come again into Tristan und Isolde (Munich, 1865), though by no means in so immediately
evident a presentation.[1] But the element of yearning is there with unprecedented urgency from the start (ex. 25).

After the intense yet spacious unfolding of the Prelude, Isolde is being
shipped back for King Marke when by every prompting of real feeling
and real honour she should be for Tristan. The story went that Morold,
Isolde's betrothed, was killed in battle by Tristan, himself then cured
by her of his own desperate wound; but when she found in Tristan's
sword a notch tallying with the fragment in Morold's head, she would
have killed him with that very sword if he had not looked into her eyes
with longing rather than fear; and neither of them, it seems, has ever
since forgotten it.

Now King Marke is a childless widower who has adopted his nephew
Tristan in place of a son, and been persuaded by him to marry the
glamorous Isolde, to the supposedly greater glory of Tristan, whose
ambition is thereby being sought at the expense of his feeling. There
is a hidden reason, which Tristan later discovers for himself; but on
shipboard now, all that becomes evident is that Tristan has a guilty conscience. It is so acute that he shares with Isolde what they both of them
believe to be a lethal poison. But Brangaene, her devoted serving maid,
has substituted a love potion, of which the startling consequences represent not so much a fresh magical event as the breaking through into
consciousness of a natural event already established in the unconscious
—namely, the love of Tristan and Isolde ever since that fateful encounter
when their eyes first met (ex. 26).

And so in Act II the horns of the royal hunting party grow distant;
and in the face of Brangaene's uneasy warning, Isolde lowers the torch
and waves to Tristan in their prearranged signal. At first the passion in
the orchestra tells us more than their wild greetings; but as they be-

(a)

## Example 25
Wagner, *Tristan und Isolde* (Munich, 1865). The seminal opening:
compare the rising minor sixth and falling semitone in app. ex. 6,
and also the yearning upward semitones in app. ex. 28; but here
the chromatic D-sharp and the altered first chord transform the
image.

## Example 26
Wagner, *Tristan und Isolde*. The muted horns preparing hauntingly
for the passion to follow. The ninth is a moderate dissonance with
its root but a pure consonance with its fifth and seventh, and may
perhaps get its elusive and dream-like suggestiveness (compare
Debussy) from this acoustic ambivalence; its romantic capabilities
are of course not in doubt.

come a little more coherent, he owns to having been dazzled by her
very radiance into a daylight vision of the honour to be won through
his dishonourable betrayal. And now?

> In the vain delusions of the day
> only one yearning remains
> for holy night, where from the beginning
> love's wonder, alone true, laughs out!

And so the long, ecstatic but quite dream-like scene unfolds, full of
such yearning in the music that love's intensity has nowhere been better expressed. But love's intensity has many dimensions. Is this music

erotic, in the sense of directly suggesting physical excitement? I think
it is; and certainly no one doubts that sex is what they urgently desire;
but so is the impassioned exchange of fantasies which (stage convention being what it then was) is all we are actually allowed to witness.
Now faithful Brangaene sings: 'Beware! Beware! Soon night gives way
to day!' They will not be warned, persuading themselves that death
will take good care of them if night does not. The music of their love
duet here will become what we customarily call Isolde's Liebestod, her
'love-death', at the end, with a symbolical ambivalence not so far to be
understood.

King Marke, brought in to discover them—with the greatest horror
—by Melot, the indispensable villain of the piece, embarks on that long
but instructive monologue, telling us very movingly how the whole
catastrophic situation had been set up at Tristan's urging. Tristan does
not even think to defend himself by explaining about the love potion;
but he is edging already towards a more insightful association which he
will later make with the mother who died in bearing him to a father
already dead.

> Where Tristan now slinks,
> are you willing, Isolde, to follow him?
> On the land that Tristan means,
> the sun's light does not shine:
> it is the dark land of night,
> from which my mother
> sent me forth
> when him, whom she had conceived by a man dead,
> in death she lay to deliver into the light.
> That which, when she bore me,
> was her love's ground,
> the wonderland of the night,
> from which I once awoke,
> this Tristan offers to you.

And she is willing. Tristan fights with Melot, lets his guard drop deliberately, and falls wounded into the arms of faithful Kurwenal.

In Act III, one hope alone draws Tristan back towards the hated light:
that somewhere it shines on Isolde. When Kurwenal tells him that she
is being fetched to heal him for the second time, he grows so deliri-
ous that he thinks he sees her ship. But the shepherd's sad piping tells
us that no ship has yet been sighted. Now memory stirs strangely, as

the tune recalls to Tristan once more the double disaster of his child-hood (ex. 27).

**Example 27**
Wagner, *Tristan und Isolde*, Act III. (a) The shepherd's sad tune which tells that the sea is still empty, but also reminds Tristan of his childhood bereavements; (b) the shepherd's happy tune when Isolde's ship comes into sight.

Doubly bereaved, Tristan must I think first have projected onto Isolde the archetypal image of the mother he never saw, and then under compulsion of the Oedipal taboo thrust her over to the ageing father-substitute whose adopted son he was. His guilt would have felt the worse because he had already killed Morold, her intended husband. But now in Act III, Tristan makes the more courageous attempt to understand, as Joseph Kerman saw long ago, and Robert Gutman more recently:[2]

> The fearful drink,
> which acquainted me with torment,
> I myself—I myself
> have brewed it!
> From father's suffering,
> and mother-woe,
> from love's tears
> from laughter and weeping,
> from delight and wounds
> have I the drink's
> poison found!

### ILLUMINATION COMES AS THE END

It was Gutman who noticed how 'fathers—vague, unidentified, vanished, dying and dead—form an important theme in Wagner's works'.[3] Siegmund bereft of his father (actually Wotan); Siegfried brooding on what his father can have been like (certainly not like little Mime); Parsifal knowing nothing much about his father till Kundry tells him —these and others are connected by Gutman with Wagner's losing his own father at six months, and his affectionate stepfather, Geyer, within eight years. And there was, too, that folk-tune played by young Wagner to Geyer on his deathbed, and repeated half a century later at a performance in Geyer's memory. Gutman thinks that Tristan's sad tune became associated with all this, and that Tristan's grief had old roots in Wagner's grief. I agree. I think that Wagner too had both a mother-problem and a father-problem, and drew strength from both of them in the devious way of genius.

It was thus self-deceiving fantasy for Tristan to seek refuge from his grief in 'the wonderland of the night': self-discovery and self-recovery to stop thinking about that fateful love potion as merely something nasty out of a bottle, and to find the source of his suffering in the traumas of his own childhood. And now once again he seems to see Isolde's ship; but this time the shepherd on the cliff's edge pipes a joyful tune; Kurwenal runs off to help with the landing; and Tristan sings, quite remarkably: 'O, this sun! Ah, this day! Ah, most sunny day of this delight!' For this moment, a blaze of sudden light on stage would match the mood, though it will soon need to sink again.

I think that Tristan, in tearing off his bandages, may be making some manic gesture towards ending all concealment. He has not a vestige of a death-wish at this moment, surely. Nevertheless, no sooner has Isolde run in than he dies, and the needless battle follows as Kurwenal and Melot fall lethally upon each other. King Marke, who because of Brangaene's confession was bringing forgiveness and reconciliation, seems to be confronted only with corpses. But Isolde next soars into that astonishing recapitulation from Act II, to words which on one level, as Bryan Magee has recently traced in detail, form the climax of Wagner's attempt to transcribe into his poetry the pessimism he found in Schopenhauer and behind that the Buddhist wish for annihilation.[4]

But did he manage it? 'His eyes are opening', Isolde assures us as she looks down at Tristan's body: 'ever more brightly see how he shines' —just as Brünnhilde talked about her dead Siegfried. Are these 'waves' or 'clouds' which 'surge' and 'roar' for her to 'dive beneath' and 'sink unconscious' into 'highest bliss'? Nirvana may be the avowed intention; yet there is something about these watery metaphors which reminds me of Senta's redeeming sea change at the optimistic conclusion of *The Flying Dutchman*.

Nirvana is at best a difficult conception for a Western mind. Schopenhauer may or may not quite have grasped it, and Wagner may by no means quite have grasped Schopenhauer. It was Magee again who remarked that Wagner evidently expected Tristan and Isolde to be blissfully united in death, whereas 'on the basis of Schopenhauer's philosophy . . . they will be united only in the sense that they will also be united with everything and everybody else'.[5] Whatever Buddhist annihilation may mean, it cannot mean that journeys end in lovers meeting.

For my Western mind, desire for annihilation looks very like the ultimate in retrogression; and Tristan's earlier invitation to Isolde to join him in 'the dark land of night, from which my mother sent me forth' could quite as well be taken for the classic longing to return to the womb. With a view to possible rebirth, then? No: rebirth is just what in Buddhist doctrine you would most hope to avert. And while Magee states correctly that Wagner 'never spelled out what he meant by it', I cannot agree that for Wagner redemption 'obviously' meant or involved 'liberation and release from this phenomenal world'.[6] I see far clearer signs of Wagner's old life-enhancing (not life-denying) yearning to become more of a whole person through growth in this mortal world rather than in release from it. However much his head may have been fascinated by the notion of a pessimistic out, I do not believe that Wagner's heart ever gave up that optimistic search.

Barry Millington (1984) has pointed out that Wagner's own term for the ending of *Tristan* was not *Liebestod* but *Verklärung*: not love-death but transfiguration. In spite of Schopenhauer, I cannot see Wagner really setting himself against the mainstream tradition that illusion and unconsciousness are of the dark, truth and consciousness of the light. It is perfectly proper to see *Tristan* as dedicated to the night so long as the lovers themselves are turned that way, convincing themselves that daylight is the illusion; but at the latter end it is the light which breaks through, and death itself must, I think, be standing in symbolically, as it so often does, for transformation and a new chance in life. Even of Tristan dead, Isolde insists that 'his eyes are opening'; that is not the language of oblivion but of illumination. The end of *Tristan* is not a nothing. The end of *Tristan* is a radiance (ex. 28).

Example 28

Wagner, *Tristan und Isolde*. The unifying recapitulation at the climax of the opera.

### HEART AND HEAD IN ART AND LIFE

The overture to *Die Meistersinger von Nürnberg* (Munich, 1868; ex. 29a) leads at the rise of the curtain, by one of the rarest strokes of operatic genius, straight into a vocal chorale eloquent of the very real faith which vitalizes this otherwise slightly conventional and closed community.[7] And Walther, newly arrived and about to open up those closed ranks eventually to mutual advantage, already has Eva inventing womanly excuses for becoming acquainted with him as the service ends. Learning that she is to be the prize for a song contest the next day, he is awarded so many faults, at the preliminary test, by Beckmesser (who is himself a candidate) that the slate has no room for any more squeaky scratches of the chalk. Yet Sachs, though aware of the faults, feels behind them an inspiration which, if brought to better order, might be just what guild and town might turn to advantage: not only, we are surely meant to appreciate, in their musical style, but in their life-style too.

In Act II, Sachs impedes the imminent elopement of Walther and Eva not in spite of but because of being so sympathetically on their side. When Beckmesser arrives to serenade Eva, it is her maidservant Magdalena who appears at the upper window, but dressed (in aid of the elopement) as Eva. David, Magdalena's impetuous follower, sets incontinently upon Beckmesser, who gets a beating he does not deserve in the riot which confusedly ensues. Sachs quells the rioters in cold fury: and at last, when the moonlit street is quiet again, the old watchman blows his horn to our uncovenanted delight before the curtain falls.

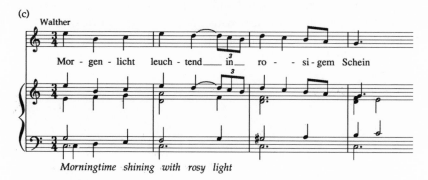

## Example 29

Wagner, *Die Meistersinger von Nürnberg* (Munich, 1868). (a) The opening of the overture, giving the solid worth, with only the most subtle hint of their pompous side, of those excellent citizens; (b) as Sachs laments that manic force without the creative impetus of which, nevertheless, Walther's prize-song at (c) did not come to him.

But in Act III, Sachs sings that sad 'Wahn, wahn' (Madness, madness—
though 'Mania, mania' might be another rendering, since this is a force
within us which can inspire as powerfully as it can dement). Sachs is
sad also for himself, loving Eva yet helping Walther because he knows
that Walther is her fitting mate and already has her heart (ex. 29b). And
when the great quintet builds up, I think perhaps we can hear in that
superlative ensemble something of the reconciliation towards which
the whole story is moving forward.

At the final contest, Beckmesser is not too unkindly laughed out of
court. Then Walther sings what he has already been heard so promis-
ingly shaping up, out of his own dream (ex. 29c). In the morning by
the golden tree of life, he sings, Eva is the poet's dream of Paradise; in
the starlit evening by the fountain of inspiration, she is his dream-muse
on Parnassus; at his waking, she is both woman and muse as his song
wins him both Parnassus and Paradise. How better could he put it for
my purpose here? But when he has been acclaimed the victor and Eva
has crowned him with the traditional laurel wreath, his pride spurns
the master's chain, until Sachs melts him by an arioso reconciling most
wonderfully, in form and content alike, the promptings of feeling with
the temperings of reason. Eva now takes the laurel wreath and sets it
from behind on Sachs's head. He starts with sudden astonishment; but
it is the music which tells us how deeply moved he is. And so are we.
For it is Sachs who, by accepting that which had to happen, has guided
it into this present reconciliation: feeling reconciled with reason, certainly; but also Sachs reconciled with Sachs. And so it is even more for
lifesmanship than it is for musicianship that we are so moved to see
him acclaimed the master of them all.

---

### ASKING QUESTIONS THE NEEDFUL ACT

In *Lohengrin*, Elsa was forbidden to ask the ultimately necessary question, but asked it. In *Parsifal* (Bayreuth, 1882), Parsifal is expected to ask questions, but does not.[1] Instead, he ends by acting as though he has found the answer to the one question which the whole opera implies. This question has to do, as great works of art so often have, with what it is really like to be a human being.

Part of what it is like to be a human being is that we have to endure a built-in component of suffering, which can nevertheless be turned round into the very dynamism of creative growth and creative achievement. This is indeed the remarkable but by no means unusual syndrome which has been so well described by so many observers as the 'creative wound'.

### THE CREATIVE WOUND

Klingsor's wound, from which we may on one level see the whole story as having taken its impetus, was his self-inflicted castration for the purpose, ostensibly, of ridding himself of his own intolerable lust. Symbolically, Klingsor descends from Attis the priest and lover of the Great Mother, who did himself this same gruesome injury, thereby submitting himself utterly to her service; for no man is more irrevocably bound to the image of the mother than the man who has rendered himself, whether by physiological or (more commonly, of course) by psychological self-injury, incapable of being unfaithful to her. It is interesting that Klingsor had himself sought to become pure enough to be acceptable into the holy brotherhood, and only when contemptuously rejected had he turned to implacable enmity. A profound ambivalence is at issue here. Klingsor became as a consequence the villain of the piece. But we have always to remember that if there were to be no villain, there would be no piece. The villain is in hard fact the initiator: he gets something going. As Alberich to the Ring, so Klingsor to Parsifal: his malevolence is necessary to the story, and leads, however indirectly, to a redemptive resolution.

Klingsor's malevolence, like Alberich's, is of enormous power. Life-force inhibited in one direction may often find all the more pressurized an outlet in another direction. Klingsor is now pouring all his pent-up energies into his bitter vendetta. That in psychological terms is the secret of the magic which he wields over his castle and his flower-maidens and above all his part-time captive and seductress-in-chief, Kundry, a personification of the eternal feminine even more ambivalent than the Queen of Night herself.

And behind all this, not directly introduced but conditioning the thoughts of the leading characters with obsessive persistence, lies the wounding, the assuredly creative wounding, of Christ on the cross. They agonize about it, but see in it the very hope of their own salvation, the very promise of their own redemption. It is very much a part of the underlying ambivalence of the situation that while the Holy Grail which caught Christ's blood is still in safekeeping, and greatly desired by Kling-sor in token of ultimate victory, the spear which wounded Christ has already been stolen by Klingsor when its all-too-human guardian Am-fortas was lying blissfully and obliviously in Kundry's arms; and with that self-same spear, Klingsor has given Amfortas a wound which in Wolfram von Eschenbach's source-version was pointedly enough in the testicles. It is apparently all one wound in principle, just as it is all one spear. Yet more pointedly, this wound in turn will not heal except by a touch of the spear which inflicted it. Which Klingsor holds. Which it will be for Parsifal to recover from Klingsor if he can.

In medieval legend, the sickness of the king is the sickness of the land, which will not heal until the pure fool, on being shown the ritual mysteries, seeks to question their meaning. It occurs to me that in some neurotic entanglements of the psyche, the truth itself may be the healing thing, and self-discovery the painful remedy. More generally, there are situations in which innocence and unconsciousness just will no longer do. It is perhaps a good beginning to start in innocence, and it is un-avoidable to start in unconsciousness. I suppose that the significance of Parsifal having to be a fool as well as pure may be that worldly wisdom and low cunning would not get him anywhere. But confronting in some manner the necessary questions will.

Parsifal shoots down the castle swan in all unconsciousness and in all seeming innocence. But there may be more behind this wanton deed than any of us, with the probable exception of Kundry, is as yet in a position to appreciate. Swans and geese and cranes and storks are all apt to figure in popular folklore as mother-symbols; and like the Ancient Mariner with his fateful albatross, Parsifal might have been impelled to his deed of violence by a deeper necessity than he knows. It is Kundry herself who now brings up the remarkable information that Parsifal had left home as the only way of getting free of his mother's over-protectiveness, following his father's death in battle before ever he was born. But, she adds, his mother now grieves for him no more, because she too is dead. Both Parsifal and we experience the sudden shock of it; but I suspect that getting free from mother may have been the deeper necessity, and killing the swan the token confirmation, in preparation for the more testing encounter later on with Kundry in her other role.

Gurnemanz, knowing the old prophecy about the pure fool coming as the predestined healer, brings Parsifal by a magical change of scene to the holy feast of the communion. And the Grail is uncovered and the light pours down from on high and Gurnemanz asks Parsifal whether he has understood. But Parsifal neither answers nor seeks to be told. So Gurnemanz pushes him out in a fury of disappointment. Thus far, thus bad. But from on high the voices of the unseen chorus repeat the hopeful promise: 'Grown wise through compassion, the pure fool'.

### THE OTHER FACE OF KUNDRY

And now in Act II, Kundry, in her other self, is greeted by Klingsor as 'nameless one' and 'first of witches'; for 'you were Herodias' (the same seductive and destructive mother-figure, appropriately enough, whom John the Baptist had denounced for incest before literally losing his head—but not his manhood—to her evil daughter Salome). When Kundry asks Klingsor by what power he compels her, he answers: 'Because only on me your power does not prevail'—and we may remember all too painfully the reason why. Klingsor has already given everything he had to the Great Mother, and is her servant anyhow. By the same token, Kundry in her destructive capacity will get free of Klingsor only when one of her intended victims resists her seduction.

Thomas Mann saw Kundry, reasonably enough, as a study in split personality; but on another level, she too is displaying the ambivalence only to be expected from so archetypal an image.[2] Like Brünnhilde with Siegfried, she claims now to have known Parsifal from a baby. Rubbing it in, she asks what else could have brought him, 'if not the wish for knowledge'. And still more insistently, she urges him by 'acknowledgement' to end his 'guilt' about his mother in 'repentance'; by 'understanding' to turn 'foolishness' into 'awareness'; and to learn from herself 'the love which Gamuret embraced when Herzeleide's flame flowed scorching over him'. Since Gamuret was Parsifal's father and Herzeleide was his mother, Kundry is inviting Parsifal to share with herself that incestuous intercourse which is at the heart of the Oedipal fantasy. 'She who once gave you love and life', insists Kundry, 'must soften death and foolishness; she offers you this day, as mother's blessing, love's last greeting, first kiss'. With that she fastens her lips on his, and the music tells us with what eagerness he responds.

Ah, but then with the utmost clarity of music and of action, Parsifal recoils. 'Amfortas!' he cries; 'Amfortas! The wound!' (ex. 30). He has made the connection. He has learnt on the instant what this most insidious of erotic fantasies entails. It entails a loss of real manhood—the spear gets stolen. It entails a wounding of the true self—only the spear recovered can restore it. Sexuality was not denied to the knights of the brotherhood: Parsifal himself became the father of Lohengrin. Mother-bound sexuality was the temptation which Parsifal had to overcome. For the psychological hazard of not sufficiently overcoming the retrogressive fascination of the mother-image does not lie in being normally attracted to women. It lies in being neurotically dependent on women.

Now for a touch of emotional blackmail as Kundry urges Parsifal to act out for her the compassionate role of the Redeemer she had once laughed at on the cross so long ago. Parsifal will indeed come to that in Act III, but here and on Kundry's present terms it would be a disaster for them both. So he repels her. So she foredooms him to long years of wandering, which I suspect he would have had to have undergone anyhow on the way to growing up. So Klingsor is recalled to hurl the spear at Parsifal, who miraculously catches it in token of manhood recovered, and making with it the sign of the cross, he sends castle and garden crumbling in token of fantasy renounced.

But in Act III, a much older and sadder Gurnemanz hears a hollow groaning which he well recalls: it is Kundry returning to consciousness in penitent mood. And Parsifal too returns, telling of the suffering and the conflict which he has certainly gone through. She washes his feet as if indeed he were Christ. Gurnemanz anoints him, calling him 'compassionate sufferer, hallowed knower'. Parsifal sprinkles Kundry with water, saying, 'Be baptized, have faith in the Redeemer'. She sinks weeping to the ground. The scene changes magically as before, but in the opposite direction, bringing us back in some altered manner to the point at which we left off before the testing adventures began of which we are now about to see the consequences.

**Example 30**

Wagner, *Parsifal* (Bayreuth, 1882), Act II. Parsifal's moment of truth
—and that grievous interval of the tritone, which we have been
watching ever since Monteverdi's *Orfeo*, does good service again.

### THE FATHER TAKES A HAND

Titurel, the father of Amfortas, having survived into an extremity of old age because the repeated sight of the Grail kept him alive,
has now died through the refusal of Amfortas to uncover the Grail, his
own wish being only for death. And Amfortas appeals to dead Titurel
to pray to the Heavenly Redeemer, in whose company he now stands,
even as He brings new life to the holy brotherhood, so for Titurel himself to grant the relief in death which he so urgently desires. I think
that Amfortas stands rather in the position of a man intolerably aware
of his own wounded state, yet unable either to ease the torment in his
damaged psyche or to delude himself that really he is perfectly normal,
perfectly all right. He knows only too well that he is not all right.

And so, rather than uncover the Grail and increase his own misery,
Amfortas pulls open his wound. The similarity to Tristan is evident
enough, and may possibly have to do once again with bringing all concealment to an end. But the outcome here is more obviously positive.
For prompt to the moment, in comes Parsifal to heal the wound with a
touch of the spear which inflicted it, and with words of absolution such
as in Tristan may in a manner be implied, but are certainly not spoken.
'Blessed be your suffering', sings Parsifal, 'which gave to the frightened
fool the highest power of compassion, and the purest might of wisdom'.
But we shall miss the whole point here unless we recall that it was Parsifal's suffering too. They are all in it together. The creative wound (and it
is indeed a hurtful suffering) is not any man's especial prerogative. Suffering is in one way or another a condition of our human state, which
we shall not escape but may hope (there can be no certainty) to turn
round at least in part to eventual advantage. Redemption was assuredly
Wagner's word for this unending search, and redemption is once more
the nub of the situation here.

So now the light streams down again and the chorus proclaims 'Redemption to the redeemer' and the Grail glows out and the dove descends. Spear and Grail are reunited as if in some far-away echo of the
sacred marriage, and possibly there is also a hint of impregnation from
the spirit-world above. The lighting is no doubt crucial here, but the
temple itself should not be too vague or abstract. It is, after all, a Christian shrine, and within reason it should look like one (fig. 18).

I see no reason to question Wagner's good faith in the matter. He
always had envisaged the symbols of religion as needing the services
of art to bring out their deep and hidden truth. And it is interesting
here that Christian symbolism has always leant somewhat towards the

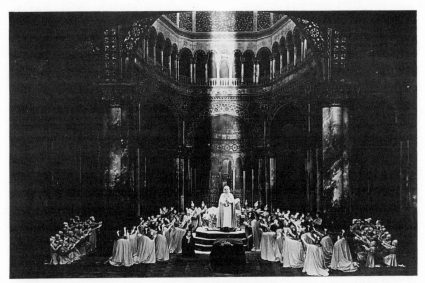

18. Paul von Joukovsky's *Romanesque Temple of the Holy Grail* graced performances of Wagner's *Parsifal* at Bayreuth for more than half a century.

masculine principle, with the three members of the Holy Trinity all depicted on the male side, and the blessed Virgin Mary contributing some, but not by any means commensurate, feminine solace. This holy brotherhood itself is proud and exclusive in its dedication to the masculine spirit and its vaunted uncontamination by that feminine allurement which always holds some vestiges of the Great Mother. There may be some positive implication here of getting free from mere animal nature: but not too free, I hope, or it might come to be rather too like the sacrifice of Attis to the Great Mother all over again.

The Heavenly Father is ritually, although not visibly, being invoked in support of Parsifal, himself the new acting father-figure of the brotherhood. It is possible in effect to assimilate the strength and authority of the father, or, come to that, the enchantment and protectiveness of the mother, not as alien introjections but as genuine growth of character, available to help both oneself and others. Nevertheless, Carl Dahlhaus quite fairly called Parsifal 'a passive hero', with particular emphasis on 'the seduction scene, which it requires the insights of psychoanalysis to interpret'.[3] True; and indeed none of the characters comes very individually to life, as people with whom we can sympathetically identify. But so archetypal are the situations that some deeper recognition stirs.

We are deeply moved by the reconciliation and the absolution in the closing scene. And throughout we are drawn along by the amazing eloquence of the music. Explain it how you will, if you are into such music you are into a numinous experience, of which the sign is an unarguable conviction that life has a meaning or is its own meaning. It is in that sense that I should call *Parsifal* a religious work (ex. 31).

But here, after so much theorizing, let me come right back to it: how we do enjoy the numinous experience! *Parsifal* is not only a beacon for the spirit. *Parsifal* is a joy to the spirit.

**Example 31**
Wagner, *Parsifal*. The serenely diatonic motive as the Holy Grail sums up Wagner's last symbol for redemption.

# 15 REALISM

## THE DESTRUCTIVE SEDUCTIVENESS OF CARMEN

Bizet's *Carmen* (Paris, 1875) has elements of the then recently fashionable 'realism', somewhat ameliorated from Mérimée's short novel on which the excellent libretto by Meilhac and Halévy is based.[1] But there remains, underneath the realism, an archetypal ambivalence. Carmen's seductiveness and Carmen's destructiveness are not two forces of nature but one force. She is dangerous to any man having the opposite side of the pattern, so that he meshes in unresistingly. Like Hedda Gabler, whom in some respects she so resembles, she is also dangerous to herself. Her opposite number is the faithful Micaela, behind whom there looms in the opera, though not in the novel, the magnetic influence of José's mother. Carmen is indeed a sex-symbol, and sex is itself an archetype, an instinct, a lure for delight as well as for entanglement. But sex in humans is liable to contamination by the mother-image, with all that this tempting fantasy promises of bliss unspeakable and in reality unattainable. That, precisely, is the fascination of the fantasy (ex. 32).

So Carmen steals that first scene with her taunting Habanera. José, loving Micaela, thinks himself immune; but Carmen nevertheless disturbs him enough for him to take her for a witch; and in that he is not so very far wrong. But now, prompt to my argument, Micaela gives José a kiss which, like Kundry, she assures him was sent to him from his mother. In Act II, José, now thoroughly besotted and compromised, so threatens Lieutenant Zuniga that José's only refuge is in the mountains with the gypsy band. And there comes that scene of strange beauty and haunting tension in which the cards foretell Carmen's death, and she with a quite genuine self-knowledge accepts it as somehow built into the very structure of her character (ex. 33). From this point onwards I think we accept her too, in the knowledge that she cannot help herself. The greatness of Carmen lies in her willingness to be Carmen. Bizet's

(a)   Allegro giocoso

(b)

(c)   Andante moderato

**Example 32**
Bizet, Carmen (Paris, 1875), Overture. (a) The taunting glitter of
Bizet's fictional Seville; (b) the brash vitality of the bullfighter
Escamillo; (c) the dangerous seductiveness of the gypsy Carmen.

greatness lies in presenting her both realistically and symbolically for
what she so remarkably is. It is a triumph of artistry and of compassion
too, and I shall presently be suggesting that it comes in part from a very
curious sort of fellow feeling. For I think that Bizet knew very well what
it feels like to be a driven character.

Escamillo arrives in search of Carmen; Micaela arrives in search of
José. Escamillo is sent packing by the gypsies, but with a meaningful
glance at Carmen he invites all who love him to his next bullfight.
Micaela just as pointedly tells José that his mother is dying, which so
gets to him that he follows her, though swearing angrily to return. By a
deliberate trick of operatic craftsmanship, the curtain comes down on
the end of Escamillo's own taunting song, and we know that trouble is
in preparation for the closing act.

The closing act raises the orchestral temperature, not so much unfeelingly as with the hard and glaring intensity of a Spanish sun and a Spanish bullfight (fig. 19). As Escamillo passes into the arena, he tells Carmen to be proud of him if she loves him, to which she replies that she loves him as she has never loved before. Other men have no doubt heard that story; but she believes it every time.

There follows what I should call a classical death-wish scene. Carmen is warned that José is around and in dangerous mood. She nevertheless lets him find her alone outside the arena. To his pleading she replies: 'Carmen has never lied' (itself a lie, but this too she believes); 'her spirit remains inflexible; between you and her everything is finished'. (Mérimée's words are: 'I will follow you to death—yes, but I will not live with you any more'.) And still talking in this oddly schizoid way of herself as if she were a third person: 'Never will Carmen yield' (how often has she not yielded?) 'for free she was born' (Mérimée has 'gypsy', which implies the same) 'and free she will die!' Free? When have her inner drives ever allowed Carmen to be free?

19. The confrontation of Carmen and Don José in Act IV of Bizet's opera is a classical death-wish scene. This is Emile Bertin's design for the 1875 première at the Opéra-Comique.

(a)

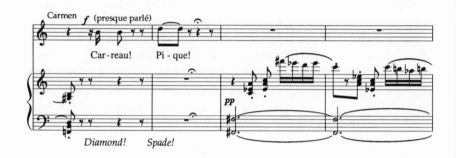

**Example 33**

Bizet, *Carmen*, Act II. Carmen reads her own death in the cards.

(b)

*In vain to shun the bitter*

*answer,   In vain you shuffle,      that does nothing,*

*the cards are honest      and do not lie!*

But as Carmen sings 'free she will *die*', the crowd inside cries 'Viva, viva'—long *live* Escamillo—with unintended irony on their part, but Bizet himself must certainly have intended this. Carmen throws José's ring contemptuously at his feet; he stabs her; the crowd pours out singing Escamillo's boastful song as if to rub it in that life has it over death; and José gives himself up for execution. Those prescient cards were certainly in the right of it.

## A CASE OF SYNCHRONICITY?

The fellow feeling which I have hinted that Bizet may have shared with Carmen would have come from quite deep down. Bizet was aware of such contributory symbolism as, for example, the flower tossed by Carmen to José and kept by him long after it had faded. He was not aware of underlying symbolism on the broad Wagnerian scale; indeed Bizet in 1867 quoted with approval a remark by Béranger that 'art is art, and that is all there is to it'.[2] That is quite a common attitude, typical of the naivety in this respect of so many artists. It is also common for art to carry symbolism without the artist knowing it. I think that Bizet was a case not so much of an artist using a symbol as of a symbol taking over an artist.

This symbol in effect was the complex and ambivalent character of Carmen herself, by which the actions of those around her were so fatefully conditioned. Bizet's actions were as I should suppose conditioned by an unconscious entanglement with his own mother. He seems to have experienced her as fascinating yet hostile, as possessive yet unloving, above all as inescapable. On receiving one letter from her bearing the address of a hospital, Bizet before even reading it fell into so acute an anxiety that he thought he had 'a sufficient pretext against the gondolier' to attack him 'with the firm intention of strangling him'. The anger thus palpably displaced may have been not so much for his mother as against her. To his mother-in-law, Mme Halévy, Bizet wrote: 'I tend to believe that I am the victim of persecution which probably exists only in my own mind. It is really an illness'.[3] An element of paranoia might be our speculation here.

As may often happen, Bizet married a second instalment of his mother-problem. He comes rather well out of this part of his story; but it shows him closely acquainted with the troubled and troubling aspects of femininity. When his mother died, Edmund Galabert reports how Bizet 'would feel an appalling agony. I [Bizet] would be compelled to throw myself into an armchair, and then I would believe that I saw my mother coming into the room. She would come across and stand next to me and put her hand on my heart. With that the agony would become more intense. I would suffocate, and it would seem to me that her hand so heavily weighing upon me was actually the cause of my suffering'.[4] The physiological cause was angina, but the psychological association with the mother was almost certainly correct. It is my suspicion that the pressure which appears to have built up within Bizet's unconscious from such contradictory impulses of love and hatred, fascination and repulsion, fear and guilt, might have been potent both for danger and for creation. There is a fairly dangerous female character in La coupe du roi de Thule, and another, in fact a mother, in Daudet's play L'Arlésienne, which Bizet set to music. Carmen is at the climax of the line, as though Bizet in his art were still feeling his way all round a theme too alarming to confront directly in consciousness, yet too urgent to leave alone: the theme of being attracted and destroyed by a woman's fascination.

Bizet composed a wonderful opera, but he could not exorcize his demon. On the very evening of his own sudden death, Galli-Marié as Carmen nearly collapsed in the scene where the cards foretell her death, and did faint in the wings.[5] No one knew why: she could only insist that 'it was not for herself that she was afraid'.[6] Jung might have taken it for a case of synchronicity, of a connection beneath consciousness which without being causal is nevertheless significant: a difficult proposition, but he had his arguments. Whatever the explanation, this strange but well-attested occurrence has a certain appropriateness as a farewell gesture. It tallies so aptly with the romantic element lingering in Bizet through every attempt at earthy realism.

### INNER OR OUTER?

The Russians, including Musorgsky and Tchaikovsky, tried hard for realism.[7] You could call it a sort of realism when Tchaikovsky so bitterly took to heart the letter scene in Eugene Onegin that it is said to have induced him into his catastrophic marriage. It is musically a realistic enough touch, again, when that needless duel is represented as a stubborn canon (ex. 34).

But it becomes more sentimental than realistic when Tchaikovsky, departing from Pushkin, tries to persuade us that Onegin still has a heart left to be broken in the last act: in Pushkin he has already killed what little heart he ever had when he killed his friend. And then again, when

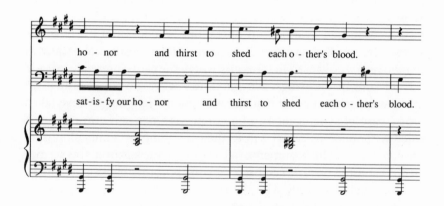

**Example 34**

Tchaikovsky, *Eugene Onegin* (Moscow, 1879), Act II, scene ii. The stubborn canon for the stubborn friends.

the hero of *The Queen of Spades* threatens the heroine's grandmother—with a pistol!—for the illicit secret which he hopes will save him at the gambling table, I call that a totally unrealistic adventure with a surrogate mother-figure which went predictably wrong.

Tchaikovsky enjoyed real-life mothering from his generous patroness Nadezhda von Meck, without either of them wanting to put their mutually beneficial projections to the test of meeting. His own childhood had been dominated by an unusually wayward mother. It was Nietzsche who commented on 'those who, being immediately allied to music, have it as it were for their mother's lap, and are connected with things almost exclusively by unconscious musical relationships'.[8] Mother-longing may certainly contribute to the intensity of musical experience. We pick up the experience where consciousness begins. But consciousness would have nowhere to begin, if consciousness were all.

So realism in music can indeed happen, but it cannot happen in isolation from unconscious symbolism. Jazz would not be jazz if it did not re-enact so urgently the tears and the laughter, the insensate rages and the unbridled joys of that formidable little narcissist, the human baby. They say that Picasso asked Rubinstein: 'How do you know how to play Spanish music?' Rubinstein to Picasso, slapping his stomach: 'I feel it here!' Picasso to Rubinstein: 'Ah, when I paint, I also feel it in the stomach!'

Gut-music, then? Yes, but also soul-music. There is always in music that strange relationship between inner emotions and outer acoustics; and connected with that, perhaps, this equally strange conviction of the body being intimately involved as well as the mind. It is not only that singers very literally and necessarily feel it that way, and that most performers make bodily movements which give an almost dance-like expression to their mental states, as well as helping small ensembles like string quartets to keep a good rapport, and conductors in particular to dance their way through their performances. That is natural, since their very deeds are physical. But even as a listener, I feel my physical state as it were swaying and pulsing along, however imperceptibly, in unison with the music. The gap, if it is a gap, between body and soul is most agreeably bridged; or perhaps it would be better to say that music is not so much of the body or the soul as of the psyche-soma, that ultimate unity within duality where all our human experiences are mysteriously melded. Music is an experience of the psyche-soma.

Music has its own symbols, and among them is that paradoxical ambiguity which runs through our lives like some fateful thread. What could be more ambivalent, for example, than that eerie cross-relation between major and minor so favoured by jazz musicians—and not only by jazz musicians (exx. 35 and 36). Of just such analogues between acoustical suggestiveness and emotional suggestibility does music's communicability consist.

Music is not only wordless communication person to person. Music is also experience of those deeper-than-personal emotions which flood the human unconscious, also wordlessly and all the more movingly on that account. Authenticity may at bottom have to do with our fidelity to those deeper emotions.

## Example 35

Coperario, 'Che pue mirarvi' (Christ Church, Oxford, MS 2,
f. 170v; short score). An early seventeenth-century cross-relation
arising from the counterpoint.

## Example 36

Vaughan Williams, Eighth Symphony, first movement (short
score). The same ambivalent cross-relation as in ex. 35, hauntingly
extended.

PUCCINI AND 'VERISMO'

Carl Dahlhaus has argued within careful limits that outer realism can come into opera, although he also quotes very fairly Busoni's
opposite view that the whole concept of *verismo* is 'untenable' because
'people performing actions while singing' can make sense only in the
realm of 'the incredible, the untrue, the improbable'.[9] That reminded
Dahlhaus of the fairy-tale context of the 'marvellous' recommended by
E. T. A. Hoffmann, and reminds me of the 'supernatural' recommended
by Dryden and Algarotti, not to mention Coleridge. The truth seems
to be that even in verismo opera there are hidden layers, where archetypes may be working assiduously enough beneath the surface in their
usual way. The images resulting may not look supernatural, but they are
certainly numinous.

Puccini is much the best of verismo, and *Tosca* (Rome, 1900) may well
be the best of Puccini.[10] Mosco Carner pointed out that Puccini lost his
father when little more than five years of age, and that he remained
obsessed with some 'concept of love as tragic guilt to be atoned for
by death'. Hence the series of doomed heroines to whom the heroes
merely act in the role of 'catalysts': a dramatic pattern which 'sprang
from an image deeply anchored in his unconscious' and which 'therefore assumed for him the force of a compulsion'.[11]

But what image? What compulsion? One possibility is that Puccini,
in fighting off some terrifying childhood fantasy of having killed his
father, took refuge in the not much less terrifying fantasy of his mother
having killed his father. Puccini's heroines had then to be doomed in
atonement for this quite specifically imagined guilt, in addition to the
more general guilt of having transgressed against the incest barrier by
their very attractiveness to their all too mother-bound and indeed rather
ill-defined heroes.

Scarpia, the villain of *Tosca*, is not ill defined. As he soars into his wonderful cantilena in Act II, he comes very near to taking over the hero's
role. Scarpia is well cast for the part of an ambivalent father-figure, and
may be doubly disturbing to Tosca on that account. In that incomparable 'Vissi d'arte, vissi d'amore', Tosca sounds more like a woman in
turmoil than the kindly young innocent she seems to be trying to make
herself out to be. Franco Zeffirelli, in his magnificent stage production,
certainly took this view of Tosca, insisting that Tosca desires Scarpia
as much as she detests him.[12] Scarpia himself insists that 'passionate in
anger is passionate in love'. Even if the director has not the insight to
bring out this crucial ambiguity, we shall in all probability pick it up that

way. It may not look that way but it will feel that way, because that is the scenario beneath the scenario; and the beauty and the poignancy of the music in this central scene confirm it to our feelings and our intuitions, if not to our thoughts.

Having resolved her conflict by stabbing Scarpia, Tosca assuages her guilt by forgiving him now that he is safely dead. But she is still a doomed heroine, and shows it by that sensational leap over the parapet, as if to return her to the unconscious from which she emerged and which may bring her likeness up again when another heroine of her formidable calibre may next be required (in *Turandot*, for example?). But it is not quite so convincing a symbol as the stabbing was. If the rest of *Tosca* were so excellent dramatically and musically as its central scene, or even if Act I and Act III were nearly so adroit as Act II, *Tosca* would be a very considerable masterpiece. If Puccini's other operas were as good as *Tosca* (perhaps *La bohème* is), he would be a more than considerable master. As it is, his lasting popularity is not undeserved. The best of his music has true quality; and out of the distresses of his childhood he wrought, as great artists do, a commensurate achievement.

## DEBUSSY AND HIS DREAM-SYMBOLS

Related to verismo only by his somewhat Musorgsky-like arioso (and I suppose by putting a murder at the end of *Pelléas et Mélisande* [Paris, 1902]), Debussy[13] himself sought to bring out as only music can 'the mysterious relationships between nature and the imagination',[14] calling Maeterlinck's 'dream-like' words 'more human' than any outer realism,[15] and following Mallarmé and Verlaine in desiring 'pas de couleur, rien que la nuance'—no colour, nothing but nuance.[16] For it was altogether the *symboliste* doctrine to say the least in order to communicate the most; and that suggestive reticence Debussy made his own. 'Love of art', Debussy insisted characteristically, 'does not depend on explanations'.[17] There are none in this opera.

Prince Golaud, lost in yet another of those poetical forests of the imagination which always have me thinking of Dante's *selva oscura*, comes upon Princess Mélisande who is equally lost by the side of a well into which she has dropped her crown; but she will not have him try to recover it. He leads her off and marries her; but all through there is such understatement in the drama and the music alike that the only purpose would seem to be to show what life may be like for those who are too cut off from their feelings to know what it might be like to have a purpose. Golaud has indeed a certain blind force without as yet knowing where it is leading him. Pelléas, his half-brother, has no force at all; his living really is no more than a dreaming; but in this he empathizes with Mélisande. The feeling, of course, is all in the music. The characters may not know much about it yet. But we do.

Mélisande, at it again, now accidentally-on-purpose drops her wedding ring into another of those symbolic wells with which the environment is so plentifully provided; at the same moment, her husband is thrown from his horse in another part of the forest; and if we take the ring for her marriage and the horse for his instinct, we shall appreciate sufficiently, if they do not, how the situation is developing. She lies to him about the ring; angry as he is, he sends the two of them together

20. The death of Pelléas, from the first production of Debussy's Pelléas et Mélisande in 1902. The forest setting is a familiar archetypal symbol, though its precise significance, like so much else in this opera, is mysterious. Perhaps it recalls the deep frustration of Dante's selva oscura.

to look for it, in the wrong place. Almost as ominously as in *Salome* or *Wozzeck*, the moon rises, to reveal three mysterious old beggars in a cave, as disconsolate as the three Norns but not nearly so communicative. In fact, they do not verbally communicate at all.

Next, radiantly and enticingly, Mélisande lets down her long golden hair from the tower for Pelléas to fondle, singing as he does so, 'It loves me'. Golaud only tells them, 'You are children'. But, taking Pelléas down by the dangerous waters in the castle vaults, Golaud shows to us, at least, how murderous his inclinations are becoming. When he lifts little Yniold up to spy on Pelléas and Mélisande, the frightened child sees nothing incriminating, but when by the fountain Golaud overhears the fey couple at last managing a shy avowal, he kills Pelléas with no least hesitation and no least resistance (fig. 20).

*It must live now, in her place*

*It is the turn of the poor little girl.*

**Example 37**
Debussy, *Pelléas et Mélisande* (Paris, 1902). The reconciling ending as Arkel, having advised Golaud not to blame himself, turns to the newly born infant in token of the as-yet-uncommitted future.

Golaud repents soon enough; and now he seems tortured by his need to know. But what is there to know? Mélisande, dying, knows nothing and can tell him nothing. Nobody does know the meaning of the tragedy; that is the meaning of the tragedy. No channel of communication opened up for the knowledge—the self-knowledge, it would have to be—which alone might have proved healing. Quietly the servants drop to their knees in the swift intuition that Mélisande is dead. But now old Arkel sings of Mélisande's tiny baby: 'It is the turn of the poor little girl' (ex. 37). No doubt, with such a start in life she will have a difficult time of it; but I find here some belated and possibly inadvertent hint that there is at least going to be a future. But no, I do not think it was inadvertent. Not in Maeterlinck.

# 16    S T R A U S S

Strauss was of the romantic essence of the late nineteenth century, which he carried miraculously forward into the twentieth.[1] Orchestral glory and unfettered feeling can go no farther than that best of all tone poems, *Also sprach Zarathustra*, which is dated 1895–96. So unfettered, in fact, was Strauss's flow and invention that there are some in our day and age who cannot go along with him at all. But I rate him very high.

*Salome* (Dresden, 1905) still sounds the most modern of his operas, worthy of its archetypal theme of the destructive seductress. *Elektra* (Dresden, 1909) strikes me as merely an interminable ranting of high sopranos, not so much archetypal as pathological. But then Hofmannsthal underwent a sea change, and Strauss with him, for that wonderfully poetical and lyrical *Rosenkavalier* (Dresden, 1911). A miracle of musicianly characterization and dramatic development, yes: but not a modern miracle. A post-dated romantic miracle, as was the whole course of Strauss's subsequent career.

It is the Marschallin whose hard-won acceptance of herself as she loses her Octavian sets the tone of *Der Rosenkavalier* just as surely as Sachs, by accepting his need to resign Eva to Walther, sets the tone of *Die Meistersinger von Nürnberg*. She must not be produced either as too old or as too pitiful. Strauss described her as 'a young and beautiful woman of thirty-two at the most who, in a bad mood, thinks herself "an old woman" as compared with the seventeen-year-old Octavian', who in any case 'is neither the first nor the last lover' of her career (fig. 21). She must therefore take her situation not 'as a tragic farewell to life but with Viennese grace and lightness, half weeping, half smiling'.[2] And the reason for this was well seen by that fine Straussian, William Mann: 'She knows that she is not ready yet to play the mother-substitute, and that he has to grow out of mother-love and discover the more positive, developing love of coeval man and woman'.[3]

In the same way, Strauss warned us not to make Baron Ochs into 'a

21. *Alfred Roller's costume designs for the original production of Strauss's* Rosenkavalier *in 1911. True to Strauss's instructions, Roller portrayed the Marschallin as a beautiful young woman, far from matronly, and Baron Ochs as a 'rustic beau'.*

disgusting vulgar monster', but on the contrary 'a rustic beau of thirty-five' who, although admittedly he is 'at heart a cad', is nevertheless entirely 'presentable'.[4] He is not of course nearly so lovable (nor indeed so old) as Falstaff. Nevertheless, he must be allowed a little of that ripe old reprobate's dignity, so that in all the fooling our sympathies do not too harshly turn against him. Here he is now getting off as he thinks with that pretty maid-servant (actually Octavian in disguise) in the very course of seeking advice from the Marschallin about a messenger to take the silver rose to his intended bride. The joke here is perhaps a little heavy-handed, but the music carries us along with it.

The opera rises to one of its finest scenes when the Marschallin sings so poignantly of her declining youth, and of how she too had once been as fresh and as innocent as Sophie now is; and although Octavian returns hotly to deny her doubts, she knows, and we know, that he is going to leave her for some younger woman, as indeed he should; and that for the sake of them both, she must take it lightly and acceptingly, as indeed she will. When Octavian brings the silver rose to Sophie as a messenger officially for Baron Ochs but prophetically for himself, into the formal dignity of the orchestra there drop those slight, pearly chords with celesta and woodwind from quite another tonality (ex. 38), and we hear for ourselves what they scarcely yet know, the stirrings of their very youthful hearts. 'Where have I once been before', each in turn sings to the other, 'that I have been so happy?' It is indeed that instant recognition, not literally of each other but of the archetypal situation, which we call love at first sight. Poetry alone could not do it quite like that; poetry and music combine their complementary symbolism. And that, as always, is opera.

As they follow up now, in an enraptured exchange of melody, this experience so old in the world, so new to them, Baron Ochs arrives to accost his bride-to-be with insulting complacency, until a quarrel works up in which Ochs receives a tiny prick in the arm from Octavian's sword. His outcry is fit for a mortal wound, but he recovers with suspicious rapidity when handed a letter purporting to be from that fascinating maidservant, but actually laying the trap for him which is going to bring down his pride and his prospects alike. The music should be telling us, if nothing else does, not to take him too puritanically; for the music floods out more joyously than ever into that transcendence of the waltz which is the ambience of the opera. A good actor will not allow us to lose a sort of amused but friendly indulgence towards the unworthy Baron.

The sly baiting and the uproarious unmasking of Baron Ochs at his ill-fated dinner party make another joke which goes on perhaps rather too

**Example 38**
Richard Strauss, *Der Rosenkavalier* (Dresden, 1911), Act II. The intoxicating harmonies from another tonality which drop into the orchestra in the silver rose scene, to express the strange sensations of those youthful hearts. The celesta predominates.

long, before the Marschallin to our relief arrives to take command of
the whole tangled situation. Octavian is overcome with shame; Sophie
with inferiority. The Marschallin, knowing better for them both, sends
Octavian across to Sophie. It had to come, only it has come a little earlier
than she had hoped. So now she calls on her own 'whole and steadfast
heart' to accept what she could not in any case have prevented; and
because she accepts, she triumphs. Her lovely music is taken up into
that trio with the other two which knits her acceptance into their happiness, with a beauty as reconciling as it is serene; and as she in her
turn quietly goes offstage, the young lovers pledge their troth in a duet
which miraculously continues the serenity and the beauty: a little more
simply, as their very freshness requires; but just as movingly (ex. 39).
And then the last touch of mastery, after they also have left, and onto the
empty stage there runs the Marschallin's little black boy to pick up the
handkerchief; and so this warm and mellow score finishes up lightly,
lightly, just as the Marschallin had always shown us that it ought to be.

### THE CONTINUING PARTNERSHIP

Ariadne auf Naxos (Stuttgart, 1912; reworked Vienna, 1916) is
a much more problematic affair.[5] The comedians are perfectly happy
to improvise their way through anything; it is the serious company
who find themselves so disconcerted by the unanticipated collabora-
tion. Hofmannsthal would have it that Ariadne and Bacchus represent 'a
world of the spirit' for which the 'merely human' comedians can have
nothing but 'incomprehension'.[6] But in fact the spiritual and the earthy
are equally human, two sides of a single coin; and insofar as Strauss was
allowed to relate them in his music, we are marvellously well contented.
Paradoxically, it was Hofmannsthal who next tried to symbolize that
very real and necessary relationship in Die Frau ohne Schatten (The woman
without a shadow; Vienna, 1919),[7] of whose distracted heroine he wrote
that 'the being human is missing: her achieving this is the essence of the
entire drama'.[8]

Getting a shadow can only mean getting to know that you have a
shadow, an earthy side as well as a spiritual side, and that you somehow
need to reconcile the two. It is only unfortunate that in his eagerness
Hofmannsthal pressed this good symbol into such inordinate complications, until Strauss himself felt driven to complain that 'the trouble is
the subject itself with its romanticism and its symbols', which 'cannot
be filled with red corpuscles', so that 'my heart is only half in it, and

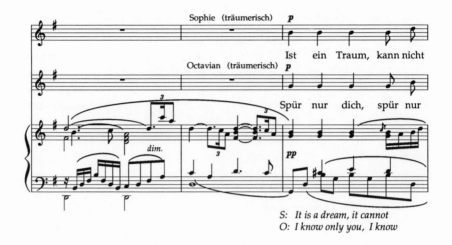

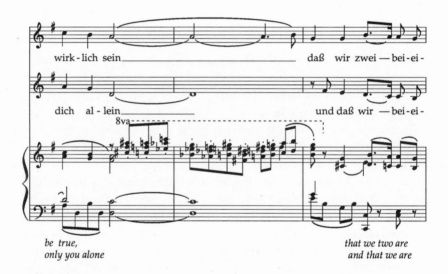

## Example 39

Richard Strauss, *Der Rosenkavalier*. The closing duet, as the young couple find their own innocent certainty at the older woman's prompting. The second verse is a little expanded to bring in, of all inspired ingenuities, the motive of the silver rose.

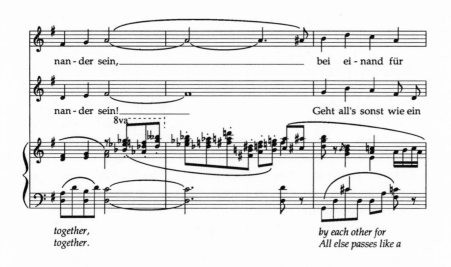

nan - der sein,_____ bei  ei - nand  für

nan - der sein!_____ Geht all's sonst wie ein

*together,*
*together.*

*by each other for*
*All else passes like a*

al - le Zeit und  E - - - - - wig - keit.

Traum da - hin  vor  mei - - - - - nem Sinn.

*all time and eternity.*
*dream before my mind.*

once the head has to do the major part of the work you get a breath of academic chill'.[9] You get, as I would prefer to put it, a synthetic replica of Straussian warmth and panache and orchestral magic, which does not quite convince us because it did not quite convince Strauss himself —until, of course, he catches fire again.

The love of Barak for his shrewish wife must have tied up for Strauss with his own loved but shrewish Pauline, and all this part of the music glows out with empathy and inspiration. So does that sudden bonus when the town's watchman, agreeably related as he is to the old night watchman in *Die Meistersinger*, sings offstage: 'You husbands and wives lying lovingly in one another's arms, you are the bridge'. The bridge is right. But opera and symbolism alike tumble into disaster when that fountain spurts up in front of the Empress, and is by context and tradition alike so evidently none other than the water of life; but by some tortuous impulse, some false logic of the head, not of the heart, she is made to turn away from it as from a guilty temptation instead of towards it as an uncovenanted blessing. Can we wonder that the Emperor now gets turned to stone (ex. 40)?

(a)  "Kaikobad"

(b)  The Messenger

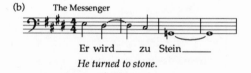

Er wird___ zu Stein___

*He turned to stone.*

## Example 40

Richard Strauss, *Die Frau ohne Schatten* (Vienna, 1919). (a) The harsh motive of the father-figure in the background, Kaikobad; (b) the still harsher motive to which the Emperor is turned to stone, with a particularly grim descent of the tritone interval very much as Hagen had it in app. ex. 21.

I cannot say what equally uncovenanted working of feminine compassion lets feeling flow once more, as the Empress casts her new-found shadow across the waterfall and makes of it a bridge indeed for all the separated characters. Not by cheating or magic or selfish clutching— that seems to be the gist of the reasoning. The symbol, anyhow, is better than the reasoning, and lifts the opera to a sudden height. After that, it goes on far too long with those unborn children sentimentalizing away, as if neither poet nor composer knew quite how to stop. A flawed masterpiece, but magnificent for all that, and suffering certainly not from a scarcity but from a surfeit of symbols.

There is less symbolism than autobiography in Strauss's own libretto for *Intermezzo* (Dresden, 1924), a splendid blend of relaxed arioso and orchestral interludes. With *The Egyptian Helen* (Dresden, 1928), Strauss and Hofmannsthal reunited in an opera of real quality, except in being much too long and complicated for its central point concerning the phantom Helen who went to Troy and the real Helen who did not; but the point is the very sound one that there can be no future in living with a fantasy, although there might be in facing up to the facts. It may be relevant here that Hofmannsthal knew Freud in Vienna. But Hofmannsthal was not so insightful when in *Die Frau ohne Schatten* he turned his Empress away from that life-giving symbol of the fountain, as if his own allegiance to life's onward flow were a little unsure. And indeed, having finished but not revised (and it needed it) that enchanting but uneven *Arabella* (Dresden, 1933), Hofmannsthal died suddenly as he was preparing for the funeral of his son who had committed suicide. So troubled a family: so splendid a poet when all is said. Yet one more example of the creative wound, I can only suppose.

All the happier, then, that *Arabella* climaxes with that superlatively life-enhancing symbol as the heroine walks down the staircase, to the very finest of Strauss, bringing to the hero the glass of clear water which so traditionally and so manifestly signifies acceptance (ex. 41). And that really was the last of Hofmannsthal, though not of Strauss.

If I were to take time here for *Daphne* (Dresden, 1938), I should admire it for its handling of that old and familiar problem of the human woman and the feminine archetype, so closely related yet so needing to be distinguished. Or if for *Die Liebe der Danae* (performed at a dress rehearsal for the cancelled Salzburg Festival of 1944, and then at Salzburg in 1952), I should remark on the symbolical ambivalence of Midas's golden touch and agree that gold in a myth may stand not only for outer wealth but for inner value, as Danae finds by losing the first in gaining the second; while Jupiter acts out, perhaps for Strauss himself, that difficult transition into old age which, if sufficiently accepted, can have its value too. 'Something for a seventy-five year old to be really proud of', was Strauss's comment on the third act; but he was not yet finished.[10] *Capriccio* was still to come, to say nothing of *Metamorphosen* and the *Four Last Songs*.

**Example 41**
Richard Strauss, *Arabella* (Dresden, 1933). The radiant climax.

AN OPERA ABOUT OPERA

*Capriccio* (Munich, 1942) is indeed a special kind of opera: *Capriccio* is an opera about opera.

There had been precedents. *Ciro*, on a libretto originally by Giulio Cesare Sorrentino and to music at least adapted and in part composed by Cavalli for performance at Venice in 1654, has a prologue with Curiosità, Architettura, Poesia and Musica wrangling over the preparations for the ensuing opera.[11] In 1713, a previous fragment of an operatic prologue by Boileau (among whose satirical targets we find Lully's librettist, Quinault) was published on the promising topic of 'a dispute between poetry and music about the relative values of these arts. At the end of the scene . . . harmony came down from heaven, and with all her graciousness and charm, reconciled the contestants [by setting] all the artists [at work on an opera]'.

Precisely; but we do not have the opera. More important, in 1934 Stefan Zweig drew Strauss's attention to a libretto by the noted wit Casti (it was composed by Antonio Salieri as an operetta and performed at the Schönbrunn orangerie in 1786): *Prima la musica e poi le parole* (First the music and then the words).[12] Here the composer himself begins some words which the poet finishes in a huff, but on being assuaged allows the composer to set to music which is then rehearsed: the germ, it seems, though no more than the germ, of Strauss's idea. His poetical colleague Joseph Gregor helped, but not much; Clemens Krauss took over, working on some dialogue by Strauss; the end result was a libretto such as Strauss wished, on a subject deeper than it looks and very much indeed to my liking.

As the curtain rises, we find that the overture, a string sextet of serene

**Example 42**
Richard Strauss, *Capriccio* (Munich, 1942). The seminal motive of the opening string sextet: Strauss's not unworthy tribute to his often expressed Mozartian ideal.

Music by Richard Strauss, libretto by Clemens Krauss. © 1942 by Richard Strauss; copyright renewed. Reprinted by permission of the Strauss family and Boosey & Hawkes, Inc., sole agents.

grace (ex. 42), is being heard through open doors by Flamand, a composer, Olivier, a poet, and—yes, but he seems to be comfortably asleep —La Roche, an impresario and stage director. And this very sextet, it seems, is a birthday present from Flamand to the Countess, a beautiful young widow, evidently visible offstage to them, although not to us. As their comments drop quietly into the orchestral texture, we learn that they are rivals in life as in art:

> *Olivier*: Enemies in love—
> *Flamand*: Friendly foes—
> *Olivier*: Words or music?
> *Flamand*: She shall decide it!
> *Olivier*: Prima le parole—dopo la musica!
> *Flamand*: Prima la musica—dopo le parole!

Ah, but so soon as that confounded sextet has finished, La Roche is ready to wake up and share in the conversation, of which he seems to have picked up enough to comment, with some asperity, that words and music would not get anywhere without his own professional ability to direct them on stage. And so it is that the third component of opera is brought into the argument. La Roche himself grumbles about that modern fellow Gluck—no proper melody, no hearing the words against 'the tumult of the orchestra'. And we in the audience, who know that Strauss in his own day had to contend with just such criticism (besides applying it quite rigorously to himself), will enjoy the sly historical double-take. A modern director who depotentiates it by mounting *Capriccio* out of period has missed a trick. Lully, Rameau, Piccini, Goldoni—all the great names of that eventful epoch are bandied about. Not 'druids and Turks and prophets from the Bible' (like the prophet in *Salome?*), demands La Roche: 'men of flesh and blood and not phantoms' (as had not Strauss once demanded from Hofmannsthal?). But now, as La Roche apologizes for having slept through Flamand's sextet, its beautiful recipient, the Countess herself, comes forward, with her amusing brother, the Count. 'But you', her brother observes to her, 'are doubly courted—do you incline to words or music?' She puts him off: 'I will not think, only delight in listening'. For him, 'beauty of living [is] the truest reward'; for her, 'truth of living the most beautiful reward'.

And now we are introduced to a sonnet finished this very morning by Olivier (it is in enchanting reality a translation from Ronsard); and Flamand, itching to compose it, goes off with it. Olivier seizes the opportunity to press the Countess for her love; but she is not yet ready to decide. When Flamand returns with his melody, she merely claims that the compounded beauty now belongs to her. Alone with her, he too attempts to press his amorous claims, to no better effect.

When the Countess describes how Olivier's sonnet had not much moved her until Flamand had composed it, 'the two together', exclaims the Count, '—stormed my heart', she finishes. The Count: 'What is to come of this?' The Countess: 'Perhaps—an opera!' And he puts it straight in front of us: 'My sister as muse!' La Roche: 'You all serve to enrich my stage!' And the Countess agrees that it is indeed the stage which 'reveals to us the secret of reality: we become aware of ourselves as in a magic mirror'; for 'the theatre is the most impressive symbol of life'. The operatic theatre, in particular; and so the Count comes up with it: 'Describe the conflict as it is moving us! The events of this day—what we have all lived through—write it and compose it! Compose it as opera!' In short, as *Capriccio*.

But suddenly, by some altogether unlooked-for inspiration, we are confronted with a sort of earthy anti-masque of servants from below stairs—though they seem not to have missed an item of the argument. 'The Countess is in love, and she does not know with which . . . perhaps with both of them . . . To get it clear, they have to write an opera'. The servants, too, are working at some humbler entertainment, some contribution as it might be from the ever-present underside; and Monsieur Taupe, the prompter, having fallen asleep and got forgotten, also emerges somehow touchingly from 'under the earth', where he is 'Lord of a magic world' and has to whisper 'the poet's deepest thoughts', and then 'everything begins to live'. But 'is it all a dream?' he wonders, 'or am I awake now?' It is a dream, although we are awake; for what is art if not a waking dream from which we must not expect too unambiguous an answer?

### STRAUSS'S LAST TESTAMENT

But here comes the Countess, to ask herself: 'The end of the opera, shall I determine it, shall I choose, decide?' And in a beautiful recapitulation she goes back to her own beautiful sonnet, but breaks off to exclaim: 'Words and music are fused in one, uniting into something new'. Then is it to be 'Flamand, the great soul?' Or is it to be 'Olivier, the strong spirit?' And there we have it. She cannot decide.

She cannot decide because she is not only a woman who might choose one or the other of the two men; she is also for both men what her brother the Count has already called her: 'my sister as muse'. *Seele*, soul, is feminine in German, like the Latin (and the Jungian) *anima*; and *Geist*, spirit, is masculine, like the Latin (and the Jungian) *animus*. We cannot *decide* between feminine and masculine, between Eros which unites and Logos which defines, between music which Wagner once imagined to be fertilized by poetry and words imagined by him as the fertilizing agent. We cannot decide because we are bisexual anyhow and have a bit of each. And so we are content here not to be told the ending of the love story because we know that on this level any ending would be the wrong ending, and that the only right ending has to be no ending. The symbol is completed even if the story is not.

Strauss put it that 'the rivalry between words and music has been the problem of my life, which *Capriccio* solves with a question mark'.[13] Deliberately, then, Strauss used the love story to symbolize an operatic speculation; intuitively, as I believe, he used the operatic speculation to symbolize a psychological insight.

The insight concerns our need to unite ourselves with ourselves by some sufficient awareness of our own polarity. I am not speaking now of intellectual awareness, which is neither probable nor necessary. I am speaking of a sort of 'as if' responsiveness which enables us to come to terms with our contra-sexed component although we may have no conscious knowledge that such a thing does or could exist. A first stage is to separate the opposites from their mere primal confusion, rather as the very earliest operas hinted with their symbolical differentiation between the woman who may be loved and the archetype which may be activated. A further stage is seeking to reunite the opposites now that it can be appreciated that they are not the same. *The Magic Flute* is a notable example of just such a sophisticated search, confirmed as the well-tested couple are indeed united in the temple which has been transformed mystically into a sun; for the sun serves there in the usual way as a symbol for illumination. Wagner, under his favourite image of redemption, returned repeatedly to 'the marriage of myself with myself'. Tippett's *Midsummer Marriage* intentionally follows the example of *The Magic Flute*, even to the point of endorsing the union of his adventurous couple with a concluding sunrise.

And so it is that in *Capriccio* there is the metaphorical marriage of words and music 'fused in one, uniting into something new'. Something new? I cannot help thinking that the something new here would be an increased awareness of the potential union of our feminine and our masculine components. The whole drift of the scenario seems to me to point that way. Of course Strauss did not plan this level, and of course we do not put it like that to ourselves, but his intuitions and ours about the basic structure of the human psyche will still show through. Planned or not, the images shape up and the message gets across. That is the normal habit of the artistic imagination, since the artist above all is the man who knows more than he knows that he knows; and nowhere more so than in opera. This is a part (although only a part) of the great service the arts can do for us.

When a man's inner femininity is in a negative mood, she can make him wayward and touchy and unreliable, just as a woman's inner masculinity can make her bossy and opinionated and falsely logical. But when the mood is positive, then we may benefit immeasurably from our contra-sexed component. We may gain a balance and an inspiration and a double vision on life's many perplexities which helps all along the line, and very particularly with our personal relationships. Mutual understanding between the sexes is made much easier, since we recognize in each other part of what we have already in ourselves. It does not matter that this process is essentially unconscious. It works all the more readily on that account.

Words and music uniting in friendly rivalry: fair enough; we need look no farther for a satisfactory experience of the opera. Yet I still believe that our satisfaction runs the deeper because of the archetypes whose luminosity is being kindled by the very content of the opera. The eternal feminine and the eternal masculine are at it again; soul and spirit are brought explicitly into the text; the perennial search is on for which, in mythology, initiation and the sacred marriage are acknowledged images; and in psychology, integration.

But now the Major-domo announces supper, and the tension lifts. Just as in *Der Rosenkavalier*, so many years and so many masterpieces ago, here too the orchestra brings down the curtain lightly, but lightly, on this opera of which Strauss, when urged by Clemens Krauss to contemplate another, said so very sufficiently, 'You can only leave one testament'.[14]

STRAVINSKY THE INSECURE

Insecurity, mounting by now to our well-justified fears of nuclear obliteration and environmental deterioration, has haunted our century at the least of it from World War I onwards. It is given to artists in some manner to sense the intimations of approaching disaster before most people so much as notice the hidden preparations for it which must nevertheless be going on beneath the surface. The German expressionist painters and writers, and even so clear-sighted a novelist as Thomas Mann, gave hints enough, subliminally or not so subliminally. And Stravinsky exploded into that forcible and prophetic Rite of Spring in 1913, just before the more lethal explosion of 1914, frightening himself so badly in the process that he never afterwards wished to or indeed could recall the emotions which, as he remained very well aware, had so possessed him at the time.

So Stravinsky took refuge in that neoclassical disposition which thereafter both supported and constrained him. He insisted that 'the more constraints one imposes, the more one frees oneself of the chains which shackle the spirit'.[1] It is a valid suggestion, which serialists in particular might endorse; but it is only half the truth. The other half concerns the courage to allow the flood of autonomous emotion to have its way, controlling it consciously as the good artist must, but not denying it or resisting it. With all his virtues and all his defects, Strauss had that courage. I am not by any means certain that Stravinsky after 1913 had. Our age became, after 1914, an age of increasingly conspicuous insecurity. Stravinsky, a glorious genius, was in his very insecurity a composer—I had almost written the composer—for our age.

When with The Rake's Progress (Venice, 1951) Stravinsky got well and truly into opera, he had the advantage of a very superior libretto by W. H. Auden (a poet of remarkable parts) and Chester Kallman; and since Auden was interested in Jung, who habitually used the term shadow for our dark human underside, I have no doubt that the double-take was intentional when Nick Shadow, clearly Old Nick the devil in very thin disguise, seduces Tom Rakewell away from reality and into fantasy along quite traditional lines. But when the devil, as was only to be expected, claims his wages in that witty graveyard scene (ex. 43), with Tom tipped to win the gentlemanly game by the Queen of Hearts who is his loving Anne, the devil, only a gentleman so long as it suits him, threatens:

> Your sins, my foe, before you go,
> Give me some power to pain:
> To reason blind shall be your mind;
> Henceforth be you insane.

And poor Tom ends up in Bedlam under the illusion that he is Adonis wounded by the boar, and that Anne compassionately visiting him is Venus, but with no suggestion that I can detect in the give-away ending that mythologically, after all, Adonis died only to be reborn. The element of musical pastiche in this clever opera makes on me rather a wry impression, but undoubtedly it is an opera of character. Twentieth-century character.

### BERG THE COMPASSIONATE

I think Schoenberg could not complete the music for Moses und Aron because he could not sufficiently reconcile in himself that vast cosmic conflict between the spiritual and the earthy components of the drama.[2] I think Berg was able to confront the more human scale of Wozzeck (Berlin, 1925) because his compassion was equal to the occasion.[3] He retained for his libretto the deliberate fragmentation of Büchner's surviving drafts, concerning which factor Ernst Křenek commented that 'the principles of the new music lead away from the closed form, and realize instead the ideal of "fragments" . . . as in Alban Berg's Wozzeck and still more distinctly, in his Lulu'. All the more, it seems, because his subject was so pitiable and his scenario so disjointed did Berg need for his music the security of the 'old and new forms', of which he pointed out 'the strict logic with which everything is worked out', although 'nobody in the audience ought to notice anything of these various Fugues and Inventions, Suite and Sonata movements, Inventions and Passacaglias— everyone should be filled only with the idea of the opera, an idea which far transcends the individual fate of Wozzeck'.[4] Not only the schizoid and hallucinated state of Wozzeck, but the schizoid and hallucinated as-

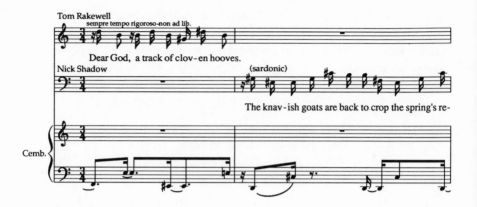

## Example 43

Stravinsky, *The Rake's Progress* (Venice, 1951). The climax of the graveyard scene where Anne's voice comes in at the unison to cap Tom's agonized appeal, so that on the word *love* they coincide—a beautiful and traditional operatic stroke.

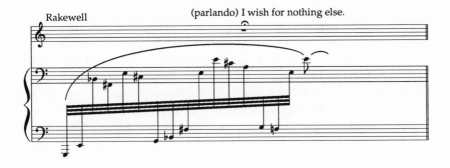

pects of our society, too, claimed Berg's compassion—that was the idea of the opera. There is an especial poignancy about that tinny piano on stage counterpointing with the wry orchestra in the pit; and so there is when Marie intersperses her hesitant speech-song, as she reads from the Bible, with the cantilena of her impassioned contrition for that pitiable infidelity of hers with the tawdry Drum-Major (ex. 44). But pity is the operative word.

But now under that archetypally blood-red moon and that hatefully obsessive B-natural ostinato, Wozzeck murders the one being who stood for something in himself of warmth and relatedness, cutting himself off at the same time from any healing through his own inner femininity. He is left by the Captain and the Doctor with diabolical unconcern to drown in the pool; but Berg's own concern glows out at us in that wonderfully Mahler-like interlude before the child's pathetic 'hoop-la, hoop-la' at the end does at least hint, by its sudden innocence in the music, that there may yet be some sort of future.

*Wozzeck* is an expressionistic opera, and a staging might well follow such expressionistic painters as Kandinsky, Kokoschka, Macke or Rouault, or indeed Schoenberg. Not too much squalor, in any case; for though this is a pitiful piece, it is not sadistic. But in *Lulu* (Zurich, 1937; in full at Paris, 1979) I do find both squalor and sadomasochism. Useless for Berg to protest that 'sensuality is not a weakness' but 'an immense strength that lies in us—the pivot of all being and thinking'.[5] What made Lulu as a woman sick and as a fantasy dangerous was not her being so sensual. It was her being so murderous.

Berg himself suffered 'a sort of nervous breakdown connected with [his] constant affliction of asthma'.[6] That sounds a little like Bizet, overcome as he may well have been by the strain of psychologically dangerous fantasies of which the glorious artistic outcome was *Carmen*. The serial rigours of *Lulu*, tighter by far even than the tight forms of *Wozzeck*, suggest a man skilful indeed and diabolically inspired, yet mortally afraid of getting for one moment out of control; and that is a stance difficult to live with. The production here should be terrible rather as the Guernica pictures of Picasso are terrible. We need for once really a nightmare quality.

## Example 44

Berg, *Wozzeck* (Berlin, 1925), Act III, scene i. The Schoenberg-like speech-song and the contrasting cantilena.

Britten's identification with the vulnerability of his flawed hero in *Peter Grimes* (London, 1945) was equally creative but far less dangerous.[7] The sea is as ever-present as in *The Flying Dutchman*, though the idiom is different. There are six orchestral interludes, the first depicting a quiet seascape as the townspeople take up the normal occupations of their working day; but there is a hint of unease in the harmony (ex. 45).

There is a raging storm in the second interlude, through which Ellen, the touching heroine, brings in the new apprentice. But though the third interlude is serene, and though we hear the bells and the church service in the background, here in front is Ellen rebuking Peter for the visible bruises he has already given the Apprentice, whom he wants to force to sea on that very sabbath, in his harsh will for the money 'to buy us a home, respect, freedom'; for he is desperately afraid that she might marry him merely out of pity. It is part of his paranoid conviction of being an outcast, which itself makes it all the more probable that he will be treated as an outcast. When she confesses now to a sense of failure, he strikes her, to her very great distress and ours. The boy runs off and Peter follows him (fig. 22).

The men having set off to hound Peter down, Auntie and her two 'nieces' remain to sing resignedly of the comfort the men so urgently require of them and then so callously dismiss. 'They are children when they weep', Ellen sings; 'we are mothers when they strive, schooling our own hearts to keep the bitter treasure of their love'. She knew, and Britten at heart must have known too, of this underlying factor in male psychology.

The fourth interlude depicts Peter's own obsessiveness in a splendid passacaglia; there are fish out to sea, and he so presses it that the boy bursts into tears, upon which Peter tries awkwardly to comfort him. But hearing now the hateful thumping of the drum as the hostile townsmen approach, Peter sends the boy out at the back—though there has recently been a landslide—warning him to go carefully; but there is a cry which must mean that he has fallen. Peter follows, and the hut is found empty. The fifth interlude is for the tranquil night and the calm light of the moon, but shrill comments from harp and flute suggest Peter's own untranquility of mind. We hear raucous dancers counterpointing from the Moot Hall offstage—not by any means the only direct reminiscence of *Wozzeck*. But here are Ellen and that wise old sea captain, Balstrode, thinking how they could best help Peter, him whose 'shadow'd life'

**Example 45**

Britten, *Peter Grimes* (London, 1945). First interlude, with a minor
third in the flutes and violins pulling quietly but uneasily against
the major third in the brass below.

22. Peter Pears as the flawed protagonist and Leonard Thompson as the hapless Apprentice in the 1945 première of Britten's Peter Grimes: another opera in which the sea offers symbolic redemption to a wounded hero.

Ellen had so wished to bring 'into the sun', and who now has sunk so deeply into the dark that help seems impossible. The cruel borough is on the hunt again; and even as we hear them near or far, the sixth interlude fills the stage with mist while Peter is seen stumbling on the shore, himself in thicker mist, and singing aimlessly in his confusion.

The foghorn adds its lugubrious repetitions. Balstrode tells Peter: 'Sail out till you lose sight of land: then sink the boat'. That these words are spoken in a sung opera gives a curious effect of finality. We do not doubt the doomful necessity. We may wonder why it has quite had to come to this.

It had to come to this because of Britten's own wounded nature. When his actual mother died, Britten showed an extremity of grief far beyond the normal tribute. Living by the sea, Britten reported, 'my life as a child was coloured by the fierce storms', to which something in his spirit must have profoundly answered. 'In writing *Peter Grimes* I wanted to express my awareness of the perpetual struggle of men and women whose livelihood depends on the sea', with which his own inner struggle must likewise already have corresponded.[8] For him the sea was indeed, as Christopher Palmer describes it, a 'sea-Mother', to which the drowned Grimes was returned in 'an image of rebirth', pre-saging redemption in 'the unconscious waters': which, as Palmer well adds, 'says as much about Britten as about Grimes'.[9] As a wartime pacifist and (more difficult then) an overt homosexual, Britten felt persecuted, as Philip Brett has suggested, not so much by society's attitude as by his own internalization of what he took to be society's attitude. His sense of alienation resembled that of Grimes all too painfully; but Brett summed it up very sympathetically when he wrote that Britten here shows us 'anew how from private pain the great artist can fashion something that transcends his own individual experience and touches all humanity'.[10] This seems to me another clear case of the creative wound.

So the first sea interlude returns full cycle as the borough takes up its habitual toil and its accustomed ways. We hear the shimmer and the mystery, the very ebb and flow of the tides of the sea and perhaps of life itself. The individual may die, but the borough goes on. So too did Britten go on, making his way from opera to opera with somnambulist assurance, never quite able to feel accepted by the borough, resenting the least criticism as if it were total rejection, earning many honours yet never comfortably relaxing into his abundant fame. All Britten's heroes lean towards the unconventional, the insecure, the victimized, as he himself at bottom so evidently felt. In reality his pacifism was widely respected, his long friendship with Peter Pears was much admired, his misgivings were needless though not valueless, since he never lost his artist's power of transmuting them into symbols of beauty and of com-passion.

The most enchanting of Britten's operas is *A Midsummer Night's Dream* (Aldeburgh, 1960); the most moving is *Death in Venice* (Aldeburgh, 1973).[11]

Already when he wrote that famous story at the age of thirty-seven, Thomas Mann knew all about genius in creating and alienation in living. Britten was not so self-aware as that, but I think he too at the end of his life caught clearer sight of the pains and the joys and the deprivations and the rewards and the whole unavoidable price of being a genius. And very eloquently he composed those visions here.

### TIPPETT THE PSYCHOLOGICAL

Tippett, under the converging influences of Jung and T. S. Eliot, reached his creative peak with *The Midsummer Marriage* (London, 1955), an opera rare indeed in using its symbols not only deliberately but with deliberately psychological intention.[12] It will for this reason suit my purpose to give it particular consideration here, as I have already given to *The Magic Flute*.

We see through the early-morning mist an eerie building which is not always there. Strephon with his flute leads out the dancers, followed by a He-Ancient and a She-Ancient of palpably archetypal stature (ex. 46). Mark runs on, singing: 'I want a new dance for my wedding day'. He then puts himself into the legendary company of all those heroes orphaned, crippled, foundlings or otherwise set apart for special tasks beyond the ordinary lot in life: 'Strange was my birth and strange my fate. My wedding should be strange. Is that not right?' Quite right. We learn, in fact, that he is 'of unknown parentage'.

Jenifer, the heroine, is also set apart, although her father is merely 'a businessman', which sounds ordinary enough until we realize that his name is King Fisher, and that Tippett connected him with that ailing Fisher King of the Grail legends around which Tippett's friend and one-time consultant T. S. Eliot built his very modern parable, *The Waste Land*. As in *The Magic Flute* (an intentional model),[13] there is a secondary couple whose integration will be less aware but instinctively sufficient. And there is the chorus, which confesses presently: 'Let Mark and Jenifer endure for us the perils of the royal way: we are the laughing children'.

The He-Ancient trips Strephon by way of showing that 'a new dance may be strange but dangerous'. As all these uncanny characters then retire, the chorus ventures out of hiding. 'Oh, Mark, who are they?' And he answers, as one whose heart knows more about it than his head: 'I don't know who they really are, but I've seen them since boyhood. I've come here on summer nights and mornings such as these. Then is the temple nearer. They are close and if I wait, eventually appear'.

**Example 46**

Tippett, *The Midsummer Marriage* (London, 1955), Act I, scene ii. The temple doors open.

Mark has been looking forward, in soaring arioso, to giving Jenifer his wedding ring. But she comes on dressed not for a wedding, but for a journey. 'Then don't you love me?' he sings. She answers that 'it isn't love I want, but truth'. So the chorus thinks, naturally enough: 'They're quarrelling—oh, what's the trouble?' Jenifer finds herself at the foot of some very strange stairs indeed; for they have no top. 'Now I know where I shall go . . . For me the light! For you the shadow. O magic staircase that I've always known in dreams since childhood at my mother's knee . . . up I climb to paradise'.

And she climbs, until suddenly, there she isn't; but Mark in his distraction, as King Fisher is heard wrathfully approaching, sings in his turn: 'Then let me go to darkness as she told me. For her the light! For me the shadow. Gates I have always longed to enter open to receive your child'. And gates no less strange, down into the hillside, open of their own accord and clang together behind Mark. For now, Tippett explained, 'the collective, magical archetypes take charge—Jung's *anima* and *animus* —the girl, inflated by the latter, rises through the stage flies to heaven, and the man, overwhelmed by the former, descends through the stage floor to hell'.[14] They go in search each of their contra-sexed component: she in those celestial regions where spirit traditionally resides; and he in those infernal regions where instinct traditionally resides.

Now Jack is a working man, respectful to his social superiors; but he has his craftsman's pride. Bella is King Fisher's practical and efficient secretary. Jack is hired by King Fisher to force open the gates; but the voice of Sosostris (another borrowing from T. S. Eliot) utters a warning which the women heed though the men do not. The wrangle ends as Jenifer returns down her mysterious staircase; and her return brings Mark up from his mysterious cavern. They are obviously changed; but not as yet so obviously for the better. They duet harshly at cross-purposes, until they are both abruptly silenced as the temple doors open and the Ancients and the dancers come out, to that same radiance in the music which seems to tell us of forces at once far-off and close at hand, conditioning us always, though we too may never give so much as a thought to what they really are.

'Prepare to justify your strife', commands the He-Ancient. 'See no hint of spiritual pride mar the contest that you now begin', warns the She-Ancient. And Jenifer relates how her soul left her body to dance with the congregation of the stars. But Mark in his turn sings of stallions stamping and the young men dancing to the springing sap and the leaping life. 'But the price for that', cries Jenifer, bringing a magic mirror for him to see himself, as the beast she thinks he has become. He counters with a golden bough (Tippett was well aware of Frazer); and the mirror shatters. 'Are you a serpent, I become a saint?' she wonders. 'Then am I Mark and go to find the beast'. She enters the gates, a red glow momentarily on her white dress. He in response climbs the stairs, a white light catching him. And the chorus sings: 'Let Mark and Jenifer endure for us the perils of the royal way. We are the laughing children'.

(a)

(b)

**Example 47**

Tippett, *The Midsummer Marriage*, Act II. (a) Preparation for the ritual dances; (b) dancers turn into trees.

In Act II, Bella takes the lead. 'Jack, don't let's go with all the others, stay behind a bit with me'. When he is still slow, she prompts him: 'For Jack, you see, I've made my mind up. It's time we married'. They court so simply and beautifully that we could be at any time, in any place where young people find each other as they always have. But when Jack and Bella go into the wood, the dancers come on; and it is as if their dancing acts out the vision which Jack and Bella are having without even knowing that they are having any vision.

The dancers are trees, but free themselves and root themselves again as if nature herself were strangely on the move. Strephon is the hare almost caught by a girl-dancer as the hound; and this is the first ritual dance, 'The Earth in Autumn'. Then Strephon is the fish wounded, this time, by a girl-dancer as the otter, in the second ritual dance, 'The Waters in Winter'. Now Strephon is the bird, his wing already broken, stalked by a girl-dancer as the hawk in the third ritual dance, 'The Air in Spring'; but as the hawk stoops for the kill, Bella screams, the stage darkens and the dancers vanish (ex. 47).

It is a nightmare climax, which I think chiefly spells it out that change cannot happen without fear and pain. These dances of the four elements (the fourth, for the fire in summer, comes in Act III) are deliberately representing a process of initiation, which however you may encounter it cannot feel safe. Traditionally, initiation is undertaken at the risk of death. Psychologically, growth in the deeper levels of the personality feels hazardous because it is hazardous, and does not necessarily come through safely for the better.

It will add greatly to our appreciation of the drama here if we accept that what the chorus called 'the perils of the royal way', by which they meant the way towards more conscious maturity, are very real and not for the great majority. Jack and Bella are not of the great majority, but neither are they leaders of the conscious way. They learn here more than they know that they learn, and Act III will show us that they learn it well. On one level, I think, Bella learns not to be a nagging woman, and Jack not to be a cringing man. She would not like it and neither would he, but it can become a downwards spiral very difficult to reverse. More broadly, it looks as though Jack and Bella pass at least through the first three stages of initiation, if no more than vicariously; and this should mean that they will be that much the better able to go along with the flow of life, wheresoever it may lead them. They will not witness the fourth ritual dance; but by then their own great moment has come, and they will have risen to it greatly (ex. 48).

**Example 48**

Tippett, *The Midsummer Marriage*, end of Act II. 'The presences are still'.

THE RITUAL UNION

In Act III, King Fisher challenges the Ancients: 'Sosostris will outwit you though the means be death'. After warning him in turn, they take up his challenge. A mock procession to intoxicating music only brings on Jack in disguise. But now the real Sosostris bemoans, in one of the most exalted solos of the opera, her destiny as a medium driven to dream always for others, never for herself (and there, thought Peter Heyworth, speaks Tippett the ever-driven creator).[15] To King Fisher, Sosostris offers 'a dream to dream himself', of Jenifer 'opening her body to the sun' and to 'the glorious lion of love, with symbol erect'. Thereupon King Fisher furiously smashes her clairvoyant's bowl. But the chorus assures him that 'she saw what happens in the soul'.

Now King Fisher has Bella help Jack to strap on a hateful black pistol—as lethal a symbol as the other was life-giving. 'Jack, unveil her',

23. *Joan Sutherland and Richard Lewis as Jenifer and Mark in the 1955 première of Tippett's Midsummer Marriage at Covent Garden. Their ritual union was enacted in hieratic poses reminiscent of Oriental imagery.*

orders King Fisher. The He-Ancient: 'Time for a man to choose his fate!' The She-Ancient: 'Time for the unborn child to speak!' The chorus: 'Ah, choose for us!' And Bella urges him: 'Speak, Jack, our moment's at its height'; and Jack replies: 'This is my choice . . . to strip the veils, not from Sosostris, but from myself'. So he throws the pistol back. 'Bella, riding on the great wave's crest I call'. She: 'Jack, before it falls like thunder in the trough I come'. This time the chorus calls after them as they go: 'He must leap and she must fall, when the sun shines bright on midsummer day'.

But King Fisher, obsessed, starts himself to strip the black veils from Sosostris, until a strange light glows through, and a great lotus-bud opens to reveal Mark and Jenifer 'transfigured as Shiva-Shakti (Shiva and Parvati). All the gestures and poses are hieratic'. It is indeed one of the world's highest symbols for ritual union, presaging in Oriental imagery the perennial theme of integration and the reconciliation of our human opposites. Yet it comes here in blatant contrast to the more or less Druidic and Celtic or possibly Grecian, but at any rate Western symbolism of the temple and the Ancients and the dancers as we have so far been accepting them. This is, I think, an inconsistency and a weakness; but given goodwill, we can certainly accept the image in the elated spirit intended. It would, in fact, be hard to think of a workable alternative in practical terms of the theatre (fig. 23).

Now King Fisher aims his black pistol at Mark, but one calm glance from the enraptured couple drops him dead. 'Carry the King to his grave', sings the He-Ancient, thus granting him his royal status in the shadow-realm; for he, too, is an archetypal figure and worthy of respect. But now, for the fourth ritual dance, Strephon and another dancer make fire in the ritual way, twirling a pointed stick in a round hole till the tinder catches and the flaming point is held aloft. So it was done of old for the renewal of the crops and of human fertility, but also, as we may imagine, still more intuitively for renewal in the human psyche. As the flames spread to conceal the hieratic couple, it is 'carnal fire', insists the chorus, 'transfigured as divine'. But when at last the dance and the fire are finished, and the moon takes over, only the chorus remain to lament the sun, 'lost on the night journey under the sea'. And then slowly, beautifully, the dawn chorus of the birds begins, and the light grows as at the start of the opera. But the temple has vanished in the early mist, or if seen, 'only as ruins and stones silhouetted against the clear sky'.

Now Mark and Jenifer are heard approaching from either wing. As they meet, he sings to her: 'Jenifer, Jenifer, my darling, after the visionary night, the senses purified, my heart's at rest'. And she: 'O Mark, truth is assumed in love so rich, I could love all, even my father, had he lived'. But in fact throwing off the father-image was part of her achievement, and Mark is quite right to sing: 'Mourn no stubborn father, but receive the ring, here in this magic wood on this midsummer day'. And then we are left with the growing sunlight and the music until the curtain falls.

But what in sober terms is it that we are left with as the curtain falls on so extraordinary an opera? The sunlight, yes, and that does traditionally stand in for illumination. The music, of which Ian Kemp, in his long and sympathetic discussion of this opera, wrote that 'music mirrors the fluidity of unconscious activity more directly than any other art and opera uses real human beings as counters'.[16] The second of these two thoughts is as crucial as the first. Human beings—or gods with human attributes —are essential to opera: actual characters upon whom the author can project his visions and the audience their identifications. For 'opera in some guise or another is the medium most suited to the projection of analogues of the inner life' (our inner life); and 'most operas, in effect if not by design, explore the world behind the external trappings of human behaviour' (our human behaviour); 'that is indeed one of the prime justifications for the genre, its very nature announcing a covenant with the strange and marvellous'.[17]

Kemp knows too about that ' "open wound" which is the hallmark of the creative mind'—the creative wound again.[18] His book is valuable about the nature of the creative process in general and of Tippett's creative process in particular. But now, sadly as I shall always think but unavoidably in view of the grittiness of Tippett's conscience and the troubled situation of our times, Tippett turned to *King Priam* in drier mood: an opera of quality, but more fragmented and less inspired; to *The Knot Garden*, more quirkily; to *The Ice Break*, more sketchily. Then, in 1984, that astonishing confrontation with the sickness and with the beauty of our world, *The Mask of Time*. Here are no actors nor even dancers to focus our identification with the great cosmic principles invoked. 'I was often asked', Tippett explained, 'if I was going to write another opera, and I knew I really wanted to write a different kind of piece'. He did.[19]

# CONCLUSION

It all depends on what you mean by opera. I mean by opera a drama with essentially human (or godly, but that is only to express quintessential humanity in yet more archetypal images) characters and situations unfolding through words, music and staging to a resolution which will be the more convincing the more inevitably it grows out of those characters and situations.

There can certainly be new ways of doing this. But unless it is being done, there may be music-theatre having much in common with opera, but there will not within the meaning of this book be opera. Some very interesting music-theatre is currently going under the name of opera which strikes me as really something different again. The name is not important, of course, but the difference is.

A certain confusion of the boundaries may, I think, be resulting from our recent tendency, which has great advantages as well as some disadvantages, to televise live or studio performances of existing operas. The disadvantages arise, although not necessarily, from the sophisticated techniques habitual now in making films. The temptation is very natural to use dissolves and close-ups and other well-tried and highly ingenious methods of the cinema. But close-ups, in particular, by showing you the whites of his eyes and the movement of his lips and his Adam's apple and every detail of his makeup, put at great hazard all that theatrical distancing which gives to the singer the magic of his otherness. The nearer we get to him, the more he begins to look like an actor and the less like an archetype. What we gain in intimacy we may lose in numinosity. Sometimes the gain may be worth the loss, but neither too often nor too close would seem to be good working rules for opera.

Another asset of the operatic stage is the proscenium arch, which is almost as valuable for concentrating the audience's magical transformation in the theatre as the alchemical container is for encouraging that transformation in the psyche which is the real search under the guise of transmuting base metal into precious metal. It is, of course, a matter of degree; but the arts in general and the art of opera in particular have it in common with alchemy that they may for the time being induce a kind of transformation.

My point is that the stylized conventions and formal expectations of the theatre are in themselves conducive. When Franco Zeffirelli had his singers wandering through all that picturesque landscape gardening in his film of *La traviata*, the scenery was beautiful and so was the singing; but landscape is nature and singing is art; and it was the singing which seemed to be diminished, the more so since you could not imagine where on earth the orchestra was supposed to be. Yet I remember a fine telecast of *Idomeneo* from the Metropolitan Opera where the cameras seemed to have settled down pretty much in the front row of the dress circle, with very little zooming in or panning round. The result was very satisfactory. Nevertheless, I still believe that no film or telecast can be quite so satisfactory as a stage performance of equal excellence, witnessed from the auditorium.

Luigi Nono did not regard his 'scenic actions' or 'actions in music' as opera, nor did Luciano Berio so regard his 'spectacle for mixed media', nor Hans Werner Henze when he dismissed opera as 'archaic and inflexible' and described the uncomfortable overlapping of three concurrent dramas and orchestras for *We Come to the River* as 'actions for music'. Philip Glass was bizarre in *Einstein on the Beach*, still remarkably in-turned in *Satyagraha*, lucid enough in *Akhnaten*, but these are too short on story and too static as music to be what I should call opera. For me, opera has to move on; and for me, I am bound to admit, minimalism resembles nothing so much as one of those nightmares in which you most wish but are least able to move your own legs and get away.

Karlheinz Stockhausen's *Donnerstag* from *Licht* struck me as rather more compulsive than inspired. That suffering mother, that yearning pianist, that old lady coming on with her toy motor car to chide them all, reminded me of the old mother found sitting at the top of the mountain when those arduous climbers made it at last in *The Ascent of F6*, except that Auden and Isherwood knew exactly the mother-bound implications of their scenario whereas Stockhausen perhaps did not, going on as he did through a great deal more purely mystical elaboration before finishing that interminably protracted, increasingly sentimental and musically diminishing Act III. The visual aspect rose indeed to a remarkable climax, but by then there was very little human and dramatic interest remaining to climax with it.

In Harrison Birtwistle's *Mask of Orpheus*, the masked actors in their mythological impersonations are eminently appropriate to opera, if only they had been allowed to develop dramatically. Instead, both characters and situations overlap in triplicate through a series of retakes, even as you might say a concurrence of retakes, 'going over the same events from different angles', as Birtwistle explained in his programme notes, 'so that a multi-dimensional object is created'. He argued that 'myths are multi-dimensional narratives containing contradictions and ambiguities'. True; but Rinuccini or Striggio or Mozart or Wagner did not need to make a sandwich out of them in order to reveal that they may carry meanings on more levels than one. Music can be multi-dimensional and in our culture normally is so: but drama? By implication, no doubt; but literally? Can we in the theatre mentally sort that one out? Is this a breakthrough in the art of theatre? Or is it an exercise in schizoid dissociation? Or just possibly both?

At least it is not opera within the definition of this book. Call it if you prefer a different kind of opera. I still think that opera of whatever kind has before it a future no less eventful than its glorious past; and I still feel certain that, in whatever new contexts, the autonomous flow of symbols will go sweeping on. Symbols arise as expressions of our basic human nature, and the basis of our human nature can hardly change. Behaviour can; and our world seems to be going through a phase of irrational violence inevitably reflected in our arts. That sort of reflection by artists not only does but ought to happen. How it is all going to turn out is not to be foreseen; but Thomas Mann put the position very nicely when he said some time ago that humanity is a cat with nine lives.

As to understanding what our symbols mean, it is not strictly necessary on any intellectual plane, though I have not myself been able to resist following up that elusive inquiry hopefully through the pages of this present book. The inquiry is elusive because it cannot possibly be completed. The answers cannot be the same for all of us, since as individuals we are not all the same. The interpretation of symbols is a little like the interpretation of dreams: you cannot do it out of any dreambook nor depend upon any rigidly preconceived theories; you have to listen to the dreamer's own associations.

And so it is that if on some level it makes sense to Jonathan Miller to associate the Mafia with *Rigoletto*, or to Patrice Chéreau to associate Marx with the *Ring*, then on that level, for them and their many admirers, it does make sense. Yet I still suspect that they may be erecting unnecessary obstacles for themselves against responding to deeper layers where archetypal insights are on offer which have little relevance to the Mafia or to Marx but great relevance to the underlying urgencies of the human spirit. I conclude therefore as I began: the fundamental mistake is to think about what the given symbols mean and then to stage whatever it may be that you think they mean. Right or wrong, thoughts are not what symbols are about. Images are, conveying meanings as they do without the distraction of intellectual mediation. In the theatre, our business is to present the symbols in words and music and staging just as we find them allied in the piece itself, trusting them to do their own interpreting.

# APPENDIX

## Musical Examples from Wagner's *Ring*

In the following excerpts from *Der Ring des Nibelungen* (in full at Bayreuth, 1876), selected leitmotifs are grouped to suggest certain of their organic relationships. See chapter 12 for a fuller discussion.

### Appendix example 1

The undoubted start of the thematic material is the simple triadic arpeggiation relating to the bottom of the Rhine and to the timeless state of nature generally.

### Appendix example 2

Slight melodic figuration and increased motion give a hint that nature's timelessness is not going to last.

### Appendix example 3

Erda the Earth-Mother as a source of intuitive, though scarcely of conscious, wisdom has a version in the minor of the original arpeggiation as modified in app. ex. 2, lower stave.

### Appendix example 4

The downfall of the gods represents on one level a return full-cycle to the unconscious for a new beginning, and the motive conveying it is for this reason, I think, an inversion of app. ex. 3.

### Appendix example 5

The motive customarily labelled *Entsagungs-Motiv* (renunciation motive) is a close variant of app. ex. 4, the link perhaps being that too wilful an attempt at controlling your life consciously has to be renounced before a new beginning in genuinely increased consciousness and maturity can be made.

## Appendix example 6

This further correlative of app. exx. 4 and 5 has also been labelled 'renunciation motive', though to call this entire group acceptance motives might really be as suitable. At (a) and at (b) the words seem negative, at (c) positive, but the common factor is acceptance of that which is in fact inevitable.

(a)

*Only he who renounces the might of desire, only he who forgoes*

*love's longing*

(b)

*So I curse love!*

(c) Siegmund

*Holiest desire, highest need*

*yearning  love,  uttermost need*

## Appendix example 7

Freia's joyful motive, standing for the joy of life itself, starts as a variant in the major of app. ex. 4, then takes an upward turn which is indeed uplifting.

## Appendix example 8

The carefree song of the Rhinemaidens is close enough to app.
ex. 7 for us to sense a common element of joy. App. ex. 2 joins in,
and behind that the original app. ex. 1, standing for the state of
nature from which indeed joy comes, though we humans must
not be enticed back to nature too irresponsibly.

## Appendix example 9

The plaint of the Rhinemaidens for their lost gold, or perhaps
more truly for its lost state of innocence, treats harmonically the
melodic added sixth shown at the end of app. ex. 8. When in the
minor, this passage links very interestingly with app. ex. 29.

### Appendix example 10

The forest bird brings to Siegfried the call of true instinct,
appropriately enough to a variant of app. ex. 8.

### Appendix example 11

The forest murmurs are linked to app. ex. 10 by the strong
suggestion of the added sixth.

### Appendix example 12

The shimmering waters of the Rhine carried something of the
same play between fifth and sixth as they reflected the light from
the sunlit gold (lower stave; see app. ex. 14).

### Appendix example 13

The added sixth provides a further link with the sleep motive
to which Brünnhilde relaxes into unconsciousness, the better to
move forward when Siegfried wakes her up again.

### Appendix example 14

Also derived from the original arpeggiation comes a group of motives whose distinctive characteristic is energy, commonly though not always endorsed by leaping intervals. This one appears (see app. ex. 12, lower stave) to suggest the immense potential force of the gold as yet undisturbed below the waters of the Rhine.

### Appendix example 15

The sword with its leaping motive, clearly in some close connection with app. ex. 14, is a primary symbol for the heroic spirit, itself a token for the force of life in full release. This motive fairly shines out at us as it rises to a more conclusive summit in keeping with its entirely positive thrust.

### Appendix example 16

There is a certain resemblance between app. ex. 15 and this, the chief of Siegfried's motives as a representative of the heroic spirit. At (a) is shown a simple version of what becomes more elaborated at (b), suggesting a further development of the hero's personality. The variant at (c) is much farther off, but is perceptibly related, besides carrying in the second complete bar an equally distant yet perhaps covertly significant hint of app. ex. 6.

(a)

(b)

(c)

## Appendix example 17

There does seem a valid link between app. ex. 16, especially as at (b), and that grand Valhalla motive which always suggests the noble quality of Wotan himself, as with all his flaws, and in rather a different sense, the ultimate hero of the *Ring*. There is an obvious connection with app. ex. 2 and thereby with the original app. ex. 1 itself; and a less expected but rather touching connection with Freia's motive of joy at app. ex. 7.

## Appendix example 18

Now comes a large group of motives whose characteristic it is to present chromatically material most of which is also operative in a diatonic treatment. The most remarkable instance is the motive of the ring itself, together with others intimately connected with it. This actual motive of the ring is in effect a chromatic version of Wotan's diatonic motive (app. ex. 17): the primary version at (a) shows the closeness of the transformation most clearly; (b) is a variant with a more plaintive aspect, and (c) is a variant with a warmer aspect; (d) shows merely the two ends of the primary motive, as used to indicate Mime's brooding on the unlikely prospect of getting his hands on the ring for himself.

(a)

(b)

(c)

(d)

## Appendix example 19

The baleful motive of Alberich's curse is a melodic unravelling of
the chromatic harmonies of the motive of the ring (app. ex. 18):
the energy shows in the leaping rise; the malice, perhaps, in
the falling close. But there is, as elsewhere in the *Ring*, a sort of
existentialist warrant for the prophecy of doom, and a chronic
ambiguity in the challenge thereby offered (compare app. ex. 6).

## Appendix example 20

The obsessive force of Alberich's will shows here as a harmonic
condensation of app. ex. 19.

### Appendix example 21

Hagen's evil parentage perhaps shows at (a), and his dark nature certainly warrants his insistent tritone, as at (b).

(a)

(b)

### Appendix example 22

The augmented triad lends an uneasy menace to those formidable Valkyries for their manic ride.

### Appendix example 23

The augmented triad confirms the mythological union of opposites between the Valkyries and the Norns, as shown here, not to mention the closely related Rhinemaidens, as is shown by the presence of their transposed arpeggiation at app. ex. 24 (b).

## Appendix example 24

At (a), the bright motive of Brünnhilde's greeting to the sun lifts
our hearts with that radiant progression to the mediant. At (b),
that same progression, darkly transposed down a semitone,
puts those shadowy Norns into an extraordinary relationship
of opposition-in-identity, showing the light and the shadow as
the two complementary poles of a single field of force; while the
arpeggiation, as from app. ex. 2, relates them to the Rhinemaidens
too.

**Appendix example 25**

Chromatic instability works for mystery in the magic of Tarnhelm, or more truly of self-deception, as at (a) and (b) here.

(a)

(b)

**Appendix example 26**

The magic of sleep standing for strategic retreat into unconsciousness shows very chromatically in this passage.

**Appendix example 27**

The withdrawn mystery of Wotan as the Wanderer on his paradoxical way towards greater self-awareness comes quite close to the chromatic indeterminacy of app. ex. 26.

## Appendix example 28

Chromatic alteration may also depict yearning, as in the upwards-seeking semitone at (a); or enchantment, as (in passing) for Freia at (b); or swelling, mounting emotion, as especially for Siegmund and Sieglinde at (c).

(a)

(b)

(c)

## Appendix example 29

The falling semitone, whether chromatic or diatonic, may have an
exactly opposite effect of downwards-drooping grief or obsession,
as in the painful motive of woe at (a), where the fall is like an
appoggiatura exacerbating the harmony; or alternatively as at (b)
and (c), where the fall occurs as part of a forcible progression in
the harmony.

(a)

*Woe's me!   Ah, woe's me!*

(b)

(c)

## Appendix example 30

There can be a more complex effect, perhaps as of grief courageously accepted, when the falling semitone is balanced by a
subsequent rise. At (a), the symbol, complete in itself, has to do
with destiny. At (b), the semitone of the bass line merely falls in
parallel with the melody as the harmony subsides, so that the
sense of destiny courageously encountered is not so evident. But
at (c), the motive as at (a) becomes the continuation of a longer
motive, itself complete including this expansion into (a); and
here the spaciousness of the handling, and the presence of the
compensating rise after the falling semitone, give yet more the
impression of unavoidable destiny accepted with undefeated
courage.

(a)

(b)

(c)

## Appendix example 31

Also connected with the falling semitone of app. ex. 30, and likewise balancing the fall by an almost immediately rising interval, (a) is commonly regarded as a motive of anxiety, which it may often be; but at (b) a prolonged version of (a) grows out of Freia's own joyfully rising motive (app. ex. 28 [b]). And at (c), out of two bars of Siegmund's motive (app. ex. 34), there grows a completely tender yet note-perfect rendering for which yearning gives a better description, as he and Sieglinde gaze so raptly into each other's eyes—although I would certainly not doubt that agitation of the sweetest kind is also contributing to their unforeseen and mingled feelings.

(a)

(b)

(c)

## Appendix example 32

The falling semitone, as at app. ex. 29 (a), but here preceded by an aggressive little cluster of changing notes, marks as at (a) Mime's nasty little will frustrated; but this very same motive expanded, as at (b), marks Wotan's equally obstinate but far-from-little will frustrated.

(a)

(b)

## Appendix example 33

Divested of its changing notes and continued still more obsessively downwards, app. ex. 32 (b) looms conspicuously behind
this motive for the formidable spear which is the symbol for all
that is most blindly and egocentrically assertive in Wotan's will.

## Appendix example 34

Siegmund, brought up to be the ill-starred agent of Wotan's will,
has a motive only a little modified and softened off from app.
ex. 33; but at (a) the augmented second, and at (b) the implied
diminished seventh, do beautifully suggest Siegmund's own
lovable courage and inherent vulnerability.

(a)

(b)

## Appendix example 35

Sieglinde's motive has an interesting trace of app. ex. 1, hinting
at the natural side of her passion for Siegmund; but again its
sadness shows in the diminished seventh as it counterpoints so
wonderfully with his.

## Appendix example 36

As Sieglinde brings to Siegmund that highly symbolic drink, the music confirms the beautiful mingling of their destinies.

## Appendix example 37

Gutrune's vulnerability shows at (a), with a hint of app. ex. 7 for the joy which in the event so heart-rendingly failed her: an irony which (b) condenses into almost unbearable poignancy; while (c) shows Gunther as on the surface quite acceptably heroic, yet weak enough at heart to fail so soon as circumstances really put him to the test.

(c)

## Appendix example 38

At (a) there might be some vaguely prophetic thought among others which Brünnhilde is sharing with Siegfried, as yet so happily. At (b), there can be no doubt about Sieglinde being told prophetically that she is pregnant with Siegfried. At (c), as the last motive heard in the *Ring*, the prophecy is to confirm, as at this late stage only the music could confirm, that redemption is Brünnhilde's purpose, so that those shattering modulations herald not only an utter disintegration in the present, but also a veiled promise for the future.

(a)

(b)

(c)

# NOTES

CHAPTER 2. WORDS, MUSIC, STAGING

1. Quoted by Carner in *Grove* 6, s.v. 'Puccini'.
2. By contrast with Deryck Cooke's pragmatic enquiry, Carl Dahlhaus's impressive *Musikästhetic* (Cologne, 1967; translated by William Austin as *Esthetics of Music* [Cambridge, 1980]) traces the leading theories about what art in general and music in particular can be expected to express, from Plato through Platonists including Plotinus and Ficino, and from Aristotle through Aristotelians including Lessing and Herder, down to our own times. Since I shall not be returning systematically to this philosophic plane, I recommend his book the more strongly to readers whose interests lie in that direction. I am still favourably impressed by Leonard Meyer (1956, 1968), with his keen awareness of psychological considerations, and by Susanne Langer (esp. 1942), with her suggestive notion of 'isomorphic' analogues between common experience and musical experience. Natasha Spender and Rosamund Shuter-Dyson in *Grove* 6 cover the field from Plato to Helmholtz, from behaviourism to depth-psychology, adding a bibliography which is a small treatise in itself. Ian Bent in *Grove* 6 does as much for the technical analysis of musical design: its symmetries and its asymmetries, its repetitions and its developments, as we take them in whether awarely or subliminally, and as a good musical analyst like Arnold Whittall or Carl Dahlhaus is able to reveal them helpfully.

CHAPTER 3. COMPATIBILITY ON STAGE

1. *Times Literary Supplement*, 25 April 1986.
2. Ibid., 4 April 1986.

CHAPTER 4. THE START OF OPERA

1. See Panofsky (1939), Seznec (1953), Wind (1958), Gombrich (1972), and Donington (1981). Also Nesca A. Robb, *Neoplatonism of the Italian Renaissance* (London, 1935), esp. on the Neoplatonic poetry of Michelangelo; B. Weinberg, *History of Literary Criticism in the Italian Renaissance* (Chicago, 1961); and Baxter Hathaway, *The Age of Criticism: The Late Renaissance in Italy* (Ithaca, N.Y., 1962). For some of the relevant

classical sources, see Plato *Rep.* 3.398ff., 10.595ff., 3.400Dff.; *Laws* 7640E; Aristotle *Pol.* 8.1340A; *Poet.* 1447Aff.; and, on the 'unities', *Poet.* 1415A.35 and 1449B.12ff. (for which see note 3 to chap. 6 below). And see Claude Palisca's compendious survey *Humanism in Italian Renaissance Musical Thought* (New Haven, 1985).

2. Dante Alighieri, *Inferno* 9.61–63.

3. Giovanni Boccaccio, *Genealogia deorum gentilium* (Venice, 1472), ed. Vincenzo Romano (Bari, 1951), 14.7.

4. Pierre de Ronsard, *Oeuvres complètes*, ed. H. Vaganay, vol. 4 (Paris, 1924), p. 159.

5. Paul Oscar Kristeller, *The Philosophy of Marsilio Ficino*, trans. Virginia Conant (New York, 1943). Consult the facsimile edition of *Marsilii Ficini opera omnia* (Basel, 1576), ed. P. O. Kristeller (New York, 1959), esp. pp. 20, 208–09, 241ff., 250ff., 255ff., 263ff., 399, 638. And see D. P. Walker, 'Orpheus the Theologian and Renaissance Platonists', *Journal of the Warburg and Courtauld Institutes* 16 (1953): 100–120.

6. Pico della Mirandola, *Opera omnia* (Bologna, 1496; facs. ed., Turin, 1971–72), ed. Eugenio Garin, pp. 580 and 162.

7. Angelo Poliziano, *La favola di Orfeo* (Mantua, 1480?). See Nino Pirrotta in Austin (1968) and Pirrotta (1969).

8. Bembo (1525). See D. Mace, 'Pietro Bembo and the Literary Origins of the Italian Madrigal', *Musical Quarterly* 1969: 65ff.; and James Haar's article on Bembo in *The New Grove Dictionary of Music and Musicians* (London, 1980; hereafter cited as *Grove 6*).

9. Zarlino (1558), 4.32, 4.71 and 7.xi.

10. Thomas Morley, *A Plaine and Easie Introduction to Practicall Musicke* (London, 1597), pp. 177ff.

11. Galilei (1581).

12. See Palisca (1954, 1960).

13. Galilei (1581), p. 89.

14. See Donington (1981) and references therein. The edition by Carol and Lander MacClintock (Rome, 1971) is excellent. For Conti's Neoplatonic interpretation, see Natale Conti (Natalis Comes), *Mythologiae sive explicationis fabularum libri decem* (Venice, 1567; I consulted the edition published in Venice in 1581), 'De Circe', pp. 374–80.

15. For those interested in the immediate prehistory of opera, a good starting point is David Nutter, 'Intermedio', in *Grove 6*. A very solid study is Wolfgang Osthoff, *Theatergesang und darstellende Musik in der italienischen Renaissance* (Turin, 1969). Sternfeld (1963) is insightful and wide-ranging. The line from sixteenth- to seventeenth-century theatrical practice is the subject of research reported in *Studi sul teatro veneto fra rinascimento ed età barocca* (Florence, 1971) and in *Venezia e il melodramma nel seicento* (Florence, 1976), edited by Maria Teresa Muraro; the latter includes contributions by Bruno Brizi, Marie-Françoise Christout, William Holmes, Giovanni Morelli, Pierluigi Petrobelli and Thomas Walker. Consult also Iain Fenlon, 'Music and Spectacle at the Gonzaga Court, c. 1580–1600', *Proceedings of the Royal Musical Association* 103 (1976–77): 90–105; Federico Ghisi, *Feste musicali della Firenze medicea* (1480–1589) (Florence, 1939); Henry Kaufmann, 'Music for a Noble Florentine Wedding (1539)', in Laurence Berman, ed., *Words and Music: The Composer's View* (Cambridge,

Mass., 1972); Andrew C. Minor and Bonner Mitchell, eds., *A Renaissance Entertainment . . . in 1539* (Columbia, Mo., 1968); Cesare Molinari, *Le nozze degli dei: Un saggio sul grande spettacolo italiano nel seicento* (Rome, 1968; traces Neoplatonic influences on Bardi's interludes of 1585/86); A. M. Nagler, *Theater Festivals of the Medici, 1539–1677* (New Haven, 1964; standard on plots and scenery, not much on music); D. P. Walker, 'La musique des intermèdes florentins de 1589 et l'humanisme', in *Les fêtes de la renaissance*, vol. 1 (Paris, 1955), and *Les fêtes du mariage de Ferdinand de Medicis et de Christine de Lorraine, Florence, 1589*, vol. 1, *Musique des intermèdes de 'La pellegrina'* (Paris, 1963). For Bardi's deliberate depiction in the 1589 interludes of 'one of the most profound allegories of Plato', see Aby Warburg's *Gesammelte Schriften* (Leipzig and Berlin, 1932), pp. 259–300; and his 'Costumi teatrali per gli intermezzi di 1589', in *Atti del'Accademia del R. Istituto Musicale di Firenze* (Florence, 1895). Further recommended are Leo Schrade, ed., *La représentation d'Edipo tiranno au Teatro Olimpico* (Paris, 1960), Pirrotta (1969), and Sternfeld (1974). And see the very detailed and musicianly study in Howard Mayer Brown, *Sixteenth-Century Instrumentation: The Music for the Florentine Intermedii* (Rome, 1973), with especial reference to those of 1589, including the methods of using the actual instruments, and reproductions from the Buontalenti stage settings. Also Donington (1981).

16. Plato *Rep.* 10.614ff.

17. Buontalenti's designs are in the Harry R. Beard Collection at the Theatre Museum, London.

18. Lilio Gregorio Giraldi, *De deis gentium . . .* (Basel, 1548); Vincenzo Cartari, *Le imagini, con la spositione de i dei de gli antichi* (Venice, 1556); Conti, *Mythologiae*. For Boccaccio, see n. 3 above.

19. Ottavio Rinuccini, *L'Euridice*, libretto (Florence, 1600), dedication. For Rinuccini, see Hanning (1980). For some of the large literature on the libretti as literature, see Donington (1981), pp. 329–330, n. 1. See esp. Carlo Calcaterra, *Poesia e canto: Studi sulla poesia melica italiana e sulla favola per musica* (Bologna, 1951); Aldo Caselli, *Catalogo delle opere liriche publicate in Italia* (Florence, 1969); Conrad (1978); Freeman (1981); Girdlestone (1972); Ulderico Rolandi, *Il libretto per musica attraverso i tempi* (Rome, 1951); Smith (1970); and Sonneck (1914).

   For Peri's dedication and other contemporary documents of the kind, a convenient modern source is Angelo Solerti, *Le origini del melodramma* (Turin, 1908). For English translations, see Strunk (1950).

20. Jacopo Peri, *L'Euridice*, dedication to score (Florence, 1601/02). For this opera, see Palisca (1968), Donington (1981) and Carter (1982). For its connections with Monteverdi's *Orfeo*, see Tomlinson (1987), pp. 131ff., a study in depth of words, music and cultural background, though uninformative on the symbolical associations in Petrarchan tradition between images for 'sensual' and 'divine' love.

21. See Hanning (1980) on Rinuccini in particular, as well as the general poetic background of the interludes and the early librettos. On *Dafne*, Sonneck's pioneering entry (1914) remains valuable. F. W. Sternfeld, 'The First Printed Opera Libretto', *Music and Letters* 59, no. 2 (1978): 121ff., has front-line research on the developing states and probable performances of *Dafne*. William V. Porter is equally impor-

tant on what can be gleaned from surviving fragments of the music, in 'Peri and Corsi's *Dafne*: Some New Discoveries and Observations', *JAMS* 18, no. 2 (1965): 170–96. The *Dafne* librettos of Rinuccini and Busenello are very richly discussed by Yves F.-A. Giraud, *La fable de Daphné* (Geneva, 1969). See also Federico Ghisi, *Alle fonti della monodia* (Milan, 1940), pp. 10ff.; Donington (1981), pp. 115–25; and esp. Howard Mayer Brown, 'How Opera Began: An Introduction to Jacopo Peri's *Euridice* (1600)', in Eric Cochrane, ed., *The Late Italian Renaissance (1525–1630)* (London, 1970).

22. First performance 1597, or 1598 in Florentine old-style dating. For this and other complications of dating at various times and places, see Donington (1981), Appendix: 'Opera and the Calendar'.

23. Conti, *Mythologiae*, pp. 227–43. On love as cause of both good and ill, compare Dante, *Purgatory* 18.103–05; on love's 'dictation', 24.52–54.

24. Plato *Symp.* 180Dff.

25. See Palisca (1968, 1972) and esp. Carter (1982).

26. See Ficino, *Opera omnia*, p. 119. It must be understood that the sonnet from which this line comes (Francesco Petrarcha, *Rime*, no. 245) refers to 'divine' love under the image of 'sensual', in the usual Neoplatonic manner, as is confirmed by *Il Petrarca con l'espositione de M. Giovanni Andrea Gesualdo* (Venice, 1533; edition of 1573), pp. 263 ff. And see esp. A. Quitslund, 'Spenser's *Amoretti VIII* and Platonic Commentaries on Petrarch', *Journal of the Warburg and Courtauld Institutes* 36 (1973): 256–76. On 'Petrarchism', see Tomlinson (1987).

CHAPTER 5. MONTEVERDI

1. See Arnold (1963) and in Grove 6; Arnold and Fortune (1985); Donington (1981); Palisca (1968); Stevens (1980); and Tomlinson (1987). Also Anna Amalie Abert, *Claudio Monteverdi und das musikalische Drama* (Lippstadt, 1954); Wolfgang Osthoff, *Das dramatische Spätwerk Claudio Monteverdis* (Tutzing, 1961); Domenico de' Paoli, *Claudio Monteverdi* (Milan, 1945); and very particularly Whenham (1986).

2. Ficino, *Opera omnia*, p. 86.

3. Conti, *Mythologiae*, p. 241; and for the Heraclitan and Orphic doctrine 'deum esse diem et noctem', there is a contemporary citation in Bartolomeo Delbene, *Civitas veri* (Paris, 1609), pp. 244ff.

4. On the symbolism of the snake, see Donington (1981), pp. 167ff.

5. On scene changes in baroque theatre, consult P. Bjurström, *Giacomo Torelli and Baroque Stage Design*, rev. ed. (Stockholm, 1962); C. Molinari, *Le nozze degli dei: Un saggio sul grande spettacolo italiano nel seicento* (Rome, 1968); and Manfred Boetzkes, 'Opera', §8, in Grove 6, an excellent survey of this crucial dimension all through the history of opera.

6. Conti, *Mythologiae*, p. 505.

7. Dante, *La vita nuova*, closing passage. For Beatrice in the role of mother-image, see *Purgatory* 30.79 and 74; and *Paradise* 1.101 and 22.4.

8. Iain Fenlon, in a very able article entitled 'Monteverdi's Mantuan *Orfeo*: Some New Documentation' (*Early Music*, May 1984: 163–72), takes the more mundane view that diplomatic or social considerations caused the ending to be changed, for a projected third performance, and regards the substituted ending as poetically inferior, and conjecturally by Ferdinando Gonzaga. Barbara Hanning (1983), on the other hand, argues for Rinuccini by comparing his methods of distributing free and rhyming verse forms. But still more, in that case, would the Neoplatonic intentions of the altered symbolism seem plain to me. On this and much else of crucial importance, see Whenham (1986).

9. Margaret Murata, *Operas for the Papal Court, 1631–1668* (Ann Arbor, Mich., 1981) is important on the Roman sequel.

10. *The Letters of Claudio Monteverdi*, edited and translated by Denis Stevens (London, 1980), p. 117.

11. See Tacitus *Annals* 12–16 and Suetonius *Lives of the Caesars*.

12. Ellen Rosand, 'Seneca and the Interpretation of L'incoronazione di Poppea', *JAMS* 38, no. 1 (Spring 1985): 34–71. See also Kurt von Fischer, 'Petit essai sur les opéras de Monteverdi', *Annuario musical* 37 (1982): 8, for his interesting view of the ending of *Poppea* as 'an allusion to the mystical texts of Christian love'.

13. On the disputed authorship of this duet, see A. Chiarelli, 'L'incoronazione di Poppea o Il Nerone': Problemi di filologia testuale', *Rivista italiana di musicologia* 9 (1974): 117–51.


## CHAPTER 6. THE AGE OF REASON

1. For Cavalli and his setting, Glover (1978) is excellent; so is Walker, 'Cavalli', in *Grove 6*. For Cavalli in Paris, see Prunières (1913). The manuscript of *Ormindo* is in the Marciano Library in Venice; see the modern edition by Raymond Leppard (London, 1969), although this version leaves out the discovery that Ormindo is Ariadeno's son.

2. For the three 'unities' so important to the French dramatic school, Aristotle (*Poet.* 1415A) recommended confining the plot to a single action in the general interests of intelligibility and effectiveness; he also recommended keeping the duration of that action within twenty-four hours if possible, while pointing out that this limit was not in fact observed by early Greek tragedians (*Poet.* 1449B.12ff.). The recommendation to restrict the action to a single place is not in Aristotle, but was added by Castelvetro in his edition of the *Poetics* in 1570, on the grounds of Aristotle's general insistence on 'probability'—after which it became erroneously accepted as part of the Aristotelian canon, with its diverse but extensive influence on dramatic structure. For his earlier, more philosophical significance, see Eugenio Garin, 'Aristotelismo e Platonismo del Rinascimento', *La Rinascita* 2 (1939). For the by then equally influential Horace, consult D. A. Russell, 'Ars poetica', in C. D. N. Costa and J. W. Binns, eds., *Horace* (London and Boston, 1973), p. 120. Horace's *De arte poetica* is a late epistle, ostensibly written to one of the Piso sons, as a discouragement against taking up poetry, but giving instructions on how to acquire

the rules of good composition if it should come to that. The epistle was left unfinished, but acquired a vast and indeed disproportionate reputation, as a guide to dramatic conduct, in particular, especially for the Age of Reason. All this was in the background of French opera, though not so directly as in French poetic drama.

3. Pierre Corneille, *Andromède*, Preface. See Margaret M. McGovan, 'Corneille', in *Grove* 6; and J. Ecorcheville, *Corneille et la musique* (Paris, 1906). The legacy of classical French drama to French tragic opera in general could hardly be exaggerated.

4. Charles Marguetel de Saint-Denis, Seigneur de Saint-Evremond, 'Sur les opéra: A Monsieur le duc de Bouquinquant [Buckingham]' (1677?). For the text and its very complicated history, see René Ternois in *Oeuvres en prose de Saint-Evremond*, 4 vols. (Paris, 1962–66), 2:195–98 and 3:127–64. And see I. Lowens, 'St. Evremond, Dryden, and the Theory of Opera', in *Criticism* 1 (1959): 226; Ternois, 'Saint-Evremond, gentilhomme normand', *Annales de Normandie* 1960: 3; and the brief but informative article by Albert Cohen, 'Saint-Evremond', in *Grove* 6.

5. John Dryden, *Albion and Albanus* (London, 1685), Preface.

6. John Hughes, *Calypso and Telemachus* (London, 1712). Last page of preface to 1717 edition of libretto, in *Poems on Several Occasions with Some Select Essays in Prose* (London, 1735).

7. Samuel Johnson, *Lives of the English Poets* (1779–81); ed. G. B. Hill (Oxford, 1905), p. 160.

8. Samuel Johnson, ed., *The Plays of William Shakespeare* (London, 1765), Preface.

9. Quotations cited and well discussed by Gloria Flaherty (1978): see esp. pp. 94ff.; but the book is of great interest and value throughout. For Mattheson in this connection, see *Der musikalische Patriot* (Hamburg, 1728), pp. 117–18; for Goethe, 'Über Wahrheit und Wahrscheinlichkeit der Kunstwerke', in *Die Propyleen* (1798).

10. Flaherty (1978), p. 113.

11. Charles Henri Blainville, *L'esprit de l'art musical* (Geneva, 1754), p. 14.

12. Freeman (1981) is extremely valuable; Smith (1970) is good for the whole history of the libretto as such: Jacques Joly's dissertation 'Les fêtes théâtrales de Métastase à la cour de Vienne (1731–1767)' (Univ. of Clermont-Ferrand, 1978) takes up the story very well on the literary aspects, less reliably on the musical, but should be consulted.

13. See Prunières (1910); but still more Prunières (1913), a magnificent study of the antecedents. Christout (1967) is highly relevant; Grout (1947) still extremely useful; Lesure (1972) especially good on visual aspects; Yates (1947) splendid on the general context; Mellers (1951) brief but good; Anthony (1973), and his *Grove* 6 article on Lully, both important. Donington (1981) has considerable detail. See also Isherwood (1973) and Girdlestone (1972). For a musical view of Lully's recitative, see Joyce Newman, *Jean-Baptiste Lully and His Tragédies Lyriques* (Ann Arbor, Mich., 1979); on its interpretation, see Robert Donington, *Baroque Music: Style and Performance* (London, 1982), pp. 24–26; and esp. R. Peter Wolf, 'Metrical Relationships in French Recitative', *Recherches sur la musique française classique* 18 (1978): 29–49. Also George Houle, *Meter and Music, 1600–1800* (Bloomington, Ind., 1987).

14. Yates (1947), with her Neoplatonic expertise and her keen psychological awareness, is of the first importance here. For Quinault, Girdlestone (1972) is excellent.
See also Etienne Gros, *Philippe Quinault: Sa vie et son oeuvre* (Paris, 1926), a sympathetic
study; and James R. Anthony, 'Quinault', in *Grove 6*.

15. Winton Dean (1959), p. 365. Dean (1969, and 'Handel' in *Grove 6*) and Dean and
Knapp (1987) are also essential reading. See Bryan Trowell, 'Congreve and the
1744 Libretto', *Musical Times* 111 (Oct. 1970): 993, and Jon Solomon's adventurous
article 'Reflections of Ovid in Semele's Mirror', *Music and Letters* 63 (July–Oct. 1982):
226–41. For a criticism of the latter, decidedly hostile, see Anthony Hicks, *Music
and Letters* 65 (April 1984): 213–16. See Dean (1959) esp. pp. 369, 395–97, 993–94.

16. Thomas Mann, 'On Schiller', in *Last Essays* (1956), trans. Richard and Clara Winston
(New York, 1958), p. 71. And see Mann, trans. Blunden (1985).

17. John C. Hodges, *The Library of William Congreve* (New York, 1955), p. 77.


CHAPTER 7. THE ENLIGHTENMENT

1. Denis Diderot and Jean le Rond d'Alembert, *Encyclopédie* (Lausanne and Berne,
1751–80), s.v. 'Foible'. See Heartz, 'Diderot' and esp. 'Enlightenment', in *Grove 6*;
Flaherty (1978); Le Huray and Day (1982); and Oliver (1947). Anna Amalie Abert,
'Die Oper zwischen Barock und Romantik' (*Acta musicologica* 49, no. 2 [July–Dec.
1977]: 137–93) is an invaluable survey of recent literature on the subject. For other
quotations in this paragraph, see Flaherty (1978). Kant's influential essay 'Zur
Beantwortung der Frage: Was ist Aufklarung?' appeared in the last issue in 1784 of
the *Berlinische Monatschrift*.

2. Algarotti (1755).

3. Goethe to J. P. Eckermann, in Richard Friedenthal, *Goethe: His Life and Times* (London, 1965), p. 493.

4. Gerald Croll and Winton Dean, 'Gluck', in *Grove 6*, is a good introduction, and has
an extensive bibliography. Petrobelli (1971) is insightful.

5. Quoted with relish by Eduard Hanslick, *Vom Musikalisch-Schönen* (1854), edited and
translated by G. Cohen (New York, 1957), p. 32.

6. See, for example, Donald Tovey's comments on the scene in his article on Gluck
in the *Encyclopedia Brittanica*, 11th ed.

7. The best summary discussion is Stanley Sadie's article on Mozart in *Grove 6*. For a
personal view, see R. B. Moberly's *Three Mozart Operas: Figaro, Don Giovanni, The
Magic Flute* (London, 1967) and 'Mozart and His Librettists', *Music and Letters* 54
(1973): 161ff.; and for another, F. Noske, *The Signifier and the Signified: Studies in the
Operas of Mozart and Verdi* (The Hague, 1977). And see H. C. Robbins Landon and
Donald Mitchell, eds., *The Mozart Companion*, rev. ed. (London, 1965).

8. Daniel Heartz, 'The Genesis of Mozart's *Idomeneo*', *Mozart-Jahrbuch* 1967: 150ff. (also
in the *Musical Quarterly* 55 [1969]: 1ff.), and his 'Mozart, His Father and "Idomeneo" ',
*Musical Times* 119 (1978): 228ff.

9. Mozart to his father, 26 Sept. 1781, in E. Anderson, ed., *Letters of Mozart and His
Family*, 2d ed., revised by A. Hyatt King and M. Carolan (London, 1966).

10. See S. Levarie, *Mozart's 'Le Nozze di Figaro': A Critical Analysis*, rev. ed. (Chicago, 1977); F. Noske, 'Social Tensions in "Le Nozze di Figaro" ', *Music and Letters* 50 (1969): 45ff. (also in Noske, *The Signifier and the Signified*); Eric Blom, 'The Literary Ancestry of Figaro', *Musical Quarterly* 13 (1927): 528ff.; and Carter (1988).

11. See Moberly, 'Mozart and His Librettists'.

12. See S. Kunze, *Don Giovanni vor Mozart . . . in italienischen Buffo-Theater des 18. Jahrhunderts* (Munich, 1972); and Nino Pirrotta (1980–81), a most excellent article on *Don Giovanni* and its precursors. See also Egon Wellesz, 'Don Giovanni and the Dramma Giocoso', *Music Review* 4 (1943): 121ff.; and Anne Livermore, 'The Origins of Don Juan', *Music and Letters* 44 (1963): 257ff. Alfons Rosenberg, *Don Giovanni: Mozarts Oper und Don Juans Gestalt* (Munich, 1968) is an original study of rare insight; and see Nino Pirrotta, 'The Traditions of Don Juan Plays and Comic Operas', *Proceedings of the Royal Musical Association* 107 (1980–81): 60–70. See also Rushton (1981), excellent both for context and for content, and Jonathan Miller, ed., *The Don Giovanni Book* (London, 1987).

CHAPTER 8. A MASONIC VISION

1. Stanley Sadie in 'Mozart', *Grove* 6, sums up well. Brophy (1964) cannot be wholly accepted, but should not be wholly dismissed. E. M. Batley, 'Textual Unity in *Die Zauberflöte*' (*Music Review* 27, no. 2 [May 1966]: 81–92) argues effectively against the quite unsupported and unnecessary hypothesis of a 'break in the libretto', and is altogether good on the popular tradition of magic plays with music; and see his full discussion in *A Preface to the Magic Flute* (London, 1969). Alfons Rosenberg, 'Die Symbolik von Mozarts Zauberflöte' (*Symbolon* 3 [1962]: 64–76) is highly suggestive, as is his uncommonly insightful *Zauberflöte: Geschichte und Deutung von Mozarts Oper* (Munich, 1964). On the crucial element of Masonic symbolism, a little overstated, see Jacques Chailley, *'La flûte enchantée': Opéra masonique* (Paris, 1968; Eng. trans. 1972). Landon (1983) is brief and to the point. P. Nettl, *Mozart and Masonry*, rev. ed. (New York, 1970) remains valuable. K. Thomson, 'Mozart and Freemasonry' (*Music and Letters* 57 [1976]: 25ff.) and *The Masonic Thread in Mozart* (London, 1977) are important. But for looking beyond Masonry itself to what its symbols may mean more generally, I recommend Jocelyn Godwin, 'Layers of Meaning in *The Magic Flute*' (*Musical Quarterly* 65, no. 4 [Oct. 1979]: 471–92) and D. Koenigsberger, 'A New Metaphor for Mozart's *Magic Flute*', in *European Studies Review* 5 (1975): 229–75. Also Eric Werner, 'Leading or Symbolic Formulas in the "Magic Flute": A Hermeneutic Examination', *Musical Review* 18 (1957): 286ff.

2. Pico della Mirandola, *Opera omnia* (Bologna, 1496; facs. ed., Turin, 1971–72), ed. Eugenio Garin, pp. 162 and 580.

3. Dent (1913), 2d ed. (London, 1947), p. 218.

4. Koenigsberger, 'A New Metaphor'.

5. Buelow's 'Rhetoric and Music' in *Grove* 6 is excellent on that doctrine of musical figures or affections to which such number symbolism in part relates.

6. MS notebook no. 21, cited by Humphry House in his valuable *Coleridge: The Clark Lectures, 1951–52* (London, 1969), p. 47.

CHAPTER 9. THE ROMANTIC MOVEMENT

1. Johann Adam Hiller, 'Abhandlung über die Nachahmung der Natur in der Musik', in F. W. Marpurg's *Historisch-kritische Beyträge*, vol. 1 (Berlin, 1754). For Hiller, Schlegel and Möser, see Flaherty (1978), who cites them and many others, and tells a very good story.

2. Christoph Martin Wieland, 'Versuch über das teutsche Singspiel' in *Der teutsche Mercur* for 1775 (nos. 3–4).

3. From 'Der Dichter und der Componist', in the collection of stories titled *Die Serapionsbrüder* (4 vols., 1819–21); extract in Strunk (1950), p. 788.

4. William Wordsworth, *The Prelude* (London, 1850), 6.602 and 6.639. J. H. Shorthouse, *On the Platonism of Wordsworth* (Birmingham, 1881) follows up this (to me) interesting aspect. See n. 5 below on Coleridge's Platonism.

5. *The Statesman's Manual* (1816), in W. G. T. Shedd, ed., *The Complete Works of Samuel Taylor Coleridge* (New York, 1884), 1: 437. Coleridge's Neoplatonic affinities are even clearer than Wordsworth's: see, for example, the references to the Hellenistic Neoplatonist Plotinus in A. E. Powell, *The Romantic Theory of Poetry* (London, 1926), pp. 90–91. Also C. Howard, *Coleridge's Idealism: A Study of Its Relationship to Kant and to the Cambridge Platonists* (Boston, 1924); J. D. Rea, 'Coleridge's Intimations of Immortality from Proclus', *Modern Philology* 26 (1928); A. D. Snyder, *The Critical Principle of the Reconciliation of Opposites as Employed by Coleridge* (Ann Arbor, Mich., 1918) and his 'Coleridge and Giordano Bruno', *Modern Language Review* 42 (1927).

6. See *Biographia Literaria* (London, 1817), chap. 9, where Coleridge tells us that he had been going through Plato and Plotinus with the aid of Ficino's commentaries and his *Theologia Platonica*. For Ficino, see Donington (1981), pp. 31 and 319, n. 19.

7. Richard Wagner, *The Art-work of the Future* (1849), trans. W. Ashton Ellis, in *Richard Wagner's Prose Works* (London, 1892), 1:9.

8. Ernest Hartley Coleridge, ed., *Anima Poetae: From the Unpublished Notebooks of Samuel Taylor Coleridge* (London, 1895), p. 115. See James Gillman, *The Life of Samuel Taylor Coleridge* (London, 1838), p. 311; also cited and discussed by Humphry House, *Coleridge* (London, 1969), p. 27.

9. See Coleridge, *Biographia Literaria*, vol. 2, p. 6.

10. Letter to W. Sotheby, 10 Sept. 1802; in Kathleen Raine, ed., *The Letters of Samuel Taylor Coleridge* (London, 1950), p. 116.

11. The great study here is John Livingstone Lowes, *The Road to Xanadu* (Boston and New York, 1927; rev. ed., London, 1931). No one has better traced the workings of that 'streamy Nature of Association' of which Coleridge himself wrote so discerningly (*Anima Poetae*, p. 55).

12. Joseph Kerman and Alan Tyson, 'Beethoven', in *Grove 6*.

13. Johann Mattheson, *Der vollkommene Capellmeister* (Hamburg, 1739), p. 219.

14. Carl Maria von Weber, *Sämtliche Schriften*, ed. G. Kaiser (Berlin and Leipzig, 1908), p. 129. Weber said the same thing more than once in almost the same words, originally when reviewing the *Undine* of E. T. A. Hoffmann; see the *Allgemeine musikalische Zeitung* 19 (1817): 201–08, translated in Strunk (1950), pp. 802–07. John Warrack, 'Weber', in *Grove 6*, is particularly valuable. See also Warrack (1968, 1977–78 and 1982); also S. Godrich, *Der deutsche romantische Oper* (Tutzing, 1975); and Ludwig Finscher, 'Weber's Freischütz: Conceptions and Misconceptions', *Proceedings of the Royal Musical Association* 101 (1983–84): 79–90.

15. In his grumbling *Freischützbuch* of 1843. Warrack (1968), chap. 11, is excellent on this and all other angles concerning the opera.

16. Warrack (1968), p. 211.

17. On opera in Paris, see Crosten (1948); Cooper (1951); Dennis Libby's contribution to the article 'Opera' in *Grove 6*; H. Becker, 'Die historische Bedeutung der Grand Opéra', in W. Salmen, ed., *Beiträge zur Geschichte der Musikanschauung im 19. Jahrhundert* (Regensburg, 1965); and Fulcher (1987).

18. There is an uncommonly informative and perceptive article on Spontini by Dennis Libby in *Grove 6*.

19. On Rossini, see Weinstock (1968) and Philip Gossett's important article 'Rossini' in *Grove 6*.

20. On Bellini, see Orrey (1969); Weinstock (1971); Friedrich Lippmann, *Vincenzo Bellini und die italienische Opera Seria seiner Zeit* (Cologne, 1969); and his article 'Bellini' in *Grove 6*.

21. On Meyerbeer, see Crosten (1948); Cooper (1955); C. Frese, *Dramaturgie der grossen Opern Giacomo Meyerbeers* (Berlin, 1970); Heinz Becker, 'Meyerbeer', in *Grove 6*; and Fulcher (1987).

CHAPTER 10. VERDI

1. Cited by Porter in 'Verdi', *Grove 6*. Frank Walker's *The Man Verdi* (London, 1962) remains after its fashion a classic. Budden (1973–81) is a monumental study; Kimbell (1981) is remarkable on the early operas, and particularly full and insightful on the middle period of *Rigoletto, Il trovatore* and *La traviata*. See also Osborne (1969). Porter's 'Verdi', in *Grove 6*, is a long and very interesting article. Noske, *The Signifier and the Signified*, is to be recommended for its highly original approach. It is also worth consulting Phyllis Hartnoll, ed., *Shakespeare in Music* (London, 1964), esp. for Winton Dean on the Boito-Verdi operas (pp. 89–175). See also W. Weaver and M. Chusid, eds., *The Verdi Companion* (New York, 1979).

2. On *Otello*, see Kerman (1956), pp. 129–67, and Winton Dean, 'Verdi's Otello: A Shakespearian Masterpiece', *Shakespeare Survey* 21 (1968): 87ff.

3. Interview on BBC 2, 9 May 1987.

4. James A. Hepokoski, ed., *Giuseppe Verdi: 'Falstaff'* (Cambridge, 1983) is now the most important discussion: predictably informative and illuminating for the most part,

as these Cambridge handbooks are; unpredictably and very excellently specu-
lative towards the end, which also includes a fascinating epilogue by Graham
Bradshaw with some agreeably way-out suggestions; though the particular Freudian possibilities there cited strike me as possibly (I do not say certainly) a little
far-fetched. A book to study, both for *Falstaff* and also for Bradshaw's further comments on *Otello*, with particular regard to Iago.

CHAPTER 11. EARLY WAGNER

1. The best starting place is *The New Grove Wagner* (London, 1984), which partly revises
   and partly replaces the composite article in *Grove 6*. John Deathridge prepared the
   new work-list in connection with his work and that of Martin Geck and Egon
   Voss for their comprehensive thematic catalogue of Wagner's musical works; he
   extended the list of Wagner's writings; and he and Carl Dahlhaus revised and
   updated the already good bibliography by Robert Bailey. The biography is now
   by Deathridge, and excellent; Dahlhaus returns with his important and original
   discussion of the aesthetics and the music. Robert Gutman (1968) is mainly very
   good, and more recently Martin Gregor-Dellin (1983) and esp. Barry Millington
   (1984). Dahlhaus (1971) has especial value for me. Jack Stein (1960, rev. ed. 1973)
   is still the best study across the disciplines. James Burnett, *Wagner and the Romantic
   Disaster* (New York and Tunbridge Wells, 1983) is a powerful book, although I take
   a different view. There is some good recent thinking in Peter Dennison, ed., 'The
   Richard Wagner Centenary in Australia' (*Miscellanea musicologica* 14 [1985]), esp. Sally
   Kester, 'The Archetypal Motives of Cosmogony and Apocalypse', pp. 99–116. We
   have at last a satisfactory edition of Wagner's autobiography by Mary Whittall,
   translated by Andrew Gray (Cambridge, 1983).
2. See 'Viviar' (V. V. Rosenfeld) on Wagner and the eternal feminine, in 'Images
   and Pictures', *Bayreuth Festival Programme* 1969. And see esp. John Deathridge, *An
   Introduction to 'The Flying Dutchman'* (London, 1982).
3. *Über die Aufführung des 'Tannhäuser'* (1852). With regard to *Tannhäuser* in this and other
   aspects, two articles by Reinhard Strohm are interesting: 'Dramatic Time and
   Operatic Form in Wagner's "Tannhäuser"', *Proceedings of the Royal Musical Association* 104 (1977–78); and 'On the History of the Opera "Tannhäuser"', *Festspielheft
   Tannhäuser* (Bayreuth, 1978).
4. Angelo Berardi, *Ragionamenti musicali* (Bologna, 1681), p. 136.
5. Sébastien de Brossard, *Dictionaire* (Paris, 1701–03), s.v. 'Recitativo'.
6. Wagner, in *Über die Benennung 'Musikdrama'* (1872), repudiated this term as mis-
   leading, but it has survived nevertheless for its obvious convenience. See Carl
   Dahlhaus, *Wagners Konzeption des musikalischen Dramas* (Regensburg, 1971).
7. Wagner, *Mitteilungen meiner Freunde* (1851).
8. Thomas Mann, 'On Schiller', in *Last Essays* (1956), trans. Richard and Clara Winston
   (New York, 1958). And see Mann, trans. Blunden (1985).

9. On the symbolical value of Elsa's brother, see Hans Grunsky, 'Totem und Tabu in Lohengrinmythos', in Wieland Wagner, ed., *Richard Wagner und das Neue Bayreuth* (Munich, 1962), pp. 94–103.

10. Richard Brinsley Sheridan, *Clio's Protest* (London, 1819).

11. Stein (1960), p. 7.

12. *Oper und Drama* (1851), part 2, chap. 3; letters to Liszt, 25 Nov. 1850, and to Röckel, 25 Jan. 1854, and 23 and 25 Aug. 1856; *Religion und Kunst* (1880).

13. Thomas Carlyle, *Sartor Resartus* (Boston, 1836; first published in *Fraser's Magazine* 1833–34). See the edition by P. C. Parr (Oxford, 1913), esp. p. 159. And see Fred Kaplan, *Thomas Carlyle: A Biography* (Cambridge, 1983).

14. Carl Dahlhaus, in 'Wagner', *Grove 6*, vol. 20, p. 118.

15. Arthur Schopenhauer, *Die Welt als Wille und Vorstellung*, book 3 (2d ed., 1844), in *Sämtliche Werke*, ed. Paul Denssen (Munich, 1911), pp. 301–03, 304, 307–12, excerpts from which will be found, very well translated, in Peter Le Huray and James Day (1982), pp. 323–30; see esp. pp. 325, 328–29. See Bryan Magee, *The Philosophy of Schopenhauer* (Oxford, 1983) for the link with Wagner.

16. Anthony Newcomb, 'The Birth of Music out of the Spirit of Drama', *19th-Century Music 5* (1981–82): 38; also his excellent contribution to the ENO/ROH Opera Guide no. 28, *Siegfried* (London, 1984).

17. Bembo (1525).


CHAPTER 12. WAGNER'S RING

1. Extensive discussions of the *Ring* come up in books mentioned in chap. 11, n. 1 above. *The New Grove Wagner* includes a separate section for the bibliographical material on the *Ring*, as it does on the other music-dramas. Bernard Shaw's one-sided *Perfect Wagnerite* (London, 1898) is, of course, marvellous reading. Donington (1963) still pleases me for a certain eager exuberance, though I have reassessed and condensed my way of putting things very substantially after all this time. Carl Dahlhaus, 'Formprinzipien in Wagners "Ring des Nibelungen" ', in A. Becker, ed., *Beiträge zur Geschichte der Oper* (Regensburg, 1969), brings Lorenz and Adorno into due proportion; see also Robert Bailey, 'The Structure of the *Ring* and Its Evolution', in *19th-Century Music 1* (1977–78): 48–61, and his detailed chapter 'Wagner's Musical Sketches for "Siegfrieds Tod" ', in H. Powers, ed., *Studies in Music History: Essays for Oliver Strunk* (Princeton, N.J., 1968). John Deathridge, 'Wagner's Sketches for the "Ring" ' (*Musical Times 118* [1977]: 383–89) is important. On the reforms embodied in the *Ring* and after, see Bailey, 'The Evolution of Wagner's Compositional Procedure after Lohengrin', *Eleventh International Musicological Society Congress Report* (Copenhagen, 1972); and Martin Gregor-Dellin, *Richard Wagner: Die Revolution als Oper* (Munich, 1973). On the mythological sources, Deryck Cooke's unfinished *I Saw the World End* (London, 1979) is full and excellent; on the broadly Jungian approach influential for a time at Bayreuth, see Wieland Wagner, ed., *Richard Wagner und das Neue Bayreuth* (Munich, 1962), particularly Iolande Jacobi, 'Archetypisches

im Ring des Nibelungen' (pp. 136–49). Michael Ewans, *Wagner and Aeschylus: The 'Ring' and the 'Oresteia'* (London, 1982) is a significant contribution, chiefly to be faulted for not making more of the reconciling ending to the *Eumenides*. Heinrich Porges, *Die Bühnenproben zu den Bayreuther Festspielen des Jahres 1876* (Leipzig, 1877), translated by Robert L. Jacobs as *Wagner Rehearsing the Ring: An Eye-Witness Account* (Cambridge, 1983), is quite fascinating, not only on production and gesture but on points of musical phrasing and expression in relation to production. See also E. Kloss and H. Weber, *Richard Wagner über den Ring des Nibelungen* (Leipzig, 1913).

2. Sally Kester, 'The Archetypal Motives of Cosmology and Apocalypse in *The Ring*', *Miscellanea musicologica* 14 (1985): 99–116.

3. *Oper und Drama* (1851), part 2, chap. 3. See chap. 11, n. 12 above.

4. See Deathridge, 'Wagner's Sketches for the "Ring" '.

5. *Das Kunstwerk der Zukunft* (Leipzig, 1849), translated by W. Ashton Ellis as *The Art-work of the Future*, in *Richard Wagner's Prose Works* (London, 1892), 1:70.

6. A weighty investigation from a psychological angle is Erich Neumann, *Ursprungsgeschichte des Bewusstseins* (Zurich, 1949), translated by R. F. C. Hull as *The Origins and History of Consciousness* (London, 1954).

7. Goethe, *Faust* 1.5.1336ff.

8. See Paul Radin, *The Trickster: A Study in American Indian Mythology*, with remarks by C. G. Jung (London, 1956), for a relevant comparison. Trickster gods are fairly familiar everywhere.

9. 'Musical Autobiography' (fragment only), in Hubert Foss, *Ralph Vaughan Williams* (London, 1950), p. 22. Quoted by kind permission of Ursula Vaughan Williams.

10. On Wagner's probable attachment to the mother-image, see Gregor-Dellin (1983), pp. 11ff.

11. Mann, trans. Blunden (1985), p. 97.

12. A marked emphasis on the subdominant is quite often what alerts us to the imminent close of any musical movement. So habitually do Wagner's heroines rise to their redeeming climaxes through plagal cadences that I wonder whether a sense of femininity may attach inherently to the subdominant regions, a sense of masculinity to the dominant regions. Elgar, whose attachment to the mother and whose projection of the mother onto his crucially supportive wife were noticed even by his friends, confessed to favouring 'a sort of plagal relationship . . . defensible on sub-dominant grounds' (see Moore [1984], esp. pp. 61 and 176). Transmuted mother-longing plays so secret a part in our psychological development; but notice well that *transmuted* is the operative word. The longing is distressful, the transmutation rewarding; and so it is that the fruits of genius may be rooted in suffering but ripen in creativeness. And that is something which ties up very closely with Wagner's own idea of redemption, here as elsewhere throughout his creative life.

CHAPTER 13. FURTHER WAGNER

1. Joseph Kerman (1956) has a chapter on Tristan, 'Opera as Symphonic Poem', of striking originality and interest. On the revolutionary aspects and effects of the harmony, especially, see E. Kurth, Romantische Harmonik und ihre Krise in Wagners 'Tristan' (Berlin, 1920); M. Vogel, Der Tristan-Akkord und der Krise der modernen Harmonie-Lehre (Düsseldorf, 1962). See also H. Truscott, 'Wagner's Tristan and the Twentieth Century', Music Review 24 (1963): 75ff.; Carl Dahlhaus, ' "Tristan"—Harmonik und Tonalität', Melos/Neue Zeitschrift für Musik 4 (1978): 215; R. Jackson, 'Leitmotive and Form in the Tristan Prelude', Music Review 36 (1975): 42ff.; Robert Bailey, 'The Genesis of Tristan and Isolde' (Ph.D. diss., Princeton Univ., 1969); and n. 8 to chap. 15 below.
2. Kerman (1956), chap. 7; Gutman (1968), pp. 9, 251ff. It should be noted that Gutman takes a more negative view of the ensuing 'love-death' than either Kerman or myself.
3. Gutman (1968), p. 9.
4. Magee (1983), esp. the appendix on Wagner. Mann, trans. Blunden (1985) is just as tortured as he is interesting here, and should not be overlooked.
5. Magee (1983), p. 363.
6. Ibid., p. 345.
7. See R. M. Raynor, Wagner and 'Die Meistersinger' (London, 1940); W. E. McDonald, 'Words, Music, and Dramatic Development in Die Meistersinger', 19th-Century Music 1 (1977–78): 246ff.

CHAPTER 14. THE LAST OF WAGNER

1. Lucy Beckett, ' "Parsifal" as Drama' (Music and Letters, July 1971: 259–71) is excellent within limits deliberately confined to the work itself; and see her important Richard Wagner: 'Parsifal' (1981), which examines both the legendary sources and the Christian ritual admirably. J. L. Weston, From Ritual to Romance (London, 1920) was very influential and is still valuable, although now old-fashioned in its Frazer-like interpretations. And see J. Chailley, 'Parsifal' de Richard Wagner: Opéra initiatique (Paris, 1979) for its unusual and interesting approach. Thomas Mann is as fascinatingly idiosyncratic as he always is on Wagner; see Mann, trans. Blunden (1985).
2. Mann, trans. Blunden (1985), pp. 98–99.
3. Dahlhaus (1971), trans. Whittall, p. 147.

CHAPTER 15. REALISM

1. Winton Dean's article 'Bizet' in Grove 6 makes an excellent introduction. His standard Bizet (London, 1948) was revised for its second edition as Georges Bizet: His Life and Work (1965), and again for its third edition (1976). See his good invective in

'The Corruption of Carmen: The Perils of Pseudo-musicology', *Musical Newsletter* 3 (7 Oct. 1973); or, more readily accessible, 'The True Carmen?', *Musical Times* 106 (1965): 846ff. See also Martin Cooper (1938) and his shorter 'Georges Bizet', in *The Heritage of Music* vol. 3 (London, 1951), pp. 108ff. Mina Curtiss, *Bizet and His World* (New York, 1958) broke new ground and is still of great interest. For source material, see esp. E. Galabert, *Georges Bizet: Souvenirs et correspondence* (Paris, 1877); Bizet, *Lettres; Impressions de Rome, 1857–60; La Commune, 1871*, ed. Louis Ganderax (Paris, 1908); and *Lettres à un ami* [Edmund Galabert], ed. Edmund Galabert (Paris, 1909). Ann Livermore, 'The Birth of Carmen', *Music Review* 27, no. 3 (Aug. 1966) is good on Mérimée's sources.

2. Bizet, article in the *Revue nationale et etrangère*, 3 Aug. 1867.

3. Cited by Curtiss, *Bizet and His World*, p. 315.

4. Edmund Galabert, 'La maladie et la mort de Bizet', *Le passant*, Feb. 1888.

5. See Charles Pigot, *Georges Bizet et son oeuvre* (1886), 2d ed. (Paris, 1911), p. 248; and Henry Blaze de Bury, *Musiciens du passé, du présent et de l'avenir* (Paris, 1880), pp. 326–27.

6. Ernest Rayer, *Quarante ans de musique* (Paris, 1910), pp. 308–09.

7. See esp. Richard Taruskin, *Opera and Drama in Russia as Preached and Practised in the 1860s* (Ealing, 1982). David Brown's article on Tchaikovsky in *Grove 6* is long and excellent; it includes a fine bibliography. His monumental *Tchaikovsky: A Biographical and Critical Study* (London, 1978–) is still in progress. K. E. Mühlendahl completed a dissertation for the Univ. of Munich (1964) with the remarkable title 'Die Psychose Tschaikowskis und der Einfluss seiner Musik auf gleichartige Psychotiker'. And see esp. John Warrack, *Tchaikovsky* (London, 1973).

8. Nietzsche, *The Birth of Tragedy from the Spirit of Music* (1872), trans. W. A. Haussmann (New York, 1924), in discussing *Tristan*. The passage continues: 'I ask the question of those genuine musicians: whether they can imagine a man capable of hearing the third act of *Tristan and Isolde* without any aid of word or scenery, purely as a vast symphonic period, without expiring . . . without flying irresistibly towards his primitive home', if there did not 'interpose between our highest musical excitement and the music in question the tragic myth and the tragic hero'.

9. Dahlhaus (1982), trans. Whittall, p. 10.

10. There is a first-rate article on Puccini in *Grove 6* by that critic of rare insight, Mosco Carner. And see his *Puccini: A Critical Biography* (1958), 2d ed. (London, 1974); and Carner (1985)—but here he uncharacteristically blurs the distinction between inner and outer realism. See also Winton Dean, 'Giacomo Puccini', in *The Heritage of Music*, ed. Hubert Foss (London, 1951), 3:153ff. Kerman (1956) disparages *Tosca*, though he softened his attitude toward Puccini in the revised edition (1988).

11. Carner, 'Puccini', in *Grove 6*, vol. 15, p. 437.

12. *Sunday Times*, 21 Sept. 1986.

13. A particularly interesting and unusual study of Debussy is Edward Lockspeiser's *Debussy: His Life and Mind* (London, 1962–65), which looks quite some way into Debussy's inner workings; see also Lockspeiser's very suggestive 'Debussy's Concept of the Dream', *Proceedings of the Royal Musical Association* 89 (1962–63): 49ff. Joseph Ker-

man (1956) has an excellent chapter on *Pelléas et Mélisande*. See also Roger Nichols's *Debussy* (London, 1973) and his article in *Grove 6*.

14. See Roger Nichols in *Grove 6*, vol. 5, p. 307.
15. Debussy, letter to the secretary general of the Opéra-Comique, 1894.
16. Cited in the *Encyclopedia Britannica*, 14th ed., 21:701, s.v. 'Symbolists'.
17. Cited in *Grove 6*, vol. 5, p. 309.

CHAPTER 16. STRAUSS

1. Norman Del Mar, *Richard Strauss: A Critical Commentary on His Life and Works* (London, 1962–72; repr. with corrections, 1978) is long, thorough and admirable; William Mann, in his insightful *Richard Strauss: A Critical Study of the Operas* (London, 1964), has great and complementary value; Michael Kennedy, *Richard Strauss* (London, 1976) is short and good. Willi Schuh, *Über Opern von Richard Strauss* (Zurich, 1947) is a foundation-piece; see also his edition of collected essays by the composer, *Richard Strauss: Betrachtungen und Erinnerungen* (Zurich, 1949; 2d ed., 1957), translated by L. J. Lawrence as *Recollections and Reflections* (London, 1953). There is a valuable article in *Grove 6* by Kennedy, with work-list and bibliography by Robert Bailey, who includes full references to the invaluable correspondence between Strauss and his librettists. The relationship between Strauss and Hofmannsthal is interestingly discussed by the Viennese composer and musicologist Egon Wellesz, who himself worked with Hofmannsthal, in *Music and Letters* 33 (1952): 239ff. And see Abert (1972) and esp. Jefferson (1986).
2. Strauss, *Recollections and Reflections*, p. 160.
3. Mann (1964), p. 119.
4. Strauss, *Recollections and Reflections*, p. 160.
5. Buelow and Daviau (1975) combine in a book of rare insight and broad-ranging interest, *The 'Ariadne auf Naxos' of Hugo von Hofmannsthal and Richard Strauss* (Chapel Hill, N.C., 1975). Critical of this, and less sympathetic to me, is Karen Forsythe, *Ariadne auf Naxos . . . Its Genesis and Its Meaning* (New York, 1982).
6. See the quotations and excellent discussion in Mann (1964), esp. pp. 164ff.
7. A particularly perceptive and sympathetic examination of this highly problematic opera will be found in Mann (1964), whose view of it is almost entirely positive and favourable. It is interesting to compare Norman Del Mar's much more critical though still appreciative study in his vol. 3 (1972), pp. 151–218. I am bound to say that this criticism, blaming Hofmannsthal's obduracy for Strauss's unequalness, seems to me a reasonable estimate. The element of greatness is not in doubt.

For the resemblances (deliberate on the author's part) between this intentionally mystical libretto and *The Magic Flute*, see Gloria Ascher, *Die Zauberflöte und die Frau ohne Schatten: Ein Vergleich zwischen zwei Operndichtungen der Humanität* (Berne, 1972).
8. Quoted by Lynn Snook in an insightful article, 'The Myth and the "Shadow" ', *Opera* 1967: 454–59.
9. See the quotations and discussion in Norman Del Mar, vol. 3 (1972), pp. 154ff. and 214ff.

10. See quotation and discussion in Mann (1964), pp. 356ff.

11. The Prologue is in Egon Wellesz, 'Cavalli und der Stil der Venezianischen Oper von 1640–1660', in *Studien zur Musikwissenschaft* 1 (1913).

12. See Edward Elmgren Swenson, 'Prima la musica e poi le parole: An Eighteenth-Century Satire', *Analecta musicologica* 9 (1970): 112–29. For a brief but informative discussion, see also Lionel Salter, 'Footnotes to a Satire', *Musical Times* 126 (1985): 21–24.

13. Strauss, *Recollections and Reflections*, p. 156.

14. See quotation in Del Mar, vol. 3 (1972), p. 245, and his full discussion in his chap. 21.

CHAPTER 17. THE TWENTIETH CENTURY

1. Igor Stravinsky, *Poétique musicale* (Cambridge, Mass., 1942); translated as *The Poetics of Music* (1947), Lecture 3. The excellent Stravinsky bibliography by Eric Walter White in *Grove 6* gives full references for the important series of talks and recollections conducted over several years with Robert Craft. White (1966; rev. ed., 1979) should also be consulted. See esp. Griffiths (1983) and Richard Middleton, 'Stravinsky's Development: A Jungian Approach', *Music and Letters* 54, no. 3 (July 1973): 289ff., which takes a more positive view than might otherwise appear probable, and makes a good though not perhaps quite conclusive case for it.

2. A very sympathetic introduction to Schoenberg will be found in O. W. Neighbour's article in *Grove 6*. H. H. Stuckenschmidt's important *Arnold Schoenberg* (Zurich, 1951; rev. ed., 1957) is available in an English translation (1959); and see his *Schoenberg: Leben, Umwelt, Werk* (Zurich, 1974). Of especial interest is Dika Newlin, *Schoenberg Remembered: Diaries and Recollections* (1938–76) (New York, 1980).

3. George Perle gives a good survey in his article for *Grove 6*; see also his bibliography there, and his valuable article 'Representation and Symbol in the Music of *Wozzeck*', *Music Review* 32 (1971): 281ff. See Douglas Jarman, *The Music of Alban Berg* (London, 1979); and esp. Mosco Carner, *Alban Berg* (London, 1975), a sympathetic study of Berg's neurotic personality and its links with his creative achievement.

4. My information and citations are from Carner's outstandingly insightful *Alban Berg*. George Perle (in *Grove 6*) and Douglas Jarman, *The Music of Alban Berg* are the twin authorities on Berg's serial techniques. Berg's own lecture on *Wozzeck* (1929) appears in translation in Hans Redlich, *Alban Berg: The Man and His Music* (London, 1957).

5. Quoted and discussed in Perle, 'Berg', *Grove 6*, vol. 2, p. 534.

6. Ibid., p. 529.

7. Peter Evans's article and bibliography on Britten in *Grove 6* are valuable. Main studies include Imogen Holst, *Britten* (London, 1966; rev. 1970); Patricia Howard, *The Operas of Benjamin Britten* (London, 1969); Eric Walter White (1970); Peter Evans, *The Music of Benjamin Britten* (London, 1979); D. Herbert, ed., *The Operas of Benjamin Britten* (London, 1979); Michael Kennedy (1981); and Arnold Whittall (1982). A

grass-roots paper is Arnold Whittall, 'The Study of Britten': Triadic Harmony and Tonal Structure', *Proceedings of the Royal Musical Association* 106 (1979–80): 27–41. See also Christopher Palmer, ed., *The Britten Companion* (London, 1984), not least for Palmer's own excellent contributions to this valuable book; and there are further contributions important for the operas by Philip Brett, John Evans, Christopher Headington, Imogen Holst, Wilfred Mellers, Donald Mitchell, Erwin Stein and, briefly, Britten himself. Donald Mitchell and J. Evans, eds., *Benjamin Britten, 1913–1976: Pictures from a Life* (London, 1978) is interesting both for its illustrations and for its information about the composer's personal life.

The best introduction to *Peter Grimes*, from which my references here are drawn, is Philip Brett (1983), especially valuable for the essays by Brett and Hans Keller. Erwin Stein, with his Viennese background, is interesting in 'Opera and "Peter Grimes"', *Tempo*, 1st ser., 12 (Sept. 1945): 2–6.

8. Palmer, *The Britten Companion*, p. 149.

9. Ibid., pp. 118–19.

10. Brett (1983), p. 190.

11. See Peter Evans, 'Britten's "Death in Venice"', *Opera* 24 (1973): 490.

12. Tippett as a man of ideas can be approached through his own *Moving into Aquarius* (London, 1958; 2d ed., 1974), a richly inconclusive but visionary medley of metaphysical, psychological and aesthetic explorations; and more recently, *Music of the Angels*, ed. Meirion Bowen (London, 1980). See the bibliography in Kemp (1984), now the major study and a highly sympathetic investigation from all angles, including the psychological. David Matthews, *Michael Tippett: An Introductory Study* (London, 1979) is brief but perceptive. And see Eric Walter White, *Tippett and His Operas* (London, 1979); Geraint Lewis, ed., *Michael Tippett: A Celebration* (Tunbridge Wells, 1985); John Warrack on 'The Knot Garden', *Musical Times* 111 (1970): 1092, and on 'The Ice Break', *Musical Times* 118 (1977): 553. See esp. Arnold Whittall (1974), which goes deep in. For this account I have thoroughly reconsidered my chapter on *The Midsummer Marriage* in Ian Kemp, ed., *Michael Tippett: A Symposium* (London, 1965).

13. See Kemp (1984), p. 231, and William Mann in Kemp, *Michael Tippett: A Symposium*, p. 116.

14. Kemp (1984), p. 218.

15. Kemp, *Michael Tippett: A Symposium*, p. 35. Peter Heyworth is brief but striking, taking Sosostris as he does for the voice of Tippett himself: 'Her account of the horrors of prophecy is his account of the torments of creation'.

16. Kemp (1984), p. 217.

17. Ibid., pp. 211 and 217.

18. Ibid., p. 61.

19. Interview with Nicholas Kenyon in the *Sunday Times*, 1 April 1984. In October 1989 Tippett's *New Year*, another opera indebted to Jungian symbolism, received its première in Houston [ed.].

# REFERENCES

This list is not a bibliography, but merely provides the references for books and articles mentioned in my text and endnotes, together with a few others which I have included for one reason or another, but without implying disparagement of anything left out. Most works of substance, including my own *Rise of Opera*, offer specialized bibliographies. The obvious first recourse is *The New Grove Dictionary of Music and Musicians* (herein cited as *Grove 6*), together with the extracts from it, often significantly revised, appearing separately in book form. 'Opera' and other related articles in *Grove 6* are of a high standard of excellence generally. For authors' names and references given in my endnotes but not in this reference list, see the index.

Two series of studies of individual operas can also be warmly recommended. The *Cambridge Opera Handbooks*, published by Cambridge University Press, are necessary reading for serious followers of opera, maintaining as they do high standards of scholarship and readability. Of special interest to me here are Beckett (1981), Rushton (1981), Brett (1982), Hepokoski (1983), Carner (1985), Jefferson (1986), Whenham (1986) and Carter (1988). The series of *Opera Guides* published jointly by the English National Opera and the Royal Opera, Covent Garden, under the general editorship of Nicholas John, are serious, short introductions for the intelligent operagoer. The volumes all include some musical breakdown with notated examples, as well as texts with translations, it being rightly suggested that some prior homework on the words can be particularly helpful. Some of the translations are a little too free for my liking, and I do not agree with all that is said in the essays, but all the more on that account do I recommend the series.

Abert, Anna Amelie. *Claudio Monteverdi und das musikalische Drama*. Lippstadt, 1954.
———. *Die Opern Mozarts*. Wolfenbüttel, 1970. English version in *The New Oxford History of Music*, vol. 7.
———. *Richard Strauss: Die Opern: Einführung und Analyse*. Hanover, 1972.
Algarotti, Francesco. *Saggio sopra l'opera in musica*. N.p., 1755. Translated anonymously as *An Essay on Opera*. London, 1767.
Anthony, James R. *French Baroque Music from Beaujoyeulx to Rameau*. London, 1973. Rev. ed., 1978. Translated, with expanded bibliographical information, as *La musique en France à l'époque baroque*. Paris, 1981.
Appia, Adolphe. *Album de réproductions*. Zurich, 1929.
———. *Mise en scène de drame Wagnérien*. Paris, 1895. Translated by Peter Loeffler as *Staging Wagnerian Drama*. Basel, 1982.
Arnold, Denis. *Monteverdi*. London, 1963.

Arnold, Denis, and Nigel Fortune, eds. *The Beethoven Companion*. London, 1971.

———. *The Monteverdi Companion*. London, 1968.

———. *The New Monteverdi Companion*. London, 1985.

Ashbrook, William. *The Operas of Puccini*. New York, 1968.

Austin, William W., ed. *New Looks at Italian Opera: Essays in Honor of Donald Grout*. Ithaca, N.Y., 1968.

Beckett, Lucy, ed. *Richard Wagner: 'Parsifal'*. Cambridge, 1981.

Bembo, Pietro. *Prose della volgar lingua*. Venice, 1525.

Bent, Ian D. 'Analysis'. In *Grove 6*.

Biacomi, Lorenzo, and Giogio Pestelli, eds. *Storia dell'opera italiana*. Vol. 5. *La spettacolarità*. Turin, 1980.

Bjurström, P. *Giacomo Torelli and Baroque Stage Design*. Stockholm, 1961. Rev. ed., 1962.

Boccaccio, Giovanni. *Genealogia deorum gentilium*. Venice, 1472.

Brett, Philip, ed. *Benjamin Britten: 'Peter Grimes'*. Cambridge, 1983.

Brophy, Brigid. *Mozart the Dramatist: A New View*. London, 1964.

Brown, David. *Tchaikovsky: A Biographical and Critical Study*. London, 1978–.

Brown, Howard Mayer, 'How Opera Began: An Introduction to Jacopo Peri's Euridice (1600)'. In Erich Cochrane, ed. *The Late Italian Renaissance, 1515–1630*. London, 1970.

———. *Music in the Renaissance*. Englewood Cliffs, N.J., 1976.

Brown, Howard Mayer, ed. *Jacopo Peri's Euridice*. Madison, Wis., 1981.

Budden, Julian. *The Operas of Verdi*. 3 vols. London, 1973–81.

Buelow, George J. 'Opera in Hamburg 300 Years Ago'. *Musical Times* 119 (1978): 26ff.

———. 'Mattheson'. In *Grove 6*.

———. 'Rhetoric and Music'. In *Grove 6*.

Buelow, George J., and Donald G. Daviau. *The 'Ariadne auf Naxos' of Hugo von Hofmannsthal and Richard Strauss*. Chapel Hill, N.C., 1975.

Bujic, Bojan. 'Music and Intellectual History: A Backward Glance to the Year 1885'. *Proceedings of the Royal Musical Association* 111 (1986): 139–54.

Burbidge, P., and R. Sutton, eds. *The Wagner Companion*. London, 1979.

Burrows, David. 'Instrumentalities'. *Journal of Musicology*, Winter 1987: 117–25.

Busch, Hans, ed. and trans. *Verdi's 'Otello' and 'Simon Boccanegra' in Letters and Documents*. Oxford, 1988.

Caccini, Giulio. Preface to *Le nuove musiche*. Florence, 1602. Edited and translated by H. Wiley Hitchcock. Madison, Wis., 1970.

Carnegy, Patrick. 'The Composer as Librettist' [conversations with Michael Tippett]. *Times Literary Supplement*, 8 July 1977: 834.

Carner, Mosco. *Puccini: A Critical Biography*. London, 1958. Rev. ed., 1975.

Carner, Mosco, ed. *Giacomo Puccini: 'Tosca'*. Cambridge, 1985.

Cartari, Vincenzo. *Le imagini, con la spositione de i dei de gli antichi*. Venice, 1556.

Carter, Tim. 'Jacopo Peri's Euridice (1600): A Contextual Study'. *Music Review* 43, no. 2 (May 1982): 83–103.

———. 'A Florentine Wedding of 1608'. *Acta musicologica* 55 (Jan.–June 1983): 89–107.

Carter, Tim, ed. *W. A. Mozart: 'Le Nozze di Figaro'*. Cambridge, 1988.

Christout, Marie-Françoise. *Le ballet de cour de Louis XIV*. Paris, 1967.

Clifton, Thomas. *Music as Heard: A Study in Applied Phenomenology*. New Haven and London, 1983.

Conrad, Peter. *Romantic Opera and Literary Form*. Berkeley, Calif., 1978.

———. *A Song of Love and Death: The Meaning of Opera*. London, 1987.

Conti, Natale. *Mythologiae, sive explicationis fabularum libri decem* (1567). Venice, 1581.

Cooke, Deryck. *The Language of Music*. London, 1959.

Cooper, Martin. *Bizet*. London, 1938.

———. *French Music . . . Berlioz to . . . Fauré*. London, 1951.

———. *Gluck*. London, 1935.

———. 'Giacomo Meyerbeer'. In *Fanfare for Ernest Newman*. London, 1955.

———. 'Opera in France'. In *The New Oxford History of Music*, 7:200–256.

———. *Opéra comique*. London, 1949.

———. *Russian Opera*. London, 1951.

———. 'Stage Works: 1890–1918'. In *The New Oxford History of Music*, 10:145–207.

Crosten, William Loran. *French Grand Opera: An Art and a Business*. New York, 1948.

Curtiss, Mina. *Bizet and His World*. New York, 1958.

Dahlhaus, Carl. *Musikästhetic*. Cologne, 1967. Translated by William Austin as *Esthetics of Music*. Cambridge, 1982.

———. *Musikalische Realismus: Zur Musikgeschichte des 19. Jahrhunderts*. Munich, 1982. Translated by Mary Whittall as *Realism in Nineteenth-Century Music*. Cambridge, 1985.

———. *Richard Wagners Musikdramen*. Velber, 1971. Translated by Mary Whittall as *Richard Wagner's Music Dramas*. Cambridge, 1979.

Dean, Winton. 'Beethoven and Opera'. In Denis Arnold and Nigel Fortune, eds. *The Beethoven Companion*. London, 1971.

———. *Bizet*. London, 1948. 3d ed., 1976.

———. 'French Opera', 'Italian Opera', and 'German Opera'. In *The New Oxford History of Music*, vol. 8.

———. *Handel and the Opera Seria*. Berkeley and Los Angeles, 1969.

———. *Handel's Dramatic Oratorios and Masques*. London, 1959.

Dean, Winton, and John Merrill Knapp. *Handel's Operas, 1704–1726*. Oxford, 1987.

Del Mar, Norman. *Richard Strauss: A Critical Commentary on His Life and Works*. London, 1962–72. Rev. ed., 1978.

Dennison, Peter, ed. 'The Richard Wagner Centenary in Australia'. *Miscellanea musicologica* 14 (1985).

Dent, Edward J. *Alessandro Scarlatti*. London, 1905. New edition, with corrections and additions by Frank Walker. London, 1960.

———. *Foundations of English Opera*. Cambridge, 1928. Rev. ed., 1965.

———. 'Libretto'. In *Grove 5*.

———. *Mozart's Operas: A Critical Study*. London, 1913. Rev. eds., 1947 and 1955.

Deutsch, O. E. *Mozart: Die Dokumente seines Lebens*. Kassel, 1961. Translated by Eric Blom, Peter Branscombe and Jeremy Noble as *Mozart: A Documentary Biography*. Stanford, Calif., 1965; supplement, 1978.

Donington, Robert. *The Opera*. New York, 1978.

———. *The Rise of Opera*. London, 1981.

————. *Wagner's 'Ring' and Its Symbols*. London, 1963. Rev. ed., 1974.

Drummond, John D. *Opera in Perspective*. London, 1980.

Dryden, John. Preface to *Albion and Albanus*. London, 1685.

Ewans, Michael. *Wagner and Aeschylus: 'The Ring' and the 'Oresteia'*. London, 1982.

Fenlon, Iain. 'Monteverdi's Mantuan Orfeo'. *Early Music*, May 1984: 163–72.

————. 'The Mantuan Stage Works'. In Denis Arnold and Nigel Fortune, eds. *The New Monteverdi Companion*. London, 1985.

Ficino, Marsilio. *Opera omnia*. Basel, 1561. Facsimile, from Basel edition of 1576, edited by Paul O. Kristeller. New York, 1959.

Flaherty, Gloria. *Opera in the Development of German Critical Thought*. Princeton, N.J., 1978.

Freeman, Robert. *Opera without Drama*. Ann Arbor, Mich., 1981.

Fulcher, Jane F. *The Nation's Image: French Grand Opera as Politics and Politicized Art*. Cambridge, 1987.

Galilei, Vincenzo, *Dialogo . . . della musica antica, et della moderna*. Florence, 1581. Partial English translation in Strunk (1950), pp. 302ff.

Giraldi, Lilio Gregorio. *De deis gentium varia et multiplex historia*. Basel, 1548.

Girdlestone, Cuthbert. *Jean-Philippe Rameau*. London, 1957. Rev. ed., 1969.

————. *La tragédie en musique (1673–1750) considerée comme genre littéraire*. Geneva, 1972.

Glover, Jane. *Cavalli*. London, 1978.

Gombrich, Ernst Hans. 'Botticelli's Mythologies: A Study in the Neoplatonic Symbolism of His Circle'. *Journal of the Warburg and Courtauld Institutes* 8 (1945): 7–60.

————. *Symbolic Images: Studies in the Art of the Renaissance*. London, 1972.

Goslich, Siegfried. *Die deutsche romantische Oper*. Tutzing, 1975.

Gregor-Dellin, Martin. *Richard Wagner*. Munich, 1980. Translated by J. Maxwell Brownjohn as *Richard Wagner: His Life, His Work, His Century*. San Diego, 1983.

Griffiths, Paul. *Igor Stravinsky: 'The Rake's Progress'*. Cambridge, 1983.

————. *Modern Music: The Avant Garde since 1945*. London, 1981.

Groos, Arthur, and Roger Parker, eds. *Reading Opera*. Princeton, N.J., 1988.

Grout, Donald Jay. *Alessandro Scarlatti: An Introduction to His Operas*. Berkeley, Calif., 1979.

————. *A Short History of Opera*. New York, 1947. 3d ed., 1988.

Gutman, Robert. *Richard Wagner: The Man, His Mind and His Music*. London, 1968.

Hanning, Barbara Russano. *Of Poetry and Music Power*. Ann Arbor, Mich., 1980.

————. Review of Donington, *The Rise of Opera*. In *Journal of the American Musicological Society* 36, no. 2 (Summer 1983): 316–22.

Hanslick, Eduard. *Vom Musikalisch-Schönen*. Leipzig, 1854. Translated by Geoffrey Payzant as *On the Musically Beautiful*. Indianapolis, 1986.

Harran, Don. *Word-Tone Relations in Musical Thought: From Antiquity to the Seventeenth Century*. Stuttgart, 1985.

Hartmann, Rudolph. *Richard Strauss: The Staging of His Operas and Ballets*. Trans. Graham Davies. New York, 1981.

Heartz, Daniel. 'The Creation of the Buffo Finale in Italian Opera'. *Proceedings of the Royal Musical Association* 104 (1977–78): 67–68.

————. 'Algarotti'. In Grove 6.

————. 'Diderot'. In Grove 6.

———. 'Enlightenment'. In *Grove 6*.

———. 'Goldoni, Don Giovanni and the Dramma Giocoso'. *Musical Times* 102 (1979): 993ff.

Hepokoski, James A., ed. *Giuseppe Verdi: 'Falstaff'*. Cambridge, 1983.

Hilleström, Gustav. *The Drottningholm Theatre: Past and Present*. Trans. P. L. Lorraine. Stockholm, 1956.

Howard, Patricia. *Gluck and the Birth of Modern Opera*. London, 1963.

———. *C. W. von Gluck: 'Orfeo'*. Cambridge, 1981.

Isherwood, Robert M. *Music in the Service of the King: France in the Seventeenth Century*. Ithaca, N.Y., 1973.

Jefferson, Alan, ed. *Richard Strauss: 'Der Rosenkavalier'*. Cambridge, 1986.

Kemp, Ian. *Tippett: The Composer and His Music*. London, 1984.

Kennedy, Michael. *Britten*. London, 1981.

———. *Richard Strauss*. London, 1976.

Kerman, Joseph. *Contemplating Music*. Cambridge, Mass., 1985. Published in England as *Musicology*.

———. *Opera as Drama*. New York, 1956. Rev. ed., 1988.

Kester, Sally. 'The Archetypal Motives of Cosmology and Apocalypse in *The Ring*'. *Miscellanea musicologica* (1985): 99–116.

Kimbell, David R. B. *Verdi in the Age of Italian Romanticism*. Cambridge, 1981.

Knapp, J. Merrill. 'Handel's Giulio Cesare in Egitto'. In Harold Powers, comp. *Studies in Music History: Essays for Oliver Strunk*. Princeton, N.J., 1968.

Koenigsberger, D. 'A New Metaphor for Mozart's *Magic Flute*'. *European Studies Review* (1975): 229–75.

Krause, Ernst. *Richard Strauss: Gestalt und Werk*. Leipzig, 1955. 5th ed., 1975. Translated by John Coombs as *Richard Strauss: The Man and His Work*. London, 1964.

Kurth, Ernst. *Romantische Harmonik und ihre Krise in Wagners Tristan*. Bern, 1920.

Landon, H. C. Robbins. *Mozart and the Masons*. London, 1983.

———. 'The Operas of Haydn'. In *The New Oxford History of Music*, 7: 172–99.

Landon, H. C. Robbins, and Donald Mitchell, eds. *The Mozart Companion*. London, 1956. 2d ed., 1965.

Langer, Susanne. *Philosophy in a New Key*. Cambridge, Mass., 1942.

Le Huray, Peter, and James Day, eds. *Music and Aesthetics in the Eighteenth and Early Nineteenth Centuries*. Cambridge, 1982.

Lesure, François. *L'opéra classique français*. Geneva, 1972.

Lewis, Geraint, ed. *Michael Tippett OM: A Celebration*. Tunbridge Wells, 1985.

Lippmann, Friedrich. *Vincenzo Bellini und die italienische Opera seria seinen Zeit*. Cologne, 1969.

Lockspeiser, Edward. *Debussy: His Life and Mind*. London, 1962–65.

———. 'Debussy's Concept of the Dream'. *Proceedings of the Royal Musical Association* 89 (1962–63): 49.

MacClintock, Carol and Lander, eds. *Le balet comique de la Royne*. Rome, 1971.

McGowan, Margaret M. *L'art du ballet de cour en France, 1581–1643*. Paris, 1963.

Magee, Bryan. *Aspects of Wagner*. London, 1968. Rev. ed., 1972.

———. The Philosophy of Schopenhauer. Oxford, 1983.

Mann, Thomas. Thomas Mann pro and contra Wagner. Trans. Allan Blunden. London, 1985.

Mann, William. The Operas of Mozart. London, 1977.

———. Richard Strauss: A Critical Study of the Operas. London, 1964.

Mellers, Wilfrid. Caliban Reborn: Renewal in Twentieth-Century Music. New York, 1967.

———. 'Lully'. In Hubert Foss, ed. The Heritage of Music, vol. 3. London, 1951.

Meyer, Leonard B. Emotion and Meaning in Music. Chicago, 1956.

———. Music, the Arts and Ideas. Chicago, 1967.

Miller, Jonathan, ed. The Don Giovanni Book. London, 1987.

Millington, Barry. Wagner. London, 1984.

Millington, Barry, and Stewart Spencer, ed. and trans. Selected Letters of Richard Wagner. London, 1987.

Moore, Jerrold Northrop. Edward Elgar: A Creative Life. Oxford, 1984.

Newcomb, Anthony. 'The Birth of Music out of the Spirit of Drama'. 19th-Century Music 5 (1981–82): 38–66.

Newman, Ernest. The Life of Richard Wagner. 4 vols. London, 1933–47.

Noble, Jeremy. 'Debussy and Stravinsky'. Musical Times 108 (1967): 22–25.

Noske, F. The Signifier and the Signified: Studies in the Operas of Mozart and Verdi. The Hague, 1977.

Oliver, Alfred R. The Encyclopedists as Critics of Music. New York, 1947.

Orrey, Leslie. Bellini. London, 1969.

———. A Concise History of Opera. London, 1972.

Osborne, Charles. The Complete Operas of Mozart. London, 1978.

———. The Complete Operas of Puccini. London, 1981.

———. The Complete Operas of Verdi. London, 1969.

Palisca, Claude. Baroque Music. Englewood Cliffs, N.J., 1968.

———. 'The "Camerata Fiorentina": A Reappraisal'. Studi musicali 1, no. 2 (1972): 203–34.

———. The Florentine Camerata: Documentary Studies and Translations. New Haven, 1989.

———. 'Girolamo Mei: Mentor to the Florentine Camerata'. Musical Quarterly 40 (1954): 1–20.

———. Humanism in Italian Renaissance Musical Thought. New Haven, 1986.

Palisca, Claude, ed. Girolamo Mei. Letters on Ancient and Modern Music. Rome, 1960. 2d ed., 1977.

Palmer, Christopher, ed. The Britten Companion. London, 1984.

Panofsky, Erwin. Studies in Iconology: Humanist Themes in the Art of the Renaissance. London and New York, 1939.

Pendle, Karin. Eugène Scribe and French Opera of the Nineteenth Century. Epping, 1979.

Petrobelli, Pierluigi. 'L'Alceste di Calzabigi e Gluck: L'illuminismo e l'opera'. Quadrivium 22 (1971): 279.

Pirrotta, Nino. Li due Orfei, da Poliziano a Monteverdi. Turin, 1969. 2d ed., 1975. Translated by Karen Eales as Music and the Theatre from Poliziano to Monteverdi. New York, 1982.

———. 'Temperaments and Tendencies in the Florentine Camerata'. Trans. Nigel Fortune. *Musical Quarterly* 40, no. 2 (April 1954): 169–89.

———. 'The Traditions of Don Juan Plays and Comic Operas'. *Proceedings of the Royal Musical Association* 107 (1980–81): 60–70.

Prunières, Henry. *Le ballet de cour en France avant Benserade et Lully*. Paris, 1914.

———. *Lully*. Paris, 1910.

———. *L'opèra italien en France avant Lully*. Paris, 1913.

Ripa, Cesare. *Iconologia*. Rome, 1593.

Rosand, Ellen. 'Seneca and the Interpretation of L'incoronazione di Poppea'. *Journal of the American Musicological Society* 38, no. 1 (Spring 1985): 34–71.

Rushton, Julian, ed. *W. A. Mozart: 'Don Giovanni'*. Cambridge, 1981.

Sadie, Stanley. *Mozart*. London, 1966.

Saint-Evremond, Charles Marguetel de Saint-Denis, Seigneur de. 'Sur les opéra: A Monsieur le duc de Bouquinquant'. London, 1677(?). In *Oeuvres*. Ed. René Ternois. Paris, 1962–66.

Schlötterer, Reinhold. *Musik und Theater im 'Rosenkavalier' von Richard Strauss*. Vienna, 1985.

Schmidgal, Gary. *Literature as Opera*. London, 1978.

Seznec, Jean. *La survivance des dieux antiques*. London, 1940. Translated by Barbara Sessions as *The Survival of the Pagan Gods*. New York, 1953.

Smith, Patrick J. *The Tenth Muse: A Historical Study of the Opera Libretto*. New York, 1970.

Sonneck, Oscar. *Library of Congress Catalogue of Opera Librettos Printed before 1800*. Washington, D.C., 1914.

Sparshott, E. E. 'Susanne Langer'. In *Grove 6*.

Spender, Natasha, and Rosamund Shuter-Dyson. 'Psychology of Music'. In *Grove 6*.

Stein, Herbert von. *Dichtung und Musik im Werk Richard Wagners*. Berlin, 1962.

Stein, Jack M. *Richard Wagner and the Synthesis of the Arts*. Detroit, 1960. Rev. ed., 1973.

Sternfeld, F. W. 'Aspects of Italian Intermedi and Early Operas'. In Heinrich Huscher, ed. *Convivium musicorum: Festschrift Wolfgang Boetticher*. Berlin, 1974.

———. 'Expression and Revision in Gluck's Orfeo and Alceste'. In J. A. Westrup, ed. *Essays Presented to Egon Wellesz*. London, 1966.

———. *Music in Shakespearean Tragedy*. London, 1963. Rev. ed., 1967.

Stevens, Denis, ed. and trans. *The Letters of Claudio Monteverdi*. London, 1980.

Storr, Anthony. *The Dynamics of Creation*. London, 1972.

Strauss, Richard. *Betrachtungen und Erinnerungen*. Ed. Willi Schuh. Zurich, 1949. 2d ed., 1957. Translated by L. J. Lawrence as *Recollections and Reflections*. London, 1953.

Stravinsky, Igor. *Poétique musicale*. Cambridge, Mass., 1942. Translated as *The Poetics of Music*. Cambridge, Mass., 1947.

Strohm, Reinhard. *Essays on Handel and Italian Opera*. Cambridge, 1985.

Strunk, Oliver, ed. and trans. *Source Readings in Music History*. New York, 1950.

Tanner, Michael. Review of *Thomas Mann pro and contra Wagner*. *Times Literary Supplement*, March, 1986.

Tippett, Michael. *Moving into Aquarius*. London, 1958. 2d ed., 1974.

———. *Music of the Angels*. Ed. Meirion Bowen. London, 1980.

Tomlinson, Gary. *Monteverdi and the End of the Renaissance.* Oxford, 1987.

Warrack, John. *Carl Maria von Weber.* New York, 1968. Rev. ed., 1976.

———. 'German Operatic Ambitions at the Beginning of the Nineteenth Century'. *Proceedings of the Royal Musical Association* 104 (1977–78): 79–88.

———. *Tchaikovsky.* London, 1973.

Warrack, John, ed. *Carl Maria von Weber: Writings on Music.* Cambridge, 1982.

Weinberg, B. *A History of Literary Criticism in the Italian Renaissance.* Chicago, 1961.

Weinstock, Herbert. *Rossini: A Biography.* New York, 1968.

———. *Vincenzo Bellini: His Life and His Operas.* New York, 1971.

Weisstein, Ulrich. *The Essence of Opera.* London, 1964.

Whenham, John, ed. *Claudio Monteverdi: 'Orfeo'.* Cambridge, 1986.

White, Eric Walter. *Benjamin Britten.* London, 1948. 3d ed., 1970.

———. *A History of English Opera.* London, 1983.

———. *Stravinsky: The Composer and His Works.* London, 1966. Rev. ed., 1979.

———. *Tippett and His Operas.* London, 1979.

Whittall, Arnold. *The Music of Britten and Tippett.* Cambridge, 1982.

———. 'The Study of Britten: Triadic Harmony and Tonal Structure'. *Proceedings of the Royal Musical Association* 106 (1979–80): 27–41.

———. 'A War and a Wedding: Two Modern British Operas' [Billy Budd, The Midsummer Marriage]. *Music and Letters* 55, no. 3 (July 1974): 299ff.

Wind, Edgar. *Pagan Mysteries in the Renaissance.* London, 1958. 2d ed., 1967.

Winternitz, Emanuel. *Musical Instruments and Their Symbolism in Western Art.* New York, 1967.

Yates, Frances A. *The French Academies of the Sixteenth Century.* London, 1947.

———. *Giordano Bruno and the Hermetic Tradition.* Chicago, 1964.

Zarlino, Gioseffo. *Le istitutioni armoniche.* Venice, 1558. Part 3 translated by G. A. Marco and C. V. Palisca as *The Art of Counterpoint.* New Haven, 1968.

———. *Sopplimenti musicali.* Venice, 1588.

# INDEX

Compiled by Judith Donington